T0271508

PROMOTING FASHION

BARBARA GRAHAM & CALINE ANOUTI

Laurence King Publishing

LAURENCE KING

Published in 2018
by Laurence King Publishing Ltd
361–373 City Road
London EC1V 1LR
Tel +44 20 7841 6900
Fax +44 20 7841 6910
E enquiries@laurenceking.com
www.laurenceking.com

A catalogue record for this book is available from
the British Library.

ISBN 978 1 78627 215 7

Front cover image © Tristan Fewings/Getty Images.
Back cover: top photograph by Barbara Graham;
(jeans) courtesy Boy Bastiaens; (model) courtesy
All Saints; (tablet and phone) courtesy Tom Walsh
Design; bottom courtesy Sephora.

Designed by John Round Design
Picture research: Heather Vickers
Printed in China

CONTENTS

INTRODUCTION

The marketing, promotion and communication of fashion are entering an extremely dynamic, fast-moving and challenging phase for both students of the subject and practitioners alike. Promotional messages must resonate in an increasingly democratic landscape of followers, style influencers, brand ambassadors, celebrities and bloggers who now demand and deserve respect as fashion commentators. Consumers want relevant, personalized fashion communications to provide a genuine reason for them to contribute to brands' activities and to feel credited and rewarded for doing so.

How to develop brands that have an immediate connection to a desired target market? How to produce campaigns that engage and involve a sophisticated and knowledgeable audience seeking a profile-boosting and rewarding journey? How to cost a communications campaign depending on available budget or sales turnover? All these questions and more are answered in this book, through industry contributions, through the examples of brands at the forefront of movements in fashion promotion and through the authors' research.

WHO IS THE BOOK FOR?

This book is aimed primarily at students of Fashion Promotion, Fashion Communication and Fashion Marketing, and at new brands that wish to explore the marketing of fashion concepts. It focuses on promotion as a specific element of the broader 'six Ps' of fashion marketing, and as such takes an in-depth look at the factors influencing promotional decision-making. The book takes both a theoretical and practical approach, intended to introduce business and marketing readers to creative approaches to the subject, while suggesting that knowledge of marketing, branding and communication theory will allow creative practitioners to make more informed decisions.

Above Carven, Autumn/Winter 2015-16. The luxury French label Carven was established in 1945, but until 2010 had produced only couture collections. Its former designer Guillaume Henry's simple formula of beautifully cut capsule pieces helped to cement the modern vision of ready-to-wear French style.

Right Many designers become known for their covetable show invitations, such as this one by Dries Van Noten in 2014.

ABOUT THIS BOOK

In this book we follow the processes of developing a promotional campaign for a brand, whether a new concept or a more established venture. Awareness of the consumer is presented as central, and the developing of an accurate profile and knowledge of the wider trend environment are suggested in order to inspire relevant, timely campaigns and trigger new innovations. We then examine the importance of brand image and identity to ensure a consistent tone of voice, before providing an overview of the available communication tools, and concluding with a communications plan.

The chapters on communication tools are not divided strictly between online and offline, since the book reflects the current desire in the industry to create a seamless experience for audiences across channels and across devices. Advertising, for example, covers both traditional (TV, print, billboard) and online opportunities (banner advertising and social media). PR reflects both offline and online opportunities, as does the chapter on direct marketing. The online-only chapters on social media and e-commerce are placed together for ease of reading. However, the art of selling, appearance at catwalk or trade shows and initiating sales promotions are not presented as lesser communication tools. All tools are discussed equally in terms of advantages and disadvantages, and can be selected to create the best mix for a given brand concept. That said, social media is discussed early in the book to reflect the opinion of the experts interviewed, that

it is essential to the building of a community of followers and creating engagement with fashion brands. In the final chapter we examine how to pull together an effective and costed marketing communications plan.

Throughout the book, theory is brought to life by interviews with industry practitioners who discuss current and future issues relevant to their areas of expertise. The chapters are illustrated with examples of striking, successful and influential campaigns across all media. Where a particular brand acts as a great example of practice, it is identified in a coloured panel or through a case study.

Authors who are referenced are introduced by their full name the first time they appear in each chapter. Subsequent uses in each chapter are shortened to the author's surname only and the date of writing, in accordance with the Harvard referencing system.

STRUCTURE

Chapter 1

Consumers and Consumer Trend-forecasting, places understanding the consumer at the forefront of planning promotional campaigns. Some of the ways in which the fashion industry profiles consumers are examined as a key part of working with a potential audience. An understanding of the consumer trend environment is given as a setting for brands and retailers to develop innovative ideas for marketing and communications.

Chapter 2

Branding for Fashion Marketing Communications, discusses the idea of developing brands that will form an immediate and lasting connection with targeted groups of consumers. The reader is introduced to the idea of developing globally recognizable, relatable, human qualities within a brand idea. The key theories of branding are introduced and illustrated with examples of successful and consistent identity, image and tone of voice across all channels.

Chapter 3

Integrated Marketing Communications, is an introduction to the various communication tools. The chapter unpicks the theory of integration, which deals with how the tools can be combined to convey the desired brand messages in a way that engages and involves the consumer most effectively. The reader is introduced to forming SMART communication objectives, essential to planning a campaign.

Chapter 4

Advertising for Fashion, discusses the dilemma of offline versus online advertising campaigns. Theories of communication are examined with regard to this well-documented communication tool. Examples are given of campaigns that extend the reach of traditional advertising methods and acknowledge the viewer experience across devices and channels.

Chapter 5

PR, Endorsement and Sponsorship, examines how brands and retailers seek to achieve credibility with potential consumers through online or offline coverage from respected third parties, such as fashion editors and influencers. Examples are given of PR-related arrangements – such as product placement, celebrity endorsement and sponsorship – that place the brand in desirable settings but where fees have been paid. The chapter focuses particularly on the widening remit of brand ambassadors.

Chapter 6

Social Media, looks at the brands that are seeking to involve followers in immersive content that inspires them and that makes them feel the experience has increased their knowledge and boosted their personal online profiles. The chapter examines how the demand for instantly available catwalk fashion is driving a new wave of e-commerce possibilities on social media, and the pioneering brands that are embracing changes to the nature of platforms.

Chapter 7

The Digital Arena: E-commerce and Online Fashion Promotion, is the first of a two-chapter examination of the retail environment for fashion. This chapter, on the online environment, shows how effective design aids the consumer's journey through e-commerce sites, but also encourages them to contribute through recommendations and to get involved in the form of retailers' own blogs or editorial copy. The role of creative copywriting is discussed in terms of its impact on search-engine optimization (SEO) and other drivers of traffic to websites, such as pay-per-click (PPC) advertising and affiliate arrangements.

Chapter 8

Personal Selling and Offline Fashion Retail, considers the impact of the rise of online shopping on the bricks-and-mortar retail of fashion. The chapter looks at selling both from a B2B perspective – whereby brands, agents or distributors sell to retailers – and a B2C scenario, in which brands and retailers employ sales staff to interface with customers. The chapter recognizes the smart retailers who are examining successful online strategies and using technology to bring these benefits on to the shop floor to create a seamless omni-channel visitor journey.

Chapter 9

Direct Marketing, presents the communication tool that works to create a personalized dialogue with a database of potential, established or lapsed customers to encourage or tempt them to try, stay with or return to the brand or retailer. The chapter looks at the more familiar methods of delivery, such as printed invitations, catalogues and emails, and how multimedia text messaging has allowed enticing content to be shared directly among a community of followers.

Chapter 10

Catwalk Fashion Shows and Trade Fairs, considers the benefits of raising awareness, meeting prospective and existing buyers, and achieving press coverage through participating in one of the global fashion weeks. The chapter examines the case for designer labels showing as part of the catwalk schedule, and the mass-, mid- and premium-market labels that choose the more interactive setting of trade fairs. The cost implications are assessed and the question is raised whether, in the light of greater access to shows, they are still relevant in the fashion diary.

Chapter 11

Sales Promotion and Packaging, looks at the global demand for discounted goods, which is fuelling a culture of discount expectation. The chapter outlines the wider context of sales promotion tools and demonstrates how retailers are seeking to add value for the consumer through more feel-good experiences, such as loyalty schemes and competitions. The chapter covers packaging as value-added, collectable, reusable items that act as a silent salesperson to reflect brand identity on the shop floor.

Chapter 12

Planning, Costing and Measuring Effectiveness, acts as a review of the book, to form a fashion marketing communications plan. A plan layout is given either as a template for a new plan, or as a tool by which to analyse an existing campaign. Methods of measuring the effectiveness of communications are discussed, so that planners can evaluate whether their chosen communications mix has been successful.

Above left A G-Star RAW lookbook image demonstrating the brand's military inspiration for Summer 2016. Many brands store press releases and accompanying images in a dedicated press zone on their websites.

Above The singer Meghan Trainor is the new face of Skechers Originals retro trainers collection, in a collaboration that ran until 2017. The star appeared in a film commercial and the #MTrainSkechers campaign on social media.

Chapter 1
CONSUMERS AND CONSUMER TREND-FORECASTING

Knowledge of consumers lies at the heart of any successful promotional campaign. How do brands know who to target? Find out how to:

- Create a consumer profile using socio-demographic groupings and psychographics
- Differentiate between consumer groups by generation and attitude
- Understand how facets of our present era act to influence trends
- Watch how trends develop, grow and fade, both seasonal fads and longer-term consumer and socio-cultural tendencies
- Create trend predictions by learning how a global trend forecasting agency researches and distills relevant material

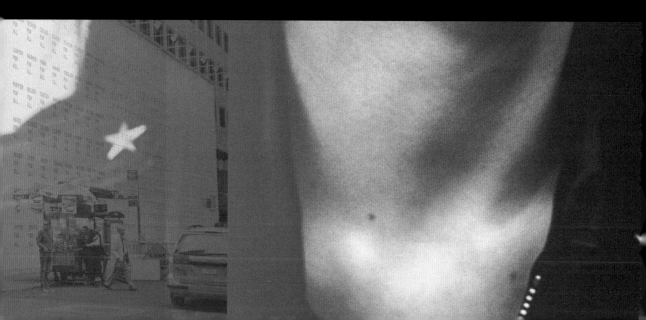

CONSUMER PROFILING

The role of consumers in the marketing industry has changed drastically since the 1950s, when people were expected to be passive consumers of product ideas from all-powerful brands. In what Philip Kotler et al. (2010) describe as the second era of marketing, it was recognized that consumers respond differently to varying products and messages. Consumers were subsequently put into market segments relating to age, location, job and lifestyle, so that they could be more effectively targeted with branded products. We are now well into what Kotler terms the third era. Promoters of fashion now need the active contribution and involvement of consumers to design credible campaigns to which they, the consumers, respond positively.

To reflect these changes there have been significant developments in the way consumers are profiled by brands and retailers. A much more detailed picture is required to suggest how consumers may behave or what they may aspire to, so that brands can assess how to engage with them.

Other factors, such as the switch to online behaviour, increasing fragmentation among consumer groups and significant improvements in data capture, have led to a questioning of the effectiveness of older methods such as socio-economic profiling. Through this system, a consumer's job and wage or salary were used to define them as a certain type of purchaser. Over time more complex methods, such as geo-demographic profiling, have taken into account a consumer's location and lifestyle, and psychographic profiling has added the measurement of attitudes and behaviour to build a more detailed picture. Today emotive segmentation provides the most detailed picture yet by adding aspiration and motivation to the behaviour of consumers.

Left Customer profile boards for fashion brands are often generated by product designers. This type of collage acts as a visual building block for the type of consumer and the influences the designer sees as ideal for the concept.

Above Total awareness of the consumer is vital for fashion brands, and can also generate campaign material. In 2015 the retailer AllSaints cast real people who 'capture the independent spirit and attitude of the brand' in a campaign entitled 'Def in Venice'. The videographer Wil Beedle shot a striking range of images and film clips that showcased the versatility of the biker jacket.

Socio-economic profiling

In the UK, academic research into market segmentation began to gather pace in the mid 1960s with the discussion of the best variables by which to define consumers. The National Readership Survey (NRS) or social grade definition was developed at this time in the attempt to classify and describe social classes.

NRS Socio-Economic Groupings or social grade definition system This model is still referred to occasionally in the fashion business, especially when dealing with media such as fashion magazines. It remains a quick way to define an upper-class, well-to-do consumer (ABC1) as distinct from the traditional, less well-off, working-class consumer (C2, D, E). See the table below.

Geo-demographic profiling

Geo-demographic based systems such as Mosaic were developed in the 1980s and designed to be updated with material from censuses. This type of profiling was introduced on the principle that understanding where and how a consumer lived was important, and that certain behaviour would be consistent with that location. Today, the global information systems company Experian takes the widest approach with its Mosaic Global classification system. Mosaic Global compiles data from 380 million households in 24 of the world's most successful economies. The system is based on the belief that there are recognizable similarities between enclaves of inhabitants globally, regardless of the country in which they live. The classification details ten distinct neighbourhood types in which consumers display similar attitudes, lifestyles and behaviour. These are:

- Sophisticated singles.
- Bourgeois prosperity.
- Career and family.
- Comfortable retirement.
- Routine service workers.
- Hard-working 'blue collar'.
- Metropolitan strugglers.
- Low-income elders.
- Post-industrial survivors.
- Rural inheritance.

Sophisticated singles, for instance, are defined as 'Young people, mostly single and well educated, who positively enjoy the variety and stimulation afforded by a life in large cities. Typically international in their outlook and with a rich network of personal contacts, they are quick to adopt and explore new social and political attitudes and are important agents of innovation, both in terms of lifestyle and consumer products.'

Consumer psychographics

Also in the 1980s, further academic research was carried out into more sophisticated, lifestyle-orientated approaches to segmentation. One significant project was the development by Arnold Mitchell, a US-based consumer futurist, of the VALS (Values and Lifestyles) model in 1978. In 1989, as the original approach of predicting consumer behaviour based on lifestyles and attitudes began to be challenged by academics, a team from the Stanford Research Institute International, Stanford University and the University of California developed VALS 2, based on the assumption that consumer psychology and demographics or psychographics were far more powerful than demographics alone. The framework identifies three primary types of motivation.

- **Ideals** Consumers who are driven by principles and values relating to what is responsible; this type contains the groups Thinkers and Believers.
- **Achievement** Consumers who are motivated by recognition of symbols of success. This group subdivides into Achievers and Strivers.
- **Self-expression** Consumers who are driven by the need for experiences, whether physical or social or risk-taking, comprising the Experiencers and Makers.

NRS SOCIO-ECONOMIC GROUPINGS OR SOCIAL GRADE DEFINITION SYSTEM

Social grade	Social status	Occupation
A	Upper middle class	Higher managerial, administrative or professional
B	Middle class	Intermediate managerial, administrative or professional
C1	Lower middle class	Supervisory or clerical, junior managerial, administrative or professional
C2	Skilled working class	Skilled manual workers
D	Working class	Semi-skilled and unskilled manual workers
E	Those at lowest level of subsistence	State pensioners or widows (no other earner), casual or lowest-grade workers

The model also recognizes a second level, a person's resources. Qualities such as energy, self-confidence, intellectualism, impulsiveness, leadership skills, novelty-seeking and vanity can enhance or restrain a consumer's primary motivators.

Briefly, the US VALS types are characterized as follows:

Innovators have the highest levels of resources and exhibit all three primary motivators, and therefore sit at the top of the model. Innovators are successful, cultivated, active consumers with high self-esteem. They enjoy change and are the most receptive to new, niche ideas and technology.

Thinkers are mature, satisfied, comfortable and reflective consumers who value order, knowledge and responsibility. They tend to be well educated and actively seek out information before making decisions. They favour durability, functionality and value in products.

Believers are strongly traditional and respect rules and authority. They are fundamentally conservative in taste, valuing family, religion, community and the nation. They choose familiar products and established brands.

Achievers have goal-orientated lifestyles and are committed to career and family. They live conventional lives, and value authority and the status quo over risk and self-discovery. They prefer premium products that convey success to their peers.

Strivers are trendy and fun-loving. They are concerned about the opinions of others and favour stylish, aspirational products that emulate the purchases of those with greater material wealth.

Experiencers are young and enthusiastic about new possibilities, but quickly lose interest. They seek variety and excitement, savouring the new, the offbeat and the risky. They spend a high proportion of their income on fast fashion, socializing and entertainment.

Makers value practicality and self-sufficiency. They choose hands-on constructive activity and spend leisure time with family and close friends. They prefer value to luxury and choose basic or functional products.

Survivors live narrow lives; they are low on resources and focus on meeting need. They do not show strong levels of the three primary motivations. They are loyal to familiar brands, and primarily concerned with good pricing, safety and security.

Anyone can take the VALS survey at www.strategic businessinsights.com/vals/presurveys.html and find their own VALS type, as well as contributing to the ongoing data capture. In 1995 UK VALS was added; it identifies slightly different primary motivators and corresponding consumer types. International VALS also operates in China, Dominica, Japan, Nigeria and Venezuela.

Emotive segmentation

Emotive segmentation, developed by VisualDNA, part of the consumer insights company Nielsen, adds more detail to psychographic profiling. The system has been developed for brands and retailers to improve the reach, performance and return on investment of their online promotional campaigns. It accepts that aspects such as location are no longer strictly relevant to the way consumers view online marketing messages, whereas aspects such as aspirations, motivation and personality traits are. Similar to the VALS system, the company has developed a series of visual quizzes by way of data capture, and they give significant insight into 12 different personality traits (see chart opposite). Emotive segmentation credits a consumer's general interests, aspirations and dreams, resourcefulness, state of mind, openness, conscientiousness, extroversion, agreeableness and neuroticism and the way they handle factors such as stress, love and finance as being relevant to the way they can be targeted with more individually tailored messages. By using subcategories of each of the 12 traits it is possible to build a detailed psychographic profile that considers consumers as individuals rather than segments. The system probably does the most to recognize that consumers of fashion can be aspirational or subject to compulsive or even irrational desires to purchase, regardless of income or location.

THE VisualDNA EMOTIVE SEGMENTATION CHART

General interests	Finances	Conscientiousness	Aspirations and dreams
Understand consumer interests and leisure activities	Understand how consumers spend their money	Understand how consumers organize their lives	Understand consumer hopes and wishes for the future
Sports fanatics	Leisure spenders	Perfectionists	Mainstream consumers
Music fanatics	Style spenders	Obsessive workers	Conventional aspirers
Bookworms	Food spenders	Life planners	Love aspirers
Gamers	Home improvers	Time keepers	Family aspirers
Auto enthusiasts	Affluent providers	Flexible thinkers	Happiness seekers
Style conscious	Careful spenders	Spontaneous workers	Idea seekers
Avant-garde		Spontaneous lifers	Nature lovers
Art and crafters		Spontaneous coasters	Career driven
Gourmet explorers		Well intentioned	Money driven
Family focused			Asset driven
			Spiritual believers
			Future champions

Resourcefulness	Extroversion	Dealing with stress	State of mind
Understand how consumers work	Understand how consumers feel about other people	Understand how consumers react to problems	Understand how consumers see the world
Experienced workers	Natural leaders	Work hard play hard	Energetic optimists
Skilled workers	Fun makers	Brush off	Wise optimists
Early stage workers	Jokers	Talk it over	Happy now
Disengaged workers	Social performers	Contemplators	Go getters
	Social listeners	Comfort seekers	Chilled out
	Story tellers	Emotional	Caring
	Conversationalists	Quick fix	Uncertain thinkers
	Supporting characters	Bottled up	Frustrated
	Frustrated extroverts	Hot and cold	Downhearted
	Measured		
	Provocative		
	Daydreamers		
	Solitary		

Agreeableness	Love	Openness	Neuroticism
Understand how interested consumers are in other people	Understand how consumers feel about love	Understand how consumers feel about new experiences	Understand how emotions drive consumer reactions
Altruists	True romantics	Expressive	Happy and secure
Positive idealists	Wavelength romantics	Creative	Self secure
Team players	Rollercoaster romantics	Curious	Self-confident
Natural collaborators	Romantic traditionalists	Nice	Sensitive
Guarded collaborators	Romantic adventurers	Intelligent	Internalizers
Researchers	Dramatic lovers	Logical	Feel the strain
Self focused	Passionate lovers	Straightforward	Self critical
Competitors	Loving companions	Sensible	Easily deflated
Control seekers	Unromantics		Internal escapists
Lone wolves	Tender hearts		Reactive escapists
Assertive	Lonely hearts		Dramatic escapists

GENERATIONAL ATTITUDES

Another method of profiling consumers works on the assumption that people behave in ways or have attitudes that are dictated by the generation in which they were born. Many authors on the subject of fashion promotion and marketing, such as Harriet Posner, Tim Jackson and David Shaw, have acknowledged the effect of generational divides on attitudes to fashion consumption, marketing and branding.

Changes in attitudes to ageing and in particular the perception of the word 'old' are now shaking up and blurring long-held generational groupings. Several factors have influenced an accelerated age compression in the younger end of the age range, and an age expansion among older consumers.

- Increased longevity, better health, increased exercise and the desire to stay young for longer has led to more active ageing populations. Working lives are becoming extended, as is the concept of 'middle age', which is lasting until the age of 55.
- Children in developed societies are maturing much earlier, causing an age-compression phenomenon known as KGOY (Kids Getting Older Younger). They are rejecting traditional children's toys, games and clothing in favour of online activities more associated with the adult world.
- Tweens (ages 10–14) are also maturing quickly; they are affected by celebrity culture and media pressure to conform to ideal body types.
- Adolescence can last until as late as the early thirties as recession-hit millennials are staying at home with their parents longer or electing to return home after expensive years at university.
- Baby boomers (born after World War II) have no intention of accepting the constraints of old age. The term 'old' may not now apply until 80. They are embracing health, fitness and stay-young beauty procedures and are enthusiastically starting businesses and learning new skills.

These changes apply to global markets and are reflected in the following updated generational breakdown:

The Swing Generation / The Silent Generation
Longer life expectancy means that this demographic, born before 1946, is expanding and comprises 8.5 per cent of the global population. This is possibly the first time this group has been of interest to developers and marketers of products and services. Now mostly pensioners, some of this group will have been born during World War II, and so they are named after the heyday of swing music. Many are on low incomes or state benefits, but some have become the wealthiest, most willing-to-spend retirees of all time. They are determined to stay healthy, live well and enjoy life. The return in product and marketing messages to local manufacture, recycling, reuse and sustainability has reignited interest in the life experiences of this previously forgotten generation, some of whom grew up with postwar deprivation and the 'make do and mend' ethos.

The Baby Boomers
Named after the global explosion in population after World War II, baby boomers make up 19.9 per cent of the world's population. As teenagers, this generation were the first to feel the benefits of extra cash and the freedom, fashion and music explosion of the 1950s and 1960s. Born between 1946 and 1964, Boomers were the first generation to raise children in a household where both parents worked. They are connected to youth, but also plan to enjoy life after their children have left home. They respond to brands and campaigns that reflect heritage values, and see brands as hard-earned social badges. However, as interest rockets in sales of cosmetics and fashion to this generation, they have found themselves the unlikely stars of campaigns such as those for Wella, Comptoir des Cotonniers and & Other Stories.

Below The then 60-year-old model Yasmina Rossi for the Dreslyn and Land of Women swimsuit collaboration, 2016.

Generation X

Generation X consists of those born between 1965 and 1980 and makes up about the same percentage globally as baby boomers, at 20.5 per cent. The X was coined by the Canadian writer Douglas Coupland in *Generation X: Tales for an Accelerated Culture* (1991) to represent a generation that wanted to avoid definition. Generation X has a reputation for being cynical and suspicious, especially when it comes to marketing and obvious marketing techniques, such as lumping consumers together in segments and running overtly commercial campaigns. Many were brought up by two working parents, and they were the first generation to reject the ideal of working all their lives, earning themselves a further title of the 'slacker generation'. They are the inventors of the gap year and of dropping out to experience the benefits of travel. They do, however, appreciate messages of exclusivity, limited editions and cool collectability. It is hoped that this difficult generation will mellow towards marketing messages in the now extended peak earning years.

Generation Y / The Millennial Generation / The Echo Boomers

Generation Y signifies those who were born between 1981 and 1990, some 17.8 per cent of the global population. Having grown up with technology, they are eager adopters of social media and other online community-forming platforms. Many members of this generation are single, stretching out their adolescence because of the difficult economic environment. They may be students or young professionals, or have young families themselves. They are happy to adopt less rigid gender roles, and so are bringing a newer, more inclusive attitude to parenting. Members of this generation are much happier to form sharing communities and will contribute actively to brands that engage them.

Generation Z / iGeneration / Boomlets / Centennials

Today's Centennials were born between 1991 and 2002 and make up 19.6 per cent of the world's population. The final name of this generation is still under debate by experts; they are also known as Next Gen or the Net Generation because of their immersion in digital technology. This generation has never known a world without video games, mobile phones or computers. Part of the KGOY phenomenon mentioned above, this generation has quickly divested itself of childlike toys and is keen to participate, consume and innovate in a digital world. This generation is expected to want to create, personalize and be credited for their own contributions to brand development and campaign material.

Above Iris Apfel (born 1921) is one of the busiest models of the moment. Her rule-breaking sense of style transcends the usual associations with older age. She was the face of the Blue Illusion Autumn/Winter 2016-17 campaign, 'Ageless'.

The Flat Age

In 2014 the global futures consultancy The Future Laboratory predicted further blurring of conventional generational divides and described attitudes to future generations in its trend release 'The Flat Age Society'. It drew attention to an engaged, technologically enabled generation of baby boomers that account for 45 per cent of spend on luxury products globally. The global population of the over-55s is set to swell by 200 million to reach 2 billion by 2050, and such a strong force is predicted to help alter remaining negative associations with being old. 'The Flat Age Society' also suggests that great intuitive design of the future should include all generation groups as society moves from a youth-driven culture to one in which age is less significant. It will become less pressing for marketers to communicate to stereotypical generational divides, and more necessary to find innovative ways of reaching consumers using messages that represent timeless or looser 'life stages'.

BUYER PERSONAS

All the profiling techniques mentioned above can be used by brands and retailers to form the basis of buyer personas. A persona is a fictional generalization of an ideal consumer based on geo-demographics, psychographics, aspirations, attitudes and personality traits. Further research – such as online behaviour in terms of engagement with brand content, shopping habits or the results of market research surveys or observation projects – can contribute to the formation of these highly detailed consumer portraits. From a marketing perspective, and in a way that is especially relevant to online communications such as newsletters and emails, consumer groups can be segmented by buyer persona and targeted with more relevant messages.

It helps promoters of fashion to realize that to appeal to consumers' lifestyles, motivation and behaviour they must analyse them in much more detail than previous profiling methods suggested. For a consumer to interact with and respond to a campaign message, it should appear as if that campaign has been constructed just for them. There have also been significant changes to conventional generational divides. This affects, for instance, producers of childrenswear, whose target market may become less responsive to childlike, cute imagery as they seek out more adult themes of celebrity and body image. Consumer futures analysts are suggesting that promoters should find ways to appeal across the generations. This is sure to have more impact on the fashion industry, which has already begun to include older models.

We turn next to the analysis of consumers for another reason: that any new behaviour, if observed in significant numbers, can suggest trends in the way future consumers may behave.

THE DEVELOPMENT OF CONSUMER TREND-WATCHING

On Boxing Day 1985, when the US-based jeans brand Levi Strauss & Co. launched its iconic 'Launderette' ad, it had been suffering flagging fortunes in the UK and was on the verge of pulling out of a trend-driven market. Created by John Hegarty and Barbara Noakes of the creative ad agency Bartle Bogle Hegarty, the ad became famous for the model Nick Kamen nonchalantly stripping down to his boxer shorts and, watched by bemused older customers and attentive young women, placing his Levi 501 jeans in the washing machine of a 1950s-style launderette. Marvin Gaye's 'Heard it Through the Grapevine' was re-released and went on to be one of four top-ten tracks that Levi's used to accompany its advertising campaigns. 'Launderette' sent UK sales soaring among both men and women, reputedly by as much as 20 times by 1987.

Without doubt, Levi's established an important advertising template and saved its reputation in a difficult market, but it is debatable whether its success was entirely down to the campaign. No other jeans brand managed to replicate this success, despite rushing to put out expensive ads in response.

In London in 1982 a series of club nights known as the Dirtbox began, hosted by Rob Milton and Phil (Dirtbox) Gray and frequented by post-punks, rockabillies and soul boys and girls. The resulting fusion of influence became

Top Nick Kamen in Levi's 'Launderette' ad.   **Above** Dirtbox rockabillies on the King's Road, London, in the early 1980s.

driven by 1950s rockabilly and was known as the Dirtbox look, later called 'hard times' style. As with punk, the look reflected the continuing recession (which had started in the 1970s), and ripped Levi's 501s, readily available at that time from second-hand shops, became a key piece of dress. They were worn rolled up, with battered brogues and no socks for boys and with vintage stilettos and fishnet tights for girls. The slim leg and cinched-in, slightly baggy front of the Levi's 501 perfectly suited the look's 1950s street-urchin ethos.

Had this key group of Innovators (see The Diffusion of Innovation, below) not already been spreading the look through clubs, music, weekend trips to the coast and styling projects, it is unlikely that Levi's could have achieved the sales figures it did. In fact – by accident or by design – it tapped into a major trend at the Early Adoption stage. Other brands found they simply did not have this grass-roots demand for a core jeans fit.

The Diffusion of Innovation

The idea of establishing a science behind predicting consumer behaviour is not new. Central to theorizing about consumers' uptake of new trends is research begun in 1962 by the American sociologist and teacher Everett M. Rogers into the uptake of a new hybrid seed corn, designed to improve yields, by a farming community in Iowa. His research measured the rate of adoption by noting both the speed of uptake and factors that increased that speed or indicated resistance to the new idea. Although now more than four decades old, the resulting types of user/consumer and the percentage of uptake of those types in the sample group still stand in trend-forecasting today.

- Innovators make up only 2.5 per cent of any given group, and although they may not invent or discover a new style or product, they translate an idea into something that others can fit into their frames of reference.

- Early Adopters are a larger group, comprising 13.5 per cent, and are usually better connected than Innovators. They are happy to observe and take the lead from Innovator friends, and to spread the word to make an idea more acceptable.
- Some 34 per cent of the group will be Early Majority. Members of this group will wait to see how Early Adopters fare with a trend, before they themselves take it on board. Highly social and able to spread a message, they are followers rather than initiators of ideas.
- A further 34 per cent will be Late Majority adopters, who need lots of acceptable examples of how something will work for them. They may seek justification or reassurance from the Early Majority that they will benefit.
- Finally, Laggards make up about 16 per cent. They are slow to adopt trends, conservative in values and reluctant to change.

This model enables trend-forecasters to keep an eye on Innovators to identify new ideas coming into the sphere of reference. They can pinpoint when a trend may 'tip' or become the next big thing by measuring reaction in the Early Adopter and Early Majority groups. A warning that an innovation's days may be numbered can be signalled in the Late Majority group, and even Laggards have a role in measuring how far an idea can be watered down before the world moves on.

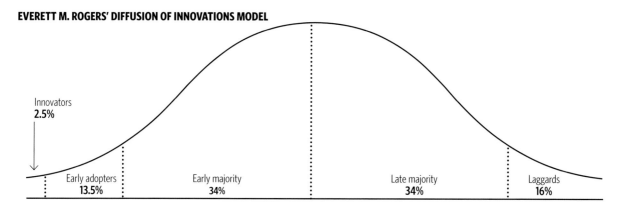

EVERETT M. ROGERS' DIFFUSION OF INNOVATIONS MODEL

Innovators
2.5%

Early adopters
13.5%

Early majority
34%

Late majority
34%

Laggards
16%

Postmodernism

That society has, since the early 1960s, been in the depths of a complex and somewhat indefinable era described as postmodern – a reaction to the progressive, optimistic spirit of the modern era (approximately 1900–60) – is in itself a subject under much debate. Some theorists argue that we have entered a post-postmodern phase, a term that is under even more discussion. One school of thought proposed by writers such as Jeffrey Nealon is that post-postmodernism is an intensification of the postmodern effect, as described below.

Key postmodern theorists were Jean Baudrillard, Fredric Jameson, Jean-François Lyotard, Roland Barthes and Jacques Derrida, although between them they held many different perspectives on the subject. The era is perhaps best summarized in relation to what modernism had represented: progress, truth and the quest for utopian ideals. Conversely, postmodernism represents exhaustion, questioning of the truth and a dystopian society. Stephen Brown, writing in Brownlie et al. (1999), perhaps best sums up Baudrillard's view of the postmodern condition:

> Every possibility in art, life, theory, politics and society has already been tried. Originality is impossible, history has ended, the future has already happened and all that remains is to play with the pieces among the anorexic ruins. In other words, the only available option is to recycle, rearrange, rediscover, recombine and reuse the forms, styles, genres, approaches, techniques and methods that already exist, usually in an ironic or irreverent manner. Thus, although postmodernism is in many ways the terminus, the outer limit, the dead-end of modernism, it is also characterized by a strange but remarkably compelling sense of playfulness, of exhilaration in the face of failure, of feeling that there's nothing we can do, so let's have a party.

This certainly goes some way towards explaining why, in fashion, decades are endlessly rehashed while to some extent nervousness of the future and of new developments and directions remains. We can adapt the marketing perspective taken by Brown to explain the facets of postmodernism.

Fragmentation The breaking down of political stability, economic theories and social organization in tandem with the increasing influence of media opinion. This term is often used to describe the breaking down of consumer groups from mass market to almost personal status.

Dedifferentiation The blending of what were once high and low cultures, such as politics and celebrity, and the blurring of once-distinct boundaries such as gender or

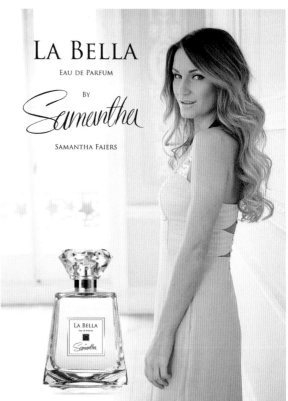

Top Comme des Garçons campaign, 1995.

Above UK Reality TV star Samantha Faiers' 'La Bella' perfume campaign, 2014.

what comprised a celebrity. In fashion, this term also explains, for example, the use of formerly disregarded 'low'-status fabrics, or the elevation of sportswear to the catwalk.

Hyper-reality The elevation of fantasy worlds and a questioning of what is 'real' and what simulation. Originally manifested through the popularity of theme parks and computer games, it has exploded into reality TV, the possibility to exist in a virtual world and ever more immersive visual gaming experiences. Through hyper-reality, society has accepted the word 'celebrity' to describe reality TV stars. It is therefore possible to market a brand created by a reality TV star using their image and standing in society, to consumers who culturally accept that message.

Pastiche/Bricolage The use of collages of existing styles and codes, assembled in a new way, often ironically or with a sense of playfulness; this may be in fashion, architecture, art, film or literature. For example, the high-end department store Harvey Nichols has established a reputation for producing ironic, cheeky, sometimes controversial ads using bricolage. In 2015 it used CCTV footage of real shoplifters, overlaid with cartoon faces to conceal their identity. The ad, for the Harvey Nichols Rewards app, used the tagline 'Love freebies? Get them legally.'

Anti-foundationalism The desire to deconstruct; to question what should be worn as outerwear and what should be concealed. Respect is often shown for the details of construction, and the function of previously accepted features such as sleeves is questioned. In a wider sense, this involves a questioning of what was once a universal truth or established point of view. Some of fashion's most progressive and intelligent contemporary designs have been based on this principle. It also explains the current desire to see 'behind the scenes' and to observe the making of a campaign.

Above right Jean Paul Gaultier, Spring/Summer 2014 campaign using a collage of catwalk shots.

Right Vivienne Westwood, Spring/Summer 2015 campaign.

HOW A TREND-FORECASTING AGENCY WORKS

Having established the importance of consumer-watching, and looked at the theory behind how trends are taken up by society and the relevance of the era on how trends may emerge, we now examine how trend-forecasting agencies formulate observed consumer behaviour into actual trends.

Each trend-forecasting agency has its own process for gathering and synthesizing research. On page 22 Victoria Loomes takes us through the process followed by trendwatching.com. A favourite of students and industry insiders alike, trendwatching.com is known and appreciated for its free publications, which include monthly trend bulletins available in nine languages, regional bulletins and a step-by-step trend canvas to help brands and retailers translate a trend idea into an innovation.

THE TRENDWATCHING.COM PERSPECTIVE

The trends below were made available as free bulletins in 2015. In subsequent chapters we will point out examples of early adopters of these longer-term consumer and socio-cultural trend ideas where they have occurred in the design of campaigns.

Subtrend: 'Post-Demographic Consumerism'

This is trendwatching.com's take on the blurring of conventional generational divides discussed earlier in the chapter; it went on to become a megatrend, replacing 'Tribes and Lives'. In a society where the flow of information is so fluid, all age groups are constructing their own identities so that consumption patterns are no longer defined by age, gender, location, income, family or status. The trend has been shaped by the global familiarity of such megabrands as Apple, Facebook, Ikea, McDonalds, Uniqlo and Nike, which promote an ageless experience worldwide.

The more liberal lifestyles in most of the world's big cities have also helped consumers to form their own identities, rather than relying on those dictated by family structures or even gender roles. An increase in the use of digital tools for personalization and experimentation has allowed more people to connect and identify with brands in more individual ways. The newer status symbols of experiences, authenticity, connections and ethical associations are opening up brands to everyone regardless of age, wealth or location. Trendwatching.com highlights four categories within this megatrend.

The new normal Brands that reduce negative impact on the well-being of the consumer. For example, Facebook Argentina has added more gender options, such as trans woman, when a profile is being created.

Heritage heresy Brands prepared to re-imagine or overturn decades of established brand history and tradition, to attract younger, wealthy, yet irreverent customers. For example, the New York skate brand Shut unveiled a luxury gold-plated skateboard.

Cross-demographic fertilization Shared taste and aspiration mean that the opportunities to transfer innovations from one core demographic to another have never been greater. For example, the CNA language school launched the Speaking Exchange Project, which connected Brazilian language students with retired Americans for English lessons via webcam.

Hyper-demographic irony Target and cater to ever smaller interest-based segments with niche products, instead of over-general traditional demographics. For example, Vogmask and Face Slap launched stylish anti-pollution face masks at Hong Kong's Spring/Summer 2015 fashion week.

Subtrend: 'Sympathetic Pricing'

This subtrend is part of the megatrend 'Human Brands'. It suggests that consumers are tired of brands telling them that they care; they would like to see some physical proof, in the form of imaginative and flexible discounting. Consumers have learned to tune out brands' messages that they care for the environment, for their workers or for their consumers, and only 5 per cent of consumers in the US and UK believe that brands are open and honest in their practices.

Continued on page 25.

Above Uniqlo's 'Made For All' campaign. A construction barricade for the launch of the New York City 5th Avenue flagship store in 2014.

Right Trendwatching.com 'Sympathetic Pricing' report.

Victoria Loomes is a Senior Trend Analyst at trendwatching.com. Set up in 2002, the organization has over 3,000 trend-spotters in more than 90 countries around the globe. Trend observations pour into five central offices, in New York, London, São Paulo, Singapore and Lagos. The organization is led by a team of 23, who are responsible for managing clients, regional offices, trend content, marketing and the look of the website. Observed trends are synthesized into Premium Service trend releases for 1,200 paying clients and the later free bulletins to over 260,000 subscribers. Clients include Diesel, Gucci, Yves Saint Laurent, Nike, Puma and Samsonite.

Anyone with an eye for local examples of consumer trends and business innovations can apply to join tw:in, trendwatching.com's trend-spotting network. Readers of the site's free publications are often recruited for this purpose. Successful contributions are rewarded with points (which can be redeemed for gifts), and may be published in one of the trend bulletins.

Trendwatching.com's trend analysts carry out global seminars and innovation workshops for clients, and also attend seminars by leading thinkers and innovators to keep at the forefront of what is happening both now and next.

Q: *How do you all compile information among the global offices?*
A: It is a challenge, but we get everyone together via Skype to exchange information. We also have a great internal chat programme called Slack, a messaging app that enables real-time comment to be pinged backwards and forwards and different people to be allowed into the conversation.

The regional offices are responsible for the regional briefings – they come back to us and go through the headers, trends and insights that they will include – but the content and direction of the briefings are signed off by each regional office. Otherwise it's a democratic process.

Q: *Do you have to do trend seminars all over the world?*
A: It's July now so we are in the middle of those (for 2015) at the moment. Amsterdam was the first one, then London, then Singapore, then a private event in Bangkok. Then Sydney and a final seminar in New York. The São Paolo event in 2016 will be a secret seminar, a more intimate, interactive experience with no set agenda. We're finding this format works better for certain markets who like the idea of a more underground event. The seminars are lots of fun, but hard work to get together. They are

Right Trendwatching.com produces free regional publications to share, like or download.

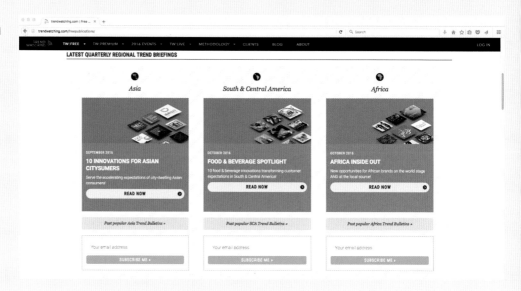

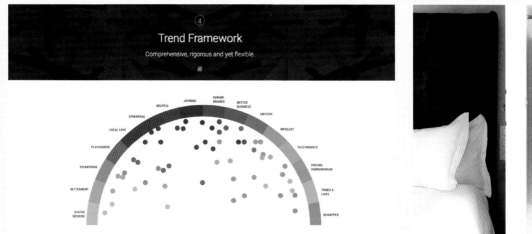

Above left
A trendwatching.com
Trend Framework.

Above right A mini fashion
bar in Antwerp, Belgium.

structured around our premium content, which is structured around our trend framework. Within this there are 16 megatrends, and within each megatrend are subtrends, which are not necessarily less important but which change more quickly and evolve more fluidly. We update the subtrends regularly and give examples of them in action. At the seminars we present the trend framework and how the subtrends will shape those over the next few years. We give ten trends that attenders should know about and be acting on now; I put a lot of that together. The travel is exciting, and we always try to tailor the content as far as possible to local markets, even if that just means changing the images to be locally relevant.

Q: *Is there any country in particular that is essential to watch at the moment?*
A: It's a difficult question. There's a lot of interesting stuff in Africa at the moment: the middle class there is growing, and they are observing, taking enjoyable ideas from people in other countries and putting their own spin on it. Because of the internet and the way information is so easily disseminated, it's difficult to say that you should watch any particular market, because now ideas and inspirations or thoughts can literally come from anywhere. I wouldn't say there is one particular market; you need to be globally aware. It's important for businesses to realize that people travel much more now, all over the world, and they take certain expectations with them and think 'Why isn't this available here?' There are a lot of global brands that are setting standards across the world, and companies like Google,

Facebook and Apple have redefined how we think about certain services and what we expect from customer service. Apple's Genius Bar is available across the world, so small start-ups are having to respond to these enhanced levels of customer service and the standards set by these big brands.

Q: *Any other particular source of interesting ideas?*
A: Good ideas can come from anywhere. Once a brand like Apple or Amazon does something, it's easier for a start-up brand to build on that idea and take its own direction from it. The barriers to entry have become lower. Digital allows you to experiment much more, more easily. For the brand – and on a personal level – it's easier to try out, or to customize; to decide to get involved with something.

It's also important to think that any channel can become a marketing channel. For instance, Banks boutique hotel in Antwerp has partnered with a German fashion store, Pimkie; now, in the hotel rooms, they have mini fashion bars of a curated selection of clothing that you can wear and pay for at the end of your trip. It saves you going to the shop, packing tons or realizing you are missing something. Marketing at every opportunity will become more and more tailored and streamlined.

Q: *Is there an example of a subtrend that became a megatrend in its own right?*
A: Maybe not something that started as a subtrend as such, but megatrends can evolve. The 'Tribes and Lives' trend has now been renamed post-demographic consumerism – the

idea that consumers don't behave as they should. People are sophisticated in their access to information and global brands; they can't be segmented by age, location or gender any more. 'Tribes and Lives' was about segmenting people by groups. We had a trend called 'Pink Profits', essentially marketing to the pink pound, and a trend relating to women. We talked a lot about how these ideas seemed outdated and clichéd. We published the idea of 'Post-Demographic Consumerism' to premium clients in November 2014. It's gone on to become even bigger than a megatrend – an overarching trend, a fundamental shift in how we need to think about people. It will be fundamental to brands to think about how they define themselves to consumers. Young people will remain the earliest adopters, but that information and that desire to adopt that information will become quicker in all generations.

Q: *Are you working on any trends now that you think will have an impact on fashion brands?*
A: The merging of fashion and technology is a really interesting one, not just for e-commerce or at point of sale. Levi's, for example, is working with Google to create smart fabric from which to manufacture jeans. The idea is that the wearer can change the volume of their music when running their hands up and down the fabric of their jeans. Responsive clothing that has technology embedded in what you are wearing is an area that looks set to grow. E-commerce possibilities are endless. Using devices can be isolating and about looking down at something; gesture technology has enabled us to be expansive and more active. Technology won't be used for its own sake: it needs to solve a problem or make something better, easier or more intuitive.

Fashion brands could think about putting consumers in touch with their contacts. Tesco ran a campaign through which customers could book tutorials with beauty bloggers, who would discuss which products would suit them. There is a lot of room for fashion brands to cash in on their contacts while helping people to improve their appearance, gain behind-the-scenes knowledge or see through the eye of a fashion insider. This considers marketing as a service – something that is useful to the consumer, rather than seeing them as passive users. Consumers are trading directly with one another and building trust with one another in other sectors, too. To stay relevant, fashion brands could look at some of those models.

Q: *Do you have any favourite brands or ideas that you have seen in trend-watching?*
A: I do watch certain brands. Domino's Pizza does amazing things by way of service marketing, such as emoji ordering. I also like Patagonia, which was very transparent with its 'Don't Buy this Jacket' campaign (2011); it was counter-intuitive, but an effective message that informed the shopper how many resources go into this bestselling jacket. I'm interested in brands that step in and help consumers to learn new skills or understand things. There's been a shift from the acquisition of goods to wanting to experience more, to collect experiences. We're not going to stop shopping, but the stories, activities and access that we can tell are associated with each purchase are becoming ever more important.

Below In the US in 2015 Domino's introduced a new pizza emoji for quick and easy ordering. Registered users who had already specified their pizza preferences could simply tweet the emoji or use the hashtag 'EasyOrder' on the @dominos account.

AT DOMINO'S, WE LOVE EMOJI TOO. ACTUALLY ONE IN PARTICULAR.

The trend covers three categories of sympathetic pricing:

Painkiller pricing Discounts that target lifestyle pain points. For example, the taxi app Uber offered discounts to travellers hit by transport disruption in London and Boston.

Compassionate pricing Discounts that offer a helping hand at difficult times. An example is the Tienda Amiga incentive in a district of Madrid, Spain, where shops offer discounts to the unemployed.

Purposeful pricing Discounts offered in support of a shared value or belief. For example, the Dutch airline Corendon offered cheaper flights to Russia for gay-rights activists.

Subtrend: 'No Interface'

This subtrend (of the megatrend 'Ubitech') involves a more natural and intuitive way of interacting with technology through speech, gesture, touch and sight. The use of the mobile phone has freed consumers, in one sense, to shop and remain connected 24/7, but it is restrictive physically. The trend has been shaped by a desire for a new approach – devices that people can talk to, notifications they can feel, rather than just looking down at a screen. The trend predicts that consumers will desire faster, more intuitive ways of dealing with the vast amount of information that comes their way.

Voice There are few interactions quicker than simply talking. For example, Amazon Echo is the smart digital service assistant that learns from your voice. It can find music, news, weather and information.

Gesture Natural gestures are a very intuitive way to interact with technology. For example, the Ring Zero, a wearable ring that allows smart devices to be controlled by gestures.

Touch Expanding on the ability to send a typed message, new touch features such as alerts or emojis are felt by the wearer. For example, the Hug app, a vibrating app that sends a hug to a receiver who can actually feel it.

Augmented reality New technology is blending digital information seamlessly with the real world. For example, RideOn augmented-reality goggles add a virtual layer of challenge or competition for skiers and snowboarders.

The nature of the consumer and the trend environment mentioned in this chapter should be at the forefront of the communication planning process. Since at least two of the trend-forecasting agencies, supported by independent published research, predict changes to how brands should view generations of future consumers, it is almost certain that this will happen and gain pace during the 2020s. More specifically, greater use of painkiller pricing would allow personalized, short-term discounts for more fun reasons than the need to sell older fashion stock. Voice- and gesture-controlled interfaces are the most immediate and likely tools that could be adopted more widely by the fashion industry. Augmented reality has also been used by Net-a-Porter and others to add depth to the shopping experience. The following chapters will highlight how these and other trends we have mentioned have been adopted as part of campaigns by forward-thinking brands.

REFERENCES

Brownlie, Douglas, et al., *Rethinking Marketing: Towards Critical Marketing Accountings*, Sage Publications 1999

Experian, 'Mosaic Global', 2007, www.experian.co.uk/assets/business-strategies/brochures/Mosaic_Global_factsheet[1].pdf

Kotler, Philip, Hermawan Kartajaya and Iwan Setiawan, *Marketing 3.0*, Wiley and Sons 2010

Strategic Business Insights, 'US Framework and VALS Types', 2015, www.strategicbusinessinsights.com/vals/ustypes.shtml

VisualDNA, 'Emotive Segmentation Methodology', 2013, www.visualdna.com/wp-content/uploads/2014/09/Emotive-Segments-White-Paper-VisualDNA.pdf

FURTHER READING

Euromonitor, 'Age Blurring: How the Breakdown of Age Boundaries Is Affecting Global Consumer Markets', Strategy Briefing, 2011

Flat Age Society, The Future Laboratory on The Flat Age Society, 2015, https://vimeo.com/85909422

Raymond, Martin, *The Trend Forecaster's Handbook*, Laurence King Publishing 2010

Retail Innovation, 'The Future of Retail with Wearable Technology', 16 March 2015, www.retail-innovation.com/the-future-of-retail-with-wearable-technology

DISCUSSION

Who are today's innovators and early adopters? How are these roles changing?

Consider how any fashion brand has successfully catered to the centennial consumer.

What three early socio-cultural trends visible today do you think will influence fashion brands and products in the next two or three years?

Chapter 2

BRANDING FOR FASHION MARKETING COMMUNICATIONS

Branding is crucial to the promotion of fashion labels. Find out how to:
- Ascribe recognizable and therefore desirable human qualities to brands, to appeal to consumers' emotions
- Identify the tangible and intangible components of a brand
- Tell the story of a brand to engage consumers
- Establish the desired brand identity using logos, colour, tone of voice and personality traits
- Measure the effectiveness and strength of brand identity using the theory of the brand identity prism
- Create and reinforce a strong, cohesive brand identity using marketing communications

FASHION BRANDS
AND BRAND MESSAGE

When consumers are asked what their favourite fashion brand is, without doubt each will answer differently, depending on their needs, wants, tastes and preferences. Most importantly, the clothes they wear and the brands they choose to identify themselves with will be based on the things they care about and the things to which they aspire. Their choices help to shape and communicate how they wish to be viewed by others.

Fashion branding is used not only to identify and differentiate one retailer's products and services from another's, but also to shape the consumer's personality, character and attitude. The message associated with a fashion brand is therefore extremely important in the fashion industry, since it becomes part of a consumer's own carefully constructed identity. This means that brands face the extremely difficult challenge of having to differentiate themselves from one another, to satisfy consumer needs, and also to create a sustained consumer desire by the way they tap into and target consumers' aspirations.

In this chapter we use the idea of humanizing a brand – affording it human traits – to examine the nature of

Opposite and above Jack Wills translates 'Fabulously British' into visual and lifestyle merchandising.

branding. Just as humans have characteristics, personality traits and a personal story, all of which combine to form a constructed sense of personal identity, so do brands. Several studies of consumer behaviour have indicated that humans generally feel first, then rationalize. It is assumed that this pattern applies to the contact we have with brands. Consequently, the messages brands use when targeting consumers are becoming more emotionally driven.

Strong fashion brands use effective branding and communication to convey their emotional message. Jack Wills, for example, has successfully built a brand around its British take on an American collegiate style of dressing. Its 'Made in Britain' and 'Fabulously British' concepts connect emotionally with its target consumers – young students and professionals – and its campaigns emphasize the younger, fresher take on British lifestyle to which they aspire.

This need to connect emotionally before thinking about function is endorsed by Ric Simcock, managing director of the branding agency Elephants Can't Jump: 'Emotion wins every time! If we don't give the consumers something to feel about us, they'll have no reason to think about us, [and] this will result in no reasons to choose us as a brand when it matters.' This view is also reflected by Kevin Roberts in his book *Lovemarks* (2006). He cites the work of the emotion researcher Dylan Evans, who identifies humans' primary emotions as joy, sorrow, anger, fear, surprise and disgust, and secondary emotions as guilt, shame, pride, envy, jealousy and, the greatest of these, love. These secondary emotions are fundamental to our ability to form relationships. We need someone or something to evoke love, and Roberts believes that 'human' brands can build this emotion into their message, fulfilling this need. From building collections of box-fresh trainers to paying out for the season's designer It bag, if a brand's message strikes a chord with the consumer, a bond similar to (if not the same as) love will be formed.

THE TANGIBLE AND INTANGIBLE COMPONENTS OF A BRAND

There are many differing definitions of branding and what the construct of a brand stands for, and it is fair to say that little agreement has been reached. One credible definition by the brand expert Kevin Lane Keller (2011) explains the tangible aspects of a brand as 'a name, term, sign, symbol or design or a combination of these intended to identify goals or services of a seller and to differentiate them from those of a competitor'. However, a brand is also said to be much more than its physical attributes, and has been identified in many sources as conveying the promise of a value to a consumer, plus a meaning and an associated image used to convey the company's message. A brand, therefore, can be described as a combination of words and images, a promise and a meaning. Together these are said to represent both the tangible and intangible elements of a brand. See the table below, modified from Paul R. Smith et al. (2000).

These tangible and intangible aspects relate to the physical and emotional attributes of a brand. They add value to generic products and allow branded products to sell at higher prices than unbranded ones. A white T-shirt by the skateboarding brand Supreme, for example, is perceived to be of much better quality because of the message the brand conveys to its consumers: 'If you wear Supreme, you're one of us, you're a skater.' Consequently, Supreme is able to charge a much higher price for its white T-shirt than would be charged for an unbranded white T-shirt of the same quality. With the power of branding, Supreme is trying to sell a promise.

Below and opposite A T-shirt bearing the Supreme logo has a much greater significance than a plain white tee. Developed by skateboarders for skateboarders, the label has become a symbol of cult underground cool.

TANGIBLE AND INTANGIBLE COMPONENTS OF A BRAND

Tangible	Intangible
Product itself (entity)	Trust, reliability (perception)
Brand name	Added value
Brand mark	A promise or idea
Distinctive features	Point of difference

The tangible components of the brand

Tangible components are physical and measurable.

Entity (product or service) The first component is known as the entity. The term is used in place of the type of product or service the brand offers, such as supplier and retailer of skateboarding garments and accessories. But it also carries a legal inference and can in addition be used to refer to the potential market value and financial worth of the product or service.

Brand name The brand name, the second component, helps consumers to identify the products and differentiate them from their competitors. Brand names are discussed in more detail in the section on brand characteristics (see p. 32).

Brand mark The third component of a brand is the brand mark. This is the element of a brand that cannot be spoken; it can be a symbol, a design or a specific type or design of packaging.

Distinctive features The final tangible components are the distinctive features. A brand may have a very distinctive product or service, such as the denim brand G-Star RAW's use of heavy, riveted denim with industrial features, or its point of distinction may be an intangible component.

The intangible components of the brand

Intangible components must manifest themselves or be expressed in a set of tangible, physical features. Using the previous example of Supreme, a white T-shirt with the brand's logo is a tangible component, but the intangible sense of rebelliousness, of cool, of belonging to a niche cult of consumers may be part of the mood portrayed by the brand in its promotion.

Trust and reliability When the mark of a known or recognized brand is added to a garment, consumers perceive trust and reliability. The Supreme T-shirt, for example, is expected to be of high quality and able to withstand the rigours of skateboarding.

Added value Value is an important element of the intangible aspects of a brand. It satisfies the consumer both rationally and emotionally, making them believe that the brand will deliver like no other. As they shop for brands, consumers are believed to be fulfilling consumption values. These could be emotional (the desire for an experience, the desire to look cool) or functional (the practical use of the product).

Promise The promise of value from a brand implies that the values attributed to the brand by the consumer will be delivered.

Point of difference This relates to the way consumers perceive the brand in relation to others in its field. For example, associations such as the credibility of the founder that make Supreme a unique skateboarding label.

BRAND CHARACTERISTICS

The examination of the tangible and intangible features of a brand shows that these are some of the factors that brands can use to differentiate themselves from their competitors. To reinforce this, they must also establish distinct characteristics from other brands. When examining brand characteristics, it is common to look at what appears inside or is core to a brand, and what appears outside or adds to or augments a brand. Chris Fill (2013) supports the idea of intrinsic attributes – the functional features of the product itself (fit, cut, performance style, and so on) – in relation to extrinsic attributes, such as the marketing communications that shape consumer associations with the brand.

The Brand Characteristic Model given by John Egan (2015) expands on this thinking to visualize a brand as a halo around a product or service. Inside the halo are the core and the augmented aspects.

Core The core aspects of the brand include functional characteristics such as basic product/service, shape/texture, performance and physical capacity.

Augmented The augmented aspects include packaging/presentation, price and terms, guarantees, extras and after-sales support.

Halo The halo itself is that aspect of the brand that is portrayed to the outside world through marketing communications. It involves image management and the promotion of the positive brand associations the consumer will make. It is the halo characteristics that the consumers use to distinguish one brand from another.

Brand characteristics can also be referred to as the characteristics of what a brand actually does. Just as humans have job titles that can define us in society, so a brand should evoke a sense of association with the product it is manufacturing. This can be achieved with the name of the brand. Micael Dahlén et al. (2010) advise that brand names need not reflect the objectives of what the brand is manufacturing, but that some suggestion of the product may help the consumer to recall the brand. In the fashion industry, certainly, for luxury and premium labels the founder's name will evoke an important association with heritage or a catwalk designer. Dahlén et al. advise that, for originality, the brand name should be different from the category name (the product group in which the brand is competing), but that a metaphor can help to make strong associations. For example, Vivienne Westwood's sub-brand Anglomania may evoke the hedonistic spirit of clothing designed to make the wearer feel heroic in the 1980s, whereas the US jeans brand Not Your Daughter's Jeans (NYDJ) made practical use of the category of jeanswear to form a clear, distinctive characteristic.

JOHN EGAN'S BRAND CHARACTERISTIC MODEL

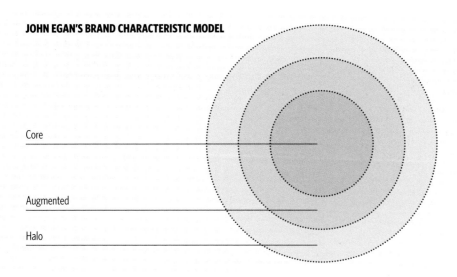

Core

Augmented

Halo

HAVAIANAS

The Brazilian shoe brand Havaianas has made a global connection with its rags-to-riches story of how a humble, government-price-controlled flip-flop, worn mostly by poor people, turned into a multi-billion-dollar global operation. The simple use of colour in the product, born of the Brazilians' penchant for turning their coloured flip-flop soles upwards, led to the development of the classic monochrome model. These worked phenomenally well in retail with the creation of merchandised walls of colour that inspired the consumer to buy into the brand. The product was relatively cheap, so lots of colour options were affordable. Havaianas is also a great example of a so-called national brand, which reflects positive aspects of the country of origin or association. In a collaboration between Havaianas and the New York-based brand Opening Ceremony, the Brazilian beach was brought to the city, giving the founders of Opening Ceremony the opportunity to create imagery that exploited the sun, sea and colour in an urban setting.

Below Opening Ceremony for Havaianas, 2013.

BRAND NARRATIVES: TELLING THE BRAND STORY

Another important reason consumers, retailers and marketers of brands engage with branding is the brand's narrative, or the story that informs the brand's reason for being. Narratives can draw on historical references or contemporary aspects of the brand's origins, or the reasons why it is of significance to the current market. This section argues that narrative should be an important consideration in creating a point of difference for a brand, and is a key part of conveying a brand's core aspects to the consumer.

Historical aspects of brand narratives have previously played an important, or even exclusive, part in luxury and premium fashion brands. For example, the use in its logo of a horse-drawn royal carriage by the French luxury house Hermès reinforces the story of its origins. Beginning life in 1837 as a saddlery in Paris, it earned a reputation for creating luxury harnesses and bridles for the nobility, and that led in 1900 to the introduction of the Haut à Courroies bag to carry saddles. The image of Hermès as a producer of impeccable-quality leather goods is thus rooted in its narrative as an artisan patronized by the aristocracy. Today, however, the contemporary aspects of brand narratives are gaining momentum and becoming of greater significance to both luxury and mainstream brands. They are conveyed as stories and can include a brand's attitude, its opinion on current lifestyle issues, its political stance and its inspirations or founding story.

Brand storytelling goes beyond the function of the product itself, opening up a connection with consumers and creating a sense of loyalty. In 2014 Christopher Bailey, chief creative and CEO of Burberry, explained with reference to building the brand in China that 'storytelling stops things from being [mere] products and starts to give it life.' Burberry itself has been able to draw on its own rich heritage. In a similar way to Hermès, its reputation as a high-quality producer of waterproof outerwear for explorers and aviators has been allied to the British reputation for fine tailored outerwear. The setting up of the Burberry Foundation, an organization that funds young people's creative ambitions and challenges, has been a large part of the translation of the brand's story for a new, younger audience. Brand narratives engage the consumer in a story that makes them want to buy as they start to identify themselves with the narrative of the brand.

There is no set formula for constructing a brand narrative, but the more credible or real the story the better the chance of connection with the target consumer, and – as will be discussed in more detail at the end of this chapter – the more chance the narrative will act as a foundation to inspire other promotional materials. Some success stories are given on the next page.

OBEY

The beginnings of Shepard Fairey's brand OBEY are not in branded clothing but in the highly credible world of street art. The brand originated in 1989, when Fairey began developing stencilled stickers of the American wrestler Andre the Giant, catching the attention of an underground following. The stickers were intended as a piece of 'non-sense', but Fairey noticed that placing them in public spaces usually given over to advertising or government signage had a certain power. Inspired by punk and skateboarding graphics, his work was also influenced by the Russian Constructivist movement and the conceptual artist Barbara Kruger, who juxtaposed text and images in meaningful ways, with dramatic use of colour. Fairey's Andre the Giant became more simplified, and included the word 'Obey', which appeared on posters from 1996. Sometimes misread as a piece of fascist indoctrination, the posters challenged the viewer's opinion of the mindless consumption that advertising promotes, and invited a questioning of their role. From this initial notoriety, OBEY grew into a clothing range from 2001, a graphic design agency and a vehicle for further art projects. Fairey continually produces public art, collaborates with other street artists and contributed the 'Hope' poster for Barack Obama's US presidential campaign in 2008. To wear OBEY is to buy into Fairey's ongoing narrative of challenge to society's dominant structures.

Narratives as straplines

Brand narratives can also inform brands' mission statements and straplines. For example, Nike's brand narrative is based on improving personal performance by hard work and tenacity, tapping into a globally held desire to be the best we possibly can be. Its strapline or slogan, 'Just Do It', implies that anyone can take this challenge, and that it's just a question of changing our behaviour and making the effort. Nike has continuously evolved all aspects of its branding in line with its story. The story of human potential in sport remains consistent throughout its brand elements, and in this way Nike keeps challenging its customers to connect with it.

Right Nike mission statement, used on campaign material and logo.

ONE TRUE SAXON

The British brand One True Saxon tapped into its target consumer's passion for the tribal nature of British football. Britain has a long tradition of connection between fashion brands and football, stemming from the continual qualification of Liverpool FC for the European Cup throughout the 1970s. Labels such as Lois, previously seen only on the continent, had found their way into British shops due to the demand created by returning fans. A rivalry exists between the north and south of England over who originated this sportswear-inspired casual look, the purist acquisition of brands from the north or the more diverse influences of the wealthier south. One True Saxon aligned itself with this story and inspired a cult following. It originally made its products available only in the north, maintaining that the north had the truly credible heritage, rather than the catwalk-driven south.

Right OBEY x Jamie Reid Be Reasonable Take It Tee, 2016. A collaboration between OBEY and Jamie Reid, a long-standing influence on Fairey and the artist behind some of the most iconic punk imagery.

Far right Shepard Fairey's OBEY project, Andre the Giant poster, post-1996.

BRAND PERSONALITY

The story of the brand with which people connect makes the purchase more 'personal' and says something about them as individuals. A brand's narrative is what helps people to define a brand for themselves, and to ascertain whether or not it belongs as part of their 'personal brand'. According to Laurence Vincent (2002), every brand should seek to establish a strong, well-drawn and promptly recognized persona. For the consumer, that persona conveys whether the brand is right for them to put on or adopt as part of the role or character they wish to portray in life. The persona is defined by attributes that express the brand's personality, such as determination, courage, honesty, flexibility and curiosity. It is to this that consumers relate and it is this that helps to create a long-lasting emotional bond with the consumers.

The idea of humanizing a brand is not a new one. In the field of brand personality, research has been conducted to attempt to align human personality traits with those of brands, in the expectation that potential consumers seek to recognize aspects of themselves in the brands they choose. As part of an extensive piece of research published in 1997, Jennifer Aaker measured the responses of 631 subjects to 37 brands against 114 human personality traits. She sought to examine the relationship between attitudes to brand personality and the big five human personality traits, which are:

- Extroversion.
- Agreeableness.
- Openness.
- Conscientiousness.
- Neuroticism.

She found that consumers perceived brands as having five distinct personality traits, and those have since become established as the main brand personality traits:

- Sincerity.
- Excitement.
- Competence.
- Sophistication.
- Ruggedness.

Aaker discovered that three traits could be considered in common, and these may directly strike a chord with the consumer when a brand represents itself as sincere (open or agreeable), exciting (extrovert) or competent (conscientious). Sophistication and ruggedness were perceived in brands although they are not among the big five human personality traits; however, the research suggested that humans may desire these traits and that they can therefore be used in marketing to provoke desire for a brand displaying these qualities.

Nicolai Schümann has brought a strong sense of planning from his native Germany to the development of an international fashion brand. He previously developed a strategy for BBC Global News mobile content, and at the engineering company ESAB he was responsible for growth, mergers and acquisitions across several regions and business channels. He became Founding Director of Alice's Pig in January 2013, creating the branding, finance and supply chain of the label, with his sister Amanda De Meleghy in charge of garment design. Although British in inspiration, growing from a love of *Alice in Wonderland* and a desire to experiment with colliding styles and cultures, Alice's Pig was designed to have internationally recognizable core values from the outset. The label now trades in over 15 international markets from its headquarters in Brixton, south London, with an additional office in Shanghai, China. This practitioner approach adds depth to the idea of establishing human qualities to form an emotional connection with brands.

Q: Do you believe that a brand can have 'human' characteristics that are transferable to an audience?
A: You should be able to perceive a brand as a person, one with its own varied personality; it helps tremendously with building all the stories around the brand – it is a good umbrella. The brand is not a product, it is more than that. I think it is important that the brand provide people with a certain lifestyle, and with a certain meaning. This is why we formed our brand almost as though we were creating a fictional character – we brought life to it.

Having profiled our customer, we used Carl Jung's archetype system, which is especially fruitful, since all 12 characteristics (Outlaw, Jester, Lover, Caregiver, Everyman, Innocent, Ruler, Sage, Magician, Hero, Creator and Explorer) are inherited in everybody around the world. If you have a good idea of what you want to convey as a brand, it is very helpful to know what archetypes your brand will represent. Often it is the combination of these archetypes that creates an interesting concept for a brand.

Barack Obama, for instance, is the Everyman but at the same time a Hero. He is somebody you could rely on, he is down to earth, but also he empowers people and encourages them to stand up and do something different, something heroic. I think it is important that you know and are aware of how your brand will help people, and if you use this archetype concept you already have very fertile ground in terms of how you want to be perceived. We chose the Explorer and the Jester for Alice's Pig: a desire to discover something different, a search for individual identity, but always with a sense of fun.

Q: Did anything else help you to establish a brand personality?
A: We carried out a word-association session to help visualize the whole personality of the brand: if it is a car it is an Alfa Romeo, if it is a book it is *Alice in Wonderland*, an element it is air, a film it is *Garden State*, an activity it is dancing, a piece of furniture it is a green velvet couch, and so on. It is tremendously helpful for internal purposes – you have a very clear picture of what the brand is about. I highly recommend everybody to carry out this association game. It helps when making decisions such as the tone of voice the brand conveys, which in our case is informal, jokey, edgy and imaginative.

Q: Where would you say the role of storytelling or brand narrative fits?
A: I hope we convey a message that people should do something different, and be themselves no matter what people say. The other thing is that it is important to be a bit funny, and that is why we include the jester. Many people lose their childlike curiosity as they grow up, but I think it is important to live a curious life and that people don't take themselves too seriously. Ultimately, however, the brand story is not what you say yourself – it's what people perceive about you.

In the development of our logo, a graphic designer took elements from the old John Tenniel illustrations for *Alice in Wonderland* and modernized them. The pig is inspired by an incident in the book, when the bad duchess is holding her crying baby and the baby transforms into a pig, which runs off into the forest. Alice says something along the lines of 'The nasty little baby has turned into a very pretty pig.' We liked the contrast, that there is beauty in everything, even a pig, that things are different from what they seem to be; it reflects the identity of the brand. In the fashion world it was different to put a pig in a logo – no one else has done it, to my knowledge. This feeds directly into our design principles: we want to add a surprising element in whatever we design. You should be brave and different in the fashion world to stand out.

Q: *How does this thinking translate into the marketing communications you carry out?*
A: We do a lot of content marketing. We have a super-visual website with witty captions that reflect the illustrative inspiration; we write a blog, run competitions and tell stories; and we make films and put them on YouTube. It is a whole mix, but it must remain consistent to the brand. We keep the core message consistent, with slight adjustments to style depending on the channel used. We cover all bases in terms of social media. We also carry out various projects, such as collaborating with illustrators

to celebrate 150 years of *Alice in Wonderland*. We gift to bloggers, and we work with about 50 bloggers a season. It is fascinating how audiences of 100,000 are being attracted by the democracy of young fashion bloggers. There is a huge power shift going on. We look at who is influencing the market and who is suitable for our brand ethos. We are wary of hitting the wrong target audience; to keep the brand intact, we target bloggers very precisely.

TONE OF VOICE

The ability of a brand to speak in a consistent tone of voice has become crucial now that brands need to be seen and heard across many different channels of communication. For a brand, tone of voice is the embodiment and expression of its personality and story across its own website, its press releases, its social media pages, its email communications with consumers and its customer service. Alice's Pig, for example, having developed such a clear personality, can put out all messages in its fun and playful way. Tone of voice is linked directly to establishing a narrative, and the passions or interests of the founders can also drive the tone of voice a brand will 'speak' in.

BRAND IDENTITY

In the same way that we distinguish ourselves to others by our name, our characteristics and our personality traits, brands evolve these facets into their products, their logos and trademarks and their marketing to define their identity and differentiate their products from those of their competitors.

Brand identity is a combination of tangible and intangible components, characteristics, narrative and the personality of the brand – a summary of all the qualities discussed so far. Strong brands stick very closely to their established identities, and their customers are crystal clear about what they are buying into. Some brands may even become identifiable by a logo or aspect of packaging alone.

Varying techniques, including moodboards and associated colour palettes, have been used to communicate brands to colleagues and to external customers. The use of logo design and colour to express identity should also be considered carefully.

1 Tiffany's little blue box defines the brand visually by packaging alone.

2 Fred Perry's famous 32-leaf laurel wreath logo is associated with both excellence in tennis and British subculture, following its uptake in the 1960s by the mod movement. A British tennis player famous in the 1930s, Perry diversified from playing the game into making sweatbands and later the polo T-shirt.

3 Fred Perry Kendrick Tipped Cuff canvas shoe. The brand identity is carried through into footwear, bags and accessories.

4 Fred Perry Re-Issue Pleated Pique tennis dress. As the range has expanded to include more fashionable items, Fred Perry has remained true to its brand identity.

5 The Original Twin-tipped Fred Perry shirt. The Pique shirt is a staple of the range.

Colour palettes

Colour is an effective, powerful and instantly recognizable medium for visual communications. Right is an example of student work set by Istituto Marangoni to BA (Hons) Fashion Business students showing the importance of identifying the core colours for a new category extension into lingerie for make-up brand Benefit. These fun and feminine colours then inform the intended identity across all the brand's communications.

Logos

A fashion brand logo can take the form of the company or brand name in a stylized typeface, such as Diesel's; it can be a designed symbol, such as the Nike swoosh; or it can be a combination of the two, such as the small C and large K used with the brand name in the Calvin Klein logo.

Logos are vital to help the consumer correctly recognize and recall the brand. According to Dahlén et al. (2010), techniques that work to make a brand distinctive, but not unnatural, include departures from symmetry, shown here in the Gas logo, and repetition of design elements. Dahlén et al. also support the power of natural, organic elements, such as plant life or depictions of animals, to help convey brand associations. The Timberland logo reflects the brand's origin as a supplier of boots, and ultimately clothing and accessories, for the outdoors. The registered trademark indicates that both devices used in the logo are registered to Timberland.

Colour is also important in a logo. Through the use of blue, Gas could be considered tranquil, forward-thinking, rational and innovative. Levi's use of red, however, is considered warm, emotional and social (Dahlén et al., 2010); yellow and white are fresh and pure, while green conveys nature, purple is regal and black suggests prominence and seriousness. Dahlén et al. also cite the work of Henderson, Giese and Cote (2004), who ranked the qualities of typefaces and how they could be combined to create different impressions. For instance, a *pleasing* effect such as that created by the Australian brand Braintree could use a natural or harmonious typeface that might include flourishes but should not be elaborate. An *engaging* logo, such as that used by Salvatore Ferragamo, can use an elaborate typeface or a natural one; it can incorporate some compression of the font but should not be too embellished. The different styles of writing the e and the r show the natural touch. A *reassuring* result, such as that used by Dior, should be harmonious and feature some flourishes but should not be elaborate. Finally, a *prominent* logotype, such as that used by Norse Projects, should emphasize weight above all other qualities and could be read as natural or harmonious.

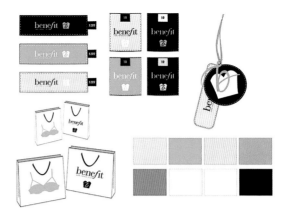

Above Brand moodboard by Fashion Business student Rea Dea Lilliard, 2015.

Diesel logo.

Timberland logo.

Braintree logo.

Nike 'swoosh'.

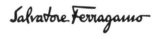

Ferragamo logo.

Gas logo.

CK logo.

Dior logo.

NORSE PROJECTS

Norse Projects logo.

THE BRAND IDENTITY PRISM

Getting the concept of their identity over to the consumer correctly is so important for brands that they must track and measure that this is happening. The strength of a brand's identity can be measured by brand managers to assess the brand's overall effectiveness. One way of measuring that strength is to use the brand identity prism as an analytical tool. Professor Jean-Noël Kapferer (2012) represents brand identity as a six-sided prism, each side of which represents one of the six aspects of brand identity.

Aspects of the brand identity prism

- *Physique* is the set of the brand's physical features, which are evoked in people's minds when the brand name is mentioned. According to Kapferer, this aspect must be considered the basis of the brand.
- *Personality*, or characteristics of the brand, can be communicated by using a specific style of writing or specific design features. A person can also be used to visualize the personality of a brand.
- *Culture* is the system of values and basic principles on which a brand has to base its behaviour (its products and communication). Many associations in this area are linked to the country of origin; Abercrombie & Fitch, for example, appeals to American values, and Chanel to French values.
- A brand can symbolize a certain *Relationship* between people. A brand manager must therefore express the relationship for which his/her brand stands. Emporio Armani, for example, differentiates itself from Armani Exchange by the price, quality and exclusivity of the product.
- *Reflection* (of the consumer) makes reference to the stereotypical user of the brand and is the source for consumer identification by the brand. In the case of Jack Wills, the ideal target market is described as university-based, fun-seeking, sporty 18-to-23-year-olds enjoying campus life, while the actual consumer group of this brand is much younger.
- *Self-image* is a mirror the target group holds up to itself. For instance, Lacoste users may see themselves as members of a sporty club, even if they do not actively play any sport.

The six aspects are then divided into four dimensions:
- The constructed sender or source (a visualization or picture of the brand, composed by the brand) versus the constructed recipient (a picture of the customer). The prism asks that the brand, as well as the consumer, be considered in the form of a person.

THE BRAND IDENTITY PRISM

The constructed source is a physique and personality; the constructed receiver is the typical buyer, who is imagined by the brand but is also a real person with their own self-image.
- Externalization versus internalization: a brand has social aspects that define its external expression (physique, relationship and reflection) and aspects that are incorporated into the brand itself (personality, culture and self-image).

Kapferer believes that strong brands are capable of weaving all aspects of the prism effectively into a whole in order to create a concise, clear and appealing brand identity. Using the dimensions to look at these aspects from both outside and inside the brand ensures that identity is assessed from a consumer's point of view and also internally. This enables a brand to establish its brand image (how the consumer sees the brand's tangible and intangible benefits), as opposed to the identity, which has been constructed by the brand. Ideally, these should match or be very close.

Brand managers can assess the strengths and weaknesses of their brand against each aspect of the prism; areas of weakness can then be worked on to establish a stronger identity. Because this involves assessing a consumer's self-image and relationship to the brand, it can also help to suggest ways of creating brand loyalty (where there will be repeat purchases). Ultimately, the stronger the brand identity the greater the resonance with target consumers, who should be more likely to buy, adding financial value to the brand.

Brand positioning

Another important consideration of the viewer's relationship to the brand is brand positioning. A positioning exercise helps the brand to analyse how viewers are likely to position the message alongside other brands in the market, and enables an examination of the competitors. For a brand, campaign objectives can also be about repositioning in the market (aiming at different consumers, introducing a sub-brand or new product category pitched at a higher level, and so on), so knowledge of the brand's existing positioning is essential. Brand positioning requires analysis of what the competitor brands are up to, awareness of which is vital in the fashion industry. In the run-up to Christmas 2015 in the UK, for example, it was unusual for a large department store or online fashion retailer not to have a memorable and visually striking TV advertising campaign, which meant that a TV ad became a force to consider.

Kevin Lane Keller (2008) proposed Points of Parity (POP) – investigating how the situation is similar to that of others – and Points of Difference (POD) – working out what the brand can do to be different – as tools to measure brand positioning. In the case of Christmas TV ads:

Points of Parity Viewers will expect a statement from large fashion brands of what Christmas means to the brand, and will wonder why it is missing from the Christmas campaign if one is not offered.

Points of Difference How can a brand make its message different from all the others? The messages in 2015 included:

- Nostalgic – yearning for the Christmases of childhood.
- Poignant – a reminder of the message of Christmas – not to forget old people, the lonely or the isolated.
- A fun-loving drink fest – a time for music, bold graphics and revelry.
- Personal identity – doing Christmas your way – anything goes.
- Identification of reality – playing on aspects we all recognize, such as receiving unwanted gifts.

Below House of Fraser's Christmas campaign 'Your Rules' (2015) gained plenty of editorial coverage. The retailer made the ad shoppable on its own site and included interviews with the singer and choreographer. The campaign prompted the creation of #YourRules and inspired over 100,000 likes on Twitter in the first week of its release.

BRANDING AND MARKETING COMMUNICATIONS

In fashion, branding is essential to marketing communications. The success of certain brands is due to effective brand communication with the consumers. Branding encourages consistency of the brand message, and following this through into marketing communications helps consumers to identify, recall, recognize, understand, feel affection for and maybe even love the brand.

A strong brand drives what is known in marketing terms as content marketing (see Chapters 6 and 7). High-quality content, such as moving or credible founding stories, a vibrant visual image or links to charitable concerns, can be used as a launch pad into all brand communications and, in highly competitive markets such as fashion, can play a key role in differentiating the brand.

For many fashion brands, editorial coverage in fashion magazines, influencers' social media feeds and blogs is the first step to spreading the story of what they do. PR-led campaigns like these will need a press release from the brand that communicates aspects such as inspirations, or the nature of the company/designer and its background. The inspiration behind fashion brands, which might include the founders' stories, the credibility of the creators, historical eras or even particular fabrics and colours,

can be used alongside more tangible attributes to brief photographers on the mood or ethos of the brand. This can translate into lookbook photographs to accompany a press release or even fashion-shoot coverage. The story of what a brand is about then feeds into campaign material. Ad campaigns from the flip-flop brand Havaianas, for example, burst with a riot of colour and tropical, often beachside, associations.

To summarize this thinking, we will examine the retail brand Cos for brand characteristics, brand personality and brand identity, and look at how this translates into marketing communications and the resulting brand image.

Cos (Collection of Style; owned by H&M) is perfectly positioned to reflect the growing interest in clean-lined, minimal Scandinavian design. In common with many high-street stores, Cos produces a range of affordable garments, accessories and footwear, and its identity is clearly reflected in its products, packaging, campaign material and selling environments. Launched in 2007, it is spreading in a careful, considered way all over the globe. Below we examine the brand using the qualities discussed in this chapter.

Tangible attributes Well-made garments with a high level of attention to detail, designed within a lifestyle concept rather than to follow high fashion. Updates are given to silhouettes, rather than offering wholly new styles each season. The clothes are presented in stripped-back, industrial shop interiors and via a clean e-commerce website. The drop-shadow design of the logo indicates the timeless, minimal ethos of the company, which is also reflected in the style of the photography.

Left Cos, Spring/Summer 2015 lookbook.   **Below** Havaianas ad campaign, 2015.

Intangible attributes The association with minimalism as a wider movement in architecture, interiors and furniture. The association with Scandinavia as a source of innovative design and garment cutting. The association with an 'intellectual', well-thought-out choice of garment design that is concerned with sculptural form over and above mindless consumption.

Characteristics Cos is functional, modernist, effortless and intelligent.

Personality Of the five brand personality traits, Cos is sincere, competent and sophisticated. As a human, Cos is confidently dressed and slightly serious, with minimal make-up and effortlessly good hair. S/he has well-informed opinions on the arts, design and society, and buys quality over quantity.

Tone of voice Informed, aware, conscious and willing to learn alongside the follower.

Identity expressed as marketing communications
Cos has constructed its colour palette, products, retail experience, logo and marketing to reflect its cool, minimal identity. It communicates with its customers primarily through lookbook photographs, which are sculptural and reflect a minimal architectural aesthetic. Through its social media, magazine-style blog and newsletters, followers are made to feel part of an artistic community via curated music collections and pieces on forthcoming exhibitions and icons of furniture and architectural design.

Brand image Cos customers feel a sense that this is right for the time. They appreciate that the garments can be mistaken for those of fellow Swedish brand Acne, Jil Sander or even Céline, i.e. those of much more expensive labels. They also appreciate that these styles will not date and need not be replaced every season. The brand image is nearly identical to the identity.

The role of fashion promotion is to communicate the brand identity and provide continuity in building the relationship between brand and consumer. Once a clear brand identity has been established and measured, the brand is ready to consider how it may best be promoted. This can be through PR, advertising or direct marketing, or through sales promotion techniques and selling techniques, or more likely a combination of some or all of these. Brand managers can then consider how the brand can be best represented in online and offline communications. Throughout this book we will explore and understand the importance of enhancing and building brands through carefully selected, integrated fashion communication campaigns.

REFERENCES

Aaker, Jennifer L., 'Dimensions of Brand Personality', *Journal of Marketing Research*, 34/3 (August 1997), p. 347

Dahlén, Micael, Fredrik Lange and Terry Smith, *Marketing Communications: A Brand Narrative Approach*, Wiley 2010

Egan, John, *Marketing Communications*, 2nd ed., Sage 2015

Fill, Chris, *Marketing Communications: Brands, Experiences and Participation*, 6th ed., Pearson 2013

Harilela, Divia, 'Storytelling Key to Burberry's China Strategy, Says Christopher Bailey', 26/4 (April 2014), www.businessoffashion.com/articles/global-currents/storytelling-key-burberrys-china-strategy

Kapferer, Jean-Noël, *The New Strategic Brand Management: Advanced Insights and Strategic Thinking*, Kogan Page 2012

Keller, Kevin Lane, Tony Apéria and Mats Georgson, *Strategic Brand Management: A European Perspective*, 2nd ed., FT Prentice Hall 2011

Roberts, Kevin, and A.G. Lafley, *Lovemarks: The Future Beyond Brands*, Powerhouse Books 2008

Smith, Paul R., Chris Berry and Alan Pulford, *Strategic Marketing Communications*, Kogan Page 2000

Vincent, Laurence, *Legendary Brands: Unleashing the Power of Storytelling to Create a Winning Market Strategy*, Dearborn Trade Publishing 2002

FURTHER READING

Hameide, Kaled K., *Fashion Branding Unraveled*, Fairchild 2011

Herskovitz, Stephen, and Malcolm Crystal, 'The Essential Brand Persona: Storytelling and Branding', *Journal of Business Strategy*, 31/3 (March 2010), pp. 21–28

Woodside, Arch G., Suresh Sood and Kenneth E. Miller, 'When Consumers and Brands Talk: Storytelling Theory and Research in Psychology and Marketing', *Psychology & Marketing*, 25/2 (February 2008), pp. 97–145

DISCUSSION

Think of one or two fashion brands and consider the following:

What are its tangible and intangible components?

What is a suitable tone of voice for this brand?

What is the brand's story, and how is this conveyed by the brand's marketing activities?

Chapter 3
INTEGRATED MARKETING COMMUNICATIONS

How can a brand create a successful promotional campaign? Find out how to:

- Use the six Ps of marketing
- Employ the communication tools, from social media to personal selling, available to marketers
- Choose Integrated Marketing Communications (IMC), by which all forms of communication and media are linked carefully together to offer a concise and effective message to the consumer
- Use the SMART model to choose campaign objectives that will optimize an integrated marketing campaign

PROMOTION AND COMMUNICATION AS PART OF THE SIX Ps

This book focuses on promotion as a specific element of the 'six Ps' of marketing. These were developed during the 1940s and 1950s and originally formalized in the early 1960s as the four Ps. This was during a time of mass consumerism, when it was necessary to market product-led features to the consumer.

The four original Ps were:
- Product – what form the product or service will take.
- Price – how much it will sell for.
- Promotion – what materials must be used to reach the consumer and how they will be used.
- Place – where and through what channels the product will be sold.

In recent years the four Ps have expanded to become six, to encompass more consumer-centric issues such as how the consumer perceives the brand and how they are influenced by it. Patrick De Pelsmacker (2007) defines the process of marketing and offers in table form (below) what he refers to as the 'instruments of the marketing mix':

Marketing is the process of planning and executing the conception, pricing, promotion and distribution of ideas, goods and services to create and exchange value, and satisfy individual and organizational objectives.

The two Ps added to De Pelsmacker's table are People and Persuasion.

In the context of the marketing mix, promotion covers all aspects of how a brand or retailer communicates its intentions to the target consumer; how a brand tempts customers with incentives to buy; how it advertises; what events it carries out; what celebrities it uses to endorse the brand; how the products are sold to the customer; and how and where the customer can read about, interact with or get involved with the brand. These promotional tools are referred to as the promotional mix, or what we also refer to in this book as the marketing communications mix.

Marketing communication involves all or some of the following:
- Advertising.
- PR, endorsement and sponsorship.
- Social media.
- Personal selling through online and offline retail.
- Direct marketing.
- Fashion catwalk and/or trade shows.
- Sales promotions.

These are carried out using a mix of digital and traditional media, which the company or brand can use to communicate with its target customers in order to promote the product and the brand or company as a whole. The elements, or tools, of the communications mix are introduced in the next section. Then we will move on to a chapter-by-chapter discussion of each tool and its current uses in the fashion industry.

PATRICK DE PELSMACKER'S INSTRUMENTS OF THE MARKETING MIX

Product	Price	Place	Promotion	People	Persuasion
Benefits	List price	Channels	Advertising	Employees	Element that will change consumer behaviour or attitude
Features	Discounts	Logistics	Public relations	Stakeholders	
Options	Credit terms	Inventory	Sponsorship	Management	Advantage over similar brands
Quality	Payment periods	Transport	Sales Promotion	Customer-facing staff	
Design	Incentives	Assortments	Direct marketing		
Branding		Locations	Point of Purchase	Culture of the company	
Packaging			Exhibitions and trade fairs		
Services			Personal selling		
Warranties			Online/offline		

THE TOOLS OF THE MARKETING COMMUNICATIONS MIX

The tools available to marketers include advertising, PR, social media, personal selling, direct marketing, trade shows and sales promotions.

Fashion advertising

In fashion, advertising is an extremely powerful and persuasive force. It uses paid-for mass media to broadcast the message, such as TV, cinema, radio, newspapers, magazines, billboards, online advertising and the social media sites where it is possible to advertise. It is the paid-for element that makes advertising distinct from other methods of communication. Advertising is considered to be mass communication, since it is broadcast to a mass audience. Depending on budget or the desire to make a great impact, brands may select one or more of the available advertising media.

Public relations for fashion, endorsement and sponsorship

In fashion, PR is considered the most credible tool of communication because its defining feature is that of third-party endorsement. Unlike advertising, PR is not paid for. Instead, it is designed to appear as if a fashion editor, celebrity or TV or film director has discovered or chosen the product to write about, be photographed in or feature in a popular film or series. Successful PR for fashion brands can include editorial coverage in a magazine; a review on a third-party blog; use of the brand's products in a magazine's fashion shoot; news coverage of the brand's campaign; a buzz or report about an event the brand has staged; or a celebrity endorsement deal. Similar to advertising, PR is considered an impersonal form of mass communication, but one that does provide more opportunities with which the consumer can interact, such as an online conversation with a blogger.

Fashion PR is concerned primarily with giving the press newsworthy information, such as details of new collections, shows, new store openings or even the appointment of a new creative director. PR can be generated by the distribution of seasonal lookbooks (brand-generated product information, usually in the form of a booklet), press releases or invitations for selected editors, journalists or bloggers to fashion shows or other events.

Celebrities bridge the gap between PR (when they are given branded products to wear) and contractual endorsement agreements, when brands sign them to appear in campaigns or at events, or to co-produce

Above Lacoste, Spring 2014, still from the film *The Big Leap* (produced by Seb Edwards), featuring the French actor Paul Hamy taking a leap of faith that represented overcoming a fear of commitment. The film was first aired on French TV to coincide with the opening of the Winter Olympics in Sochi, Russia, during which the French athletes wore Lacoste.

Below Lacoste, Spring 2014, *Life is a Beautiful Sport*. The film was at the heart of a wider billboard and print campaign shot by the photographer Jacob Sutton and featuring the models Kati Nescher and Roch Barbot confidently striding high above urban landscapes.

Left Christopher Kane's Spring/Summer 2016 collection made bold, graphic use of panels in primary colours, contrasting with fluid fringing.

Above The theme of the collection, 'Crash and Repair', inspired a similarly striking ad campaign – the first for the brand – shot by the photographer Hayley Weir and featuring the model Alice Buckingham.

ranges. Through this latter arrangement, a celebrity is said to be 'endorsing' or acting as an 'ambassador' for a brand. Sponsorship agreements work in a similar way: two companies agree to sign a contract for mutual benefit, such as increased exposure. Product placement in TV programmes and films puts the brand on or around lead characters. The film *The Devil Wears Prada* (2006) contained more than 21 instances of product placement, including references to Calvin Klein, Chanel, Dolce & Gabbana, Dior, Fendi, Hermès, Jimmy Choo and Manolo Blahnik.

PR employees also deal with crisis management. In the fashion industry, this can include negative press about allegations of drug use in the industry, the use of size zero models or the firing of creative directors. It is the job of the PR professional to issue counter-statements that show the brand in a more positive light.

It is very much part of the PR remit to establish relationships with style influencers and bloggers and encourage them to post favourable reviews of products and brands. Bloggers, particularly those who have demonstrated their influence on contemporary fashion by becoming brand ambassadors themselves, have become powerful in the fashion industry, and are considered credible experts in their own right. It is also important to identify style influencers who may not blog but who have built credible profiles through large followings on social media, especially for brands that wish to connect to younger, centennial audiences.

Social media

Previously part of the PR remit, social media is increasingly considered a marketing-communication art form in its own right. Social media has gained momentum among fashion brands as a method of promoting themselves in a more personal way in a forum that audiences have created themselves, where they are happy to like, share and exchange views. Brands that have their own pages on social media use them for content that will involve and engage followers in branded activities.

For more than 120 years Barbour has been designing clothes that offer protection in the harshest environments. Their Heritage of Adventure range was inspired by this history, and a campaign built on the theme. Barbour posted an inspirational video, created and seeded by the communications agency Cult LDN and featuring the photographer (and Adventurer of the Year) Sean Conway. His search for the perfect photo in the hills of the English Lake District was designed to get potential contributors to take action. Followers were invited to submit via Twitter or Instagram photos or videos of their own adventures in the great outdoors, with the best entry winning £500 of merchandise. Over 800 entries contributed to the campaign content, generating 8 million impressions alongside a substantial rise in e-commerce sales. The use of social media is inspiring brands to create ever more inventive ways to engage with their followers and to drive sales.

Offline and online personal selling

Successful personal selling comes from having well-trained and enthusiastic staff to give consumers the right information about the product or brand in order to motivate them to buy. The defining point about personal selling is that it is a one-to-one activity, either to another business or to the end consumer. It has the advantage that information can be tailored to suit the requirements of the end user; this can mean adjusting order quantities, arranging deliveries in timed drops through the season, or simply providing additional information. The rise of e-commerce means that brands and retailers must consider the consumer's journey carefully when he or she is engaging with their landing and shopping pages, apps and customer services.

Direct marketing

Direct marketing is a personal communication that is intended to engage with the customer individually. Central to this tool is the purchase or use of a database of targeted consumer contacts. Increasingly, this form of communication can be targeted to an individual customer, as improved methods of capturing online behaviour mean that information can be sent to customers based on previous interest in new lines, discounted lines, events or activities. Direct marketing is often used in conjunction with sales promotion to advise consumers of offers, and can also take the form of printed catalogues or invitations sent to a home address, or e-newsletters and emails.

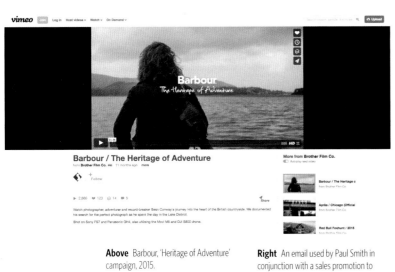

Above Barbour, 'Heritage of Adventure' campaign, 2015.

Right An email used by Paul Smith in conjunction with a sales promotion to advise a customer of a period of free shipping. The act of clicking through from this email can be tracked by the brand, and suggests a future interest in this type of incentive.

Fashion and trade shows

Fashion shows are essential in the fashion industry to create publicity and awareness, and also to keep the brand in the limelight in order to gain new customers and retain existing ones. International fashion weeks are used by luxury and premium designer brands that have the budget to show on the catwalk. Catwalk shows act as a preview for the fashion press, valued individual customers of the designer and store buyers. Their purpose is to generate publicity and orders for the range, which is then manufactured. Trade fairs are generally static exhibitions of seasonal product ranges, and are used by premium and mass-market brands. Their purpose is to create a forum for business-to-business selling between brands and interested store buyers.

Sales promotions and retail point of sale

In fashion, promotions are often used to increase sales. The most familiar form of promotion is a discounted price offer. These are used most by high-street fashion brands and in the beauty industry, although upper-end independent shops and designer brands are now feeling the pressure to start discounting earlier in the selling seasons. Promotions include all forms of incentive to buy; they can be used to introduce the consumer to new products through trials or free samples, or to increase sales by using bundle pricing, such as two for the price of one. Sales promotions can also be used to reward customers for repeated purchases, through loyalty cards. Improved methods of consumer data capture mean that promotions can be targeted specifically to an individual's shopping habits.

Retail point of sale refers to the communications at the point of purchase in the store. Branded items such as banners, posters, showcards and shelf dividers are used to separate different brands or product lines in store, and are referred to as point-of-sale materials or POS. Other point-of-sale elements could be postcards, branded lookbooks, branded carrier bags and stickers. Later we will look at the wider retail environment of merchandise presentation and store layout (see p. 153).

The communication tools that are selected depend on the message the brand wants to convey, the nature of the campaign and the budget. The selection also depends on the objectives of the message; for example, the message could be personal (which would dictate the use of personal communications such as direct marketing or personal selling), or its aim could be to raise general awareness of the brand, in which case advertising would be a quick-acting and effective choice. A successful marketing communication campaign requires the 'pick and mix' of tools that complement one another but fulfil different tasks. We will now examine integration as a concept, and then look at how to set objectives to achieve the best promotional campaign plan.

Above Constant discounting on UK high streets has led consumers to expect price reductions. Designer ranges and small independents can struggle to compete with the very short full-price selling seasons of large retailers.

Above Sales promotion also includes sales incentives such as this Charles Tyrwhitt discount , which forms a different kind of feel-good relationship with the customer.

Above Gap, Via del Corso, Rome, 2011. The US retail giant Gap is expert at placing visuals and graphics raised up above blocks of merchandise. These act as sight lines through the store, guiding shoppers to the various product lines.

DEFINITIONS OF INTEGRATED MARKETING COMMUNICATIONS

Generally speaking, the concept of integrating the elements of the communications mix involves, for marketers, matching the message they would like to broadcast to a suitable form of media. It is still accepted that exposure to messages via several media is more effective than repetition through one media channel.

According to Dahlén et al. (2010), the message becomes the focus when multiple channels are used:

> The employment of several media, and indeed several elements of the marketing communications mix, is often referred to as integrated marketing communications (IMC). An IMC approach needs to coordinate all brand encounters, medium or message, which contribute to building the brand narrative.

Fashion brands have traditionally been very good at considering how their image appears across different elements of the marketing communications mix. Integration has been practised for years by good marketers without being labelled or pigeonholed as IMC.

A more detailed definition of IMC is given by the American Association of Advertising Agencies:

> A concept of marketing communication planning that recognizes the added value of a comprehensive plan that evaluates the strategic roles of a variety of communication disciplines, e.g. general advertising, direct response, sales promotion and public relations – and combines these disciplines to provide clarity, consistency and maximum communication impact.

Current thinking on IMC recognizes the importance of a personalized approach to the customer's experience in terms of communications, and seeks to incorporate elements such as direct marketing and social media that involve and engage the viewer. The use of technology, in particular consumer-driven databases, has enabled greater interaction with the consumer as well as measurement of feedback to marketing communications.

In the next section, we look at a practitioner who pushes the concept of IMC further because of his main aim: to consider the role of the consumer in a technology-based campaign.

Above Between 1998 and 2001 the Dutch designer and art director Boy Bastiaens redesigned Pepe Jeans London's identity. The brief was to create a family of innovative packaging, branding materials, retail display items and point-of-sale material. These were to be used in store, in the environment, in print and on Pepe's website. Attention was given to even the smallest element of branding.

Below Billboards, posters and even retail shelves were placed in unlikely and often visually chaotic situations. Printed packaging pioneered the use of non-recognition photography, where the focus is on the product rather than the model's appearance. Lookbooks included artists' thoughts on what denim and the brand meant to them. The concept of 'new' was delivered using cool, industrial, cutting-edge yet fun and immersive objects and imagery.

In February 2013 Justin Cooke, as Topshop's new Chief Marketing Officer, unveiled 'The Future of the Fashion Show', his ambitious digital campaign in partnership with Google. The project showcased Topshop's appearance with its catwalk-level sub-brand Topshop Unique at London Fashion Week.

Cooke came to Topshop after six years at Burberry, where he was the worldwide PR/VIP Events Executive. His previous innovative projects for Burberry had included 'The Art of the Trench' and 'Retail Theatre'. His aim with 'The Future of the Fashion Show' was to match the digitally super-engaged customer – already active on social media channels while out shopping – to a similar experience whereby they could engage with communications used as part of a campaign. He began the process by examining the successful types of media used to broadcast past fashion shows and looking at the suite of interactive communication tools now available, before moving on to develop an exciting, interactive experience.

Topshop, a much-loved high-street brand in the UK, also has flagship stores in New York, Chicago, Las Vegas and Los Angeles, and a

further 137 international franchises. 'The Future of the Fashion Show' democratized the fashion show by providing the online viewer with a front-row experience. They had the chance to get involved by customizing products and making a buyer's selection from the catwalk, commenting on the show, chatting with its stars or viewing the catwalk from a model's perspective. According to Mashable.com, over 2 million people in 100 countries watched the show live, resulting in 200,000 social media shares on Google+, Facebook, Twitter, Pinterest, Instagram and Tumblr during the first five minutes of the show.

Running over three days, the project was designed to feature the fashion show using the functions and special features of Google+, combined with other social media platforms, and Topshop's online and physical selling environments. Three days before the show, Topshop and Google+ installed a 'Be the Model' photobooth in Topshop's flagship store on Oxford Circus, London, allowing customers to pose in outfits and share animated GIFs with friends. Two days before the show, videos of the preparations were broadcast on YouTube, and

Below Topshop's 'The Future of the Fashion Show', in collaboration with Google+.

Right A 'Be the Model' photobooth created animated GIFs for users to share on social networks.

bloggers and fans were invited to contribute to a Google+ hangout (where multiple users can contribute to a video stream in real time) with Topshop's creative director and the design team.

Just before the show, Topshop broadcast the hangout chats between bloggers and also clips of celebrities on their way to the show. The show was streamed live on Topshop's website, on its Google+ page, on Twitter and on a giant screen in the Oxford Circus store. Viewers were given a model's-eye view broadcast through micro-cameras fitted to the garments and accessories. In partnership with Facebook, users could customize certain items, order them and be alerted when their order was due. They could download music used in the show from iTunes and shop for the make-up the models were wearing. According to Cooke, sales of make-up were phenomenal, and some of the customizable outfits sold out before the show had finished. The winner of a Twitter-based 'tweet-off' review competition won tickets for the next season's Topshop show.

After the show customers were invited to 'Be the Buyer' using a Google+ custom app, which let them take swipeable versions of catwalk clips and put them into wish-list ranges of what they would most like to see in-store. This later enabled Topshop's buyers to view valuable data about items of interest from the catwalk.

It is hard to analyse if this was deliberate use of integrated marketing communications. The campaign was certainly one of many initiatives that Topshop has since taken to democratize the fashion industry for its followers. In line with the observation from Victoria Loomes at trendwatching.com (see pp. 22–24), it invited its shoppers to learn and be part of how the fashion industry works. Cooke himself cites disruption to the normal as his main source of inspiration. The seamless use of technology, however, the use of various social media platforms to their full potential, the synergy between an event, selling environments and social media, the high cross-cultural levels of consumer engagement and interactive, personalized content appears to be IMC in a nutshell.

THE FUTURE OF INTEGRATED MARKETING COMMUNICATIONS

The challenge for marketers and promoters of fashion is how to develop the latest thinking in IMC into a formula that is useful when planning a campaign. The case study from Topshop introduces the term synergy. Synergy is in fact one of the two important values in the marketing communications mix; the other is consistency.

Consistency

The term consistency recognizes that a brand's marketing mix, as well as its communications mix, should be integrated. This means that all the marketing (elements of the six Ps) and communications mixes must have the same aim if they are to be effective.

Synergy

Justin Cooke's use of an event with the sales environment, various social media platforms and specialist apps shows an incorporation of Topshop's key desire to involve consumers in communications in the way they were already liking and sharing items while shopping. The use of all tools jointly reinforced this aim, resulting in high levels of synergy.

Disruption

Cooke cites another important concept as being central to 'The Future of the Fashion Show', that of disruption. He claims that technology he had seen at London's Science Museum inspired the micro-cameras on the models' outfits, demonstrating an awareness of much wider sources of inspiration than just the fashion industry. The full-service advertising agency TBWA also cites disruption as key to the early discussion of the client's brief, defining it as 'the art of asking better questions, challenging conventional wisdom and overturning assumptions and prejudices that get in the way of imagining new possibilities and visionary ideas' (TBWA.com, 2015).

Alex Hesz (2015) defines disruption as different from newness or innovation; it should contain a genuinely unexpected principle, a fresh approach to how an audience can converse with, buy from or get involved with a brand. Opening up a channel of conversation between Topshop followers and the brand's creative director might appear illogical and unproven in its success, but it genuinely disrupted normal behaviour in the general course of purchasing clothing. At the marketing and promotional level, a disruptive element, often enabled by technology, may lend a touch of Cooke's magic to a campaign.

A FRAMEWORK FOR A PROMOTIONAL CAMPAIGN

This checklist is useful for promoters when planning an effective campaign, and is based on the latest discussions of IMC theory.

Synergy Does each method of communication and media selected provide an interesting and immersive experience in itself and also reflect the brand's core message across all the channels used?

Technology Is technology used both to engage and involve the audience and to measure reactions, degree of integration and feedback? Is technology also used to enable cost savings and lessen reliance on traditional media? Does its use link to a disruptive experience?

Disruption Is there an element within the campaign – an experience, new knowledge, a buzz – that is genuinely unexpected and disrupts the way an audience would normally behave?

Consistency Is there a consistent, cohesive message across selected suitable communication channels that works to support the brand's marketing strategy?

Continuity Can the selected communications deliver these experiences reliably?

In each chapter of this book relating to the communication instruments, the use of these IMC factors will be noted and attention drawn to the combination of communication tools used in a particular campaign.

SETTING OBJECTIVES AND THE SMART MODEL

Having established a definition of the communication tools and examined IMC, which suggests that there is an ongoing value in combining the tools and the media through which they are broadcast, it is also essential to establish how objectives for a campaign are set. These objectives will determine the choice of the communications mix and media. Marketing and communications objectives are developed from the main corporate objectives of the company or of the brand. The overall corporate objectives are generally long-term, whereas marketing and communications objectives are short-term and tactical.

Marketing and communications objectives

Currently the SMART model is the best-known of the available frameworks for setting objectives:

- Ⓢ Specific
- Ⓜ Measurable
- Ⓐ Achievable
- Ⓡ Realistic
- Ⓣ Time-related

This model states that objectives must be thought through carefully; they must be very *specific* as to what is intended to be achieved. They must also be *measurable*, to allow improvements and harness results. Objectives must be both *achievable* and *realistic* within a given *time* constraint.

Above The British casualwear brand Firetrap was launched in 1991 to near-perfect marketing-mix conditions. The holding company WDT (World Design & Trade) used extensive research from retailers of brands it had previously owned and distributed to create favourable marketing conditions for Firetrap. Having a clear, existing target market shaped the look of the promotion, which has remained consistent for more than two decades.

AIDA AND DAGMAR

Theoretical tools exist to help match the outcome of the set objectives with the selection of a communication strategy. Paul R. Smith and Ze Zook (2016) list the AIDA (Attention, Interest, Desire, Action) model, a concept believed to have been formalized by Edward Strong in 1925, alongside the DAGMAR (Defining Advertising Goals for Measuring Advertising Responses) model, developed by Russel H. Colley in 1961. Planners can use either model to help suggest types of communication.

If, for example, the desire is to raise interest (AIDA) or comprehension (DAGMAR) then PR, product placement, sponsorship and social media are the suggested tools.

AIDA AND DAGMAR AND IMPLIED SUGGESTIONS FOR TYPES OF COMMUNICATION

AIDA	DAGMAR	Suggested strategy for communications
---	Unawareness	—
Attention	Awareness	Advertising, PR, celebrity endorsement
Interest	Comprehension	PR, product placement, sponsorship, social media
Desire	Conviction	PR, product placement, sponsorship, direct marketing, sales promotion, social media
Action	Action	Sales promotion, direct marketing, personal selling

USING THE SMART MODEL TO SET OBJECTIVES FOR A COMMUNICATIONS PLAN

MARKETING COMMUNICATIONS PLAN

for Head, Heart and Base.

Left Louisa Clayden's 'Head, Heart and Base' idea for selling solid perfumes and oils online: the customer could mix their own scents from a menu of ingredients. Image by Seamless.

Second-year students on the BA (Hons) Fashion Retail Management and Fashion Marketing and Business Management courses at London Metropolitan University were set the challenge of developing a communications mix for final-year business start-up students.

Final-year student Louisa Clayden took the opportunity, while working part-time in retail with perfume and scented products, to research the market by questioning customers. She discovered a gap in the market for personalized, handbag-sized, non-spill perfumes made from plant extracts with no chemical additives, at an affordable price. She developed solid perfumes with the brand name Head, Heart and Base. Because initial retail would be online, she planned to make small samples available to shoppers before they committed to a larger

Below A Gantt chart by Seamless showing the objectives for Head, Heart and Base plotted on a timeline of events. The control element shows how each objective will be evidenced.

pot. To combat the fact that consumers would not be able to create their own products online using their sense of smell, she planned workshops both to educate the customer and to promote the product.

Second-year students Pauline Goetz and Anna Szymanska, as communications agency Seamless, developed the objectives for a suitable communications plan.

PR objectives

Objective 1: Begin a blog on the Head, Heart and Base website to be updated daily. The blog will be used to drive traffic to sign up to the website, then to promote the workshops.

COMMUNICATIONS PLAN FOR HEAD, HEART AND BASE

SUMMARY OF OBJECTIVES	APRIL	MAY	JUNE	JULY	AUGUST	SEPTEMBER	OCTOBER	NOVEMBER	DECEMBER	JANUARY	FEBRUARY	CONTROL
1 BEGIN BLOG	Create blog news posts of launch	Begin promoting subscriptions to site		Inform readers about workshop	Showcase photos and videos from the event	Start a conversation with followers about the forthcoming campaign	Experiences from the interview with the founder	Inform readers about new Christmas products	Christmas discount news	Valentine's Day products	Valentine's Day discounts	Blog to be updated daily to achieve five subscribers a month to the site and link to social media sites. Fifteen anticipated subscribers from first workshop.
2 GIFT TO EXTERNAL BLOGGERS												Gift samples to 20 external bloggers over four months with the aim of achieving seven social media and/or blog posts.
3 ORGANIZE THE WORKSHOP EVENT			Plan venue and organization	Carry out seven hour-long scent-mixing tutorials								Seven workshops aiming to attract five invited visitors each. Film and photograph event. Sell products.
4 OBTAIN EDITORIAL COVERAGE THROUGH AN INTERVIEW						Interview with *Made in Shoreditch* magazine						Interview with a creative magazine to boost social media followers by 100 on Facebook, 20 on Instagram and 20 more subscribers to the site.
5 COMPILE DATABASE			Email regarding workshops					Email regarding Christmas discount vouchers				Compile database of a target of 100 subscribers initially for mailshots.
6 SET UP AND MAINTAIN SOCIAL MEDIA PAGES	Set up and post initial images	Daily posts regarding scents, experiences, images					Instagram to promote new Christmas products					Post daily on Twitter, Facebook and Instagram. Use Instagram for discount news. Aim to reach 300 followers.
7 DISCOUNT VOUCHER CODES									Christmas discounts		Valentine's Day discounts	Limited but welcome discounts at key times of the year to increase sales by 20 per cent.

Objective 2: Send gift samples to establish relationships with 20 external bloggers over four months.

Objective 3: Organize the workshop events of seven sessions over four days. Use event photos to fuel the blog and social media feeds, and invite user-generated content.

Objective 4: In month six, achieve editorial coverage in a magazine that is sympathetic to creatives, such as *Made In Shoreditch*.

Direct marketing objectives
Objective 5: Ensure the website is able to capture data in order to build a database of subscribers who can be targeted with news of events and promotions.

Social media objectives
Objective 6: Ensure in month one that business accounts are set up with Twitter, Instagram and Facebook. Update daily, featuring visuals, or thoughts and opinions on scents and seasonal teasers.

Sales promotion objectives
Objective 7: In month nine, release discount codes to all subscribers for Christmas buys. A similar promotion can run for Valentine's Day.

These objectives are specific, detailing exactly which element of communication will be used and how. By stating in the control section of the Gantt chart (left) how these objectives will be evidenced, the objectives are then made measureable. By plotting an order of events, the objectives are made achievable within a certain time frame. All these objectives are realistic for a small-budget business start-up, since they concentrate on free and low-cost ideas. Anticipated target numbers are given each time, reflecting a slow, realistic, organic build-up of interested customers. Finally, the objectives are planned out visually over the year, giving an at-a-glance picture of how and when communications objectives may need to be reviewed.

As well as an example of SMART objective setting, the planned launch campaign is consistent in the way it is formed from the marketing plan. The suggested tools all link together to inform one another and work towards launching a start-up, demonstrating a synergy. Technology is used across social media and blogging platforms, but could in time extend to the digital scent technology that is now being developed, to make it possible to convey smell online. This could provide a future element of disruption. Continuity could easily be maintained through monitoring customer experience and generating further imagery, comment and experiences associated with smell. This is a great example to look at when planning the creative and budget elements of a communication campaign. The issues specific to each tool of the communications mix are discussed in the following chapters.

REFERENCES

Dahlén, Micael, Fredrik Lange and Terry Smith, *Marketing Communications: A Brand Narrative Approach*, Wiley 2010

De Pelsmacker, Patrick, Maggie Geuens and Joeri Van den Bergh, *Marketing Communications: A European Perspective*, 4th ed., Pearson 2007

Hesz, Alex, 'The Essay: Beyond the Myths – What Disruption Looks Like', *Marketing*, 1 July 2015, p. 1

Marketing communications definition, Thedma.org (2016), thedma.org/membership/member-groups-communities/integrated-marketing-community/integrated-marketing-definitions/

Smith, Paul Russell and Zook, Ze, *Marketing Communications: Offline and Online Integration, Engagement and Analytics*, 6th edition, Kogan Page 2016

TBWA.com, 'Disruption', accessed 8 June 2015, www.tbwa-london.com/about/disruption

FURTHER READING

Abnett, Kate, '6 Reasons the British High Street Is Struggling', 22 January 2016, www.businessoffashion.com/articles/intelligence/6-reasons-the-british-high-street-is-struggling

Allchin, Josie, 'Topshop CMO: Marketing Industry Needs Disruption', *Marketing Week*, 28 June 2013, p. 4

Diaz, Anne-Christine, 'Topshop Raises Digital Bar in Fashion World', *Advertising Age*, 84/9 (6 March 2013), p. 18, www.adage.com/article/cmo-interviews/topshop-raises-digital-bar-fashion-world/240100

Grant, Jules, 'Firetrap Restates Cred in "Deadly Denim" Ad Campaign', *Campaign*, 25 June 2004, www.campaignlive.co.uk/article/214727/firetrap-restates-cred-deadly-denim-ad-campaign

Hill, Adam, 'Client View: Justin Cooke: Fashioning the Ideal Digital Strategy', *PR Week*, 21 November 2012, www.prweek.com/article/1159282/client-view-justin-cooke-topshop-fashioning-ideal-digital-strategy

Mullany, Anjali, 'How Google+ and Topshop Co-created London Fashion Week's Most Interactive Show', *Fast Company*, 18 February 2013, www.fastcocreate.com/1682445/how-google-and-topshop-co-created-london-fashion-weeks-most-interactive-show

DISCUSSION

Which tools of the marketing communications mix do you think are the most effective at garnering publicity?

Do you think this will change in the future? Why?

Analyse a fashion promotion event similar to Topshop's 'The Future of the Fashion Show'. How does it display consistency and synergy?

Chapter 4
ADVERTISING FOR FASHION

How can a fashion brand advertise effectively to increase sales? Find out how to:

- Interpret the theory of advertising
- Attract consumers' attention and increase their involvement with brands
- Identify the advantages of different advertising media, including TV, print, celebrity-driven ads, billboards and guerrilla tactics
- Use each type of advertising, from the traditional to newer banner advertising and social media platforms, which offer greater opportunities for viewer interaction
- Optimize social media and online adverts

DEFINITIONS OF ADVERTISING

Below DKNY, Spring/Summer 2016.
A double-page magazine spread of the
print campaign shot by the photographer
Lachlan Bailey and featuring the model
Adrienne Jüliger.

In general, advertising involves the use of a medium, such as TV, print, radio, billboard or web, which is paid for by the brand to communicate a message to the desired consumer. Despite the availability of cheaper and more interactive media, the aspirational nature of fashion brands (particularly luxury brands) means that high-profile, visually impactful print and/or billboard advertising campaigns can still be the core element of a brand's marketing communications mix.

Gaynor Lea-Greenwood (2012) defines advertising as 'any form of outward-facing communication that is clearly seen to come from a company. It is usually paid for and originates with the company.' Chris Fill (2013) recommends to students and practitioners the definition proposed by Jef I. Richards and Catharine M. Curran in 2002: 'Advertising is a paid, mediated form of communication from an identifiable source, designed to persuade the receiver to take some action now or in the future.'

THE VALUE OF ADVERTISING

As a general indication of the global value of paid media for advertising, eMarketer (2016) predicted a figure of US$674.24 billion to be spent on online, magazine, newspaper, outdoor, radio and TV media in 2020. A Euromonitor report of 2014 (see below) highlighted a continuing global trend towards the sustained popularity of TV advertising, a decline in print and a steady increase in online advertising. Marketingtechnews.net (2016) estimate the amount spent on online advertising to soar to US$285 billion by 2020, nearly double the amount spent in 2016.

Below Euromonitor (2014), global adspend 1990–2013, top five markets total adspend, and top three global adspend by media type.

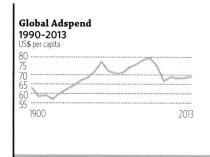

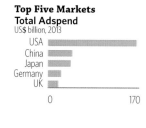

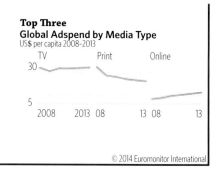

© 2014 Euromonitor International

EVALUATING THE EFFECTIVENESS OF ADVERTISING

Central to the development of an integrated communications plan is the ability to rate each type of communication for effectiveness, and therefore assess its advantages and disadvantages. Chris Fill's four Cs framework (2013, shown below with an added column for social media) summarizes the key characteristics of each marketing communication tool in terms of its effectiveness as a piece of *communication*, its *credibility*, its *cost* and the ability of the brand or retailer to *control* it. This model applies to most of the tools discussed in the following chapters and will be revisited each time it is relevant.

Advantages of advertising

- It reaches a large audience with one message, although this may be untargeted and may reach consumers who cannot afford the products.
- Although the total cost of producing an advert may be high, the cost divided by the people it reaches (cost per contact) may be low.
- The brand producing the advert has a reasonable level of control over taking the advert down should it offend or cause unwanted controversy.

Disadvantages of advertising

- With its large audience reach, its ability to deliver a personal or personalized message is low.
- There is not much opportunity to interact directly with advertising.
- Audiences tend to appreciate that it is a paid-for communication and do not afford it much credibility, particularly in the case of magazine print adverts, which are often flicked past in a desire to reach more engaging content.
- Producing a film or campaign shoot is expensive, and media costs – such as broadcasting slots, billboard rental or magazine pages – will be extra.
- Apart from a rise in sales, it is hard to measure the effects of traditional advertising.

CHRIS FILL'S 4Cs FRAMEWORK: A SUMMARY OF THE KEY CHARACTERISTICS OF MARKETING COMMUNICATIONS

	Advertising	Sales promotion	Public relations	Personal selling	Direct marketing	Social media
Communications						
Ability to deliver a personal message	Low	Low	Low	High	High	High
Ability to reach a large audience	High	Medium	Medium	Low	Medium	Medium
Level of interaction	Low	Medium	Low	High	High	High
Credibility						
Given by the target audience	Low	Medium	High	Medium	Medium	High
Cost						
Absolute costs	High	Medium	Low	High	Medium	Low
Cost per contact	Low	Medium	Low	High	High	Low
Wastage	High	Medium	High	Low	Low	Low
Size of investment	High	Medium	Low	High	Medium	Low
Control						
Ability to target particular audiences	Medium	High	Low	Medium	High	High
Management's ability to adjust the deployment of the tool as circumstances change	Medium	High	Low	Medium	High	Low

Fill's framework is a useful model for the effective combination of complementary communication tools. For instance, traditional advertising is considered expensive, reaches a large but untargeted audience, and offers limited opportunities for the consumer to interact with the campaign; but if the promoter also releases a shortened version of the television advert on their social media feed, the consumer can leave a written reaction to the message. Social media is low-cost, reaches an audience interested in a certain subject and allows consumers to comment – positively or negatively – and so the two are effective together.

Therefore, if there is a budget large enough for the campaign designer to use advertising, the challenge is to make it more interactive, more personal to the consumer and as credible as possible to overcome the disadvantages and justify the expense.

THEORIZING ADVERTISING

Advertising is the most theorized about of all the communication tools, because it has been around for much longer. There are two main theoretical traditions regarding advertising.
- Viewers see new messages and process that information in certain logical stages.
- Viewers relate and respond to various socio-cultural cues within the advertising message.

Chris Hackley (2010) expands on this dual thinking to encompass 'hard sell' messages, which see the ad purely as a sales vehicle, and 'soft sell' messages, where creative techniques are used to inspire affection, amusement, engagement and ultimately loyalty in the viewer. This duality is sometimes expressed as the *rational* approach, whereby emphasis is placed on the advertised product's features, performance or price, versus the *emotional* approach, where engagement with and the likeability of the message are the important factors.

Above right Topshop, Spring 2016 campaign, featuring Karlie Kloss. This rational message acts on the desire of Topshop's young target audience to be like Kloss: in demand, well-connected and with an admirable, inclusive attitude to technology.

Right Neil Barrett, Autumn/Winter 2015-16 campaign, shot by the photographer Matthew Stone. In this example of an emotional approach, the viewer is drawn into a narrative of the relationship between the models that they can interpret. A new viewer would become aware of the brand's reputation for considered garments.

Information-processing theory in advertising

Hackley (2010) acknowledges the effect of the information-processing model that was developed by Claude Elwood Shannon and Warren Weaver in the late 1940s to theorize communication as the transmission of information to the receiver of the information (see below). It is believed to apply not only to advertising but also to the cognitive stages humans use when interpreting any messages transmitted between a sender and a receiver.

In an advertising context, the company originates the request, which is put into a suitable format by a marketing agency and transmitted via a particular communication medium to the end receiver. Feedback is issued by the receiver to confirm that the correct interpretation has taken place and to validate the chosen media. Noise, identified as a distracting issue by Shannon and Weaver in early models, means other marketing messages.

AIDA in advertising theory

AIDA, introduced in Chapter 3 (see p. 55) as a model for matching objectives to communication strategy, can also be used to hone in on the theoretical effect of advertising. It is still used by some marketing agencies today to ensure that a campaign addresses all the stages an indifferent consumer will go through before a purchase. Sometimes referred to as a hierarchy of effects, this model describes a series of prompts from the brand that act as the trigger to buy, rather than a series of cognitive stages.

This model acknowledges the effect of marketing noise at the attention stage, and accepts that it may take many attempts before a viewer's attention is gained, the desire for the product or brand becomes rooted in the consumer's mind, and the purchase finally takes place. In other words, in this model the role of persuading the consumer is recognized. As in the Neil Barrett example pictured opposite, the viewer may need to see the campaign, see a piece from the collection on a respected actor or model, read a fashion editor enthusing about the clothes, spot a fashion entrepreneur in a piece from the collection or even read a piece about the designer before buying.

The lines of thinking are arguably blurred in fashion campaigns; many campaigns use a mixture of messages. This means that analysing the way in which advertising works and being able to apply set formulas can be very lucrative for promoters. Both Fill (2013) and Micael Dahlén et al. (2010) cite the development by O'Malley (1991) and Hall (1992) of four possible frameworks for the way advertising can work on viewers.

- The persuasion model: following the AIDA model, the viewer will move through a series of persuasive messages generated by the brand based on how unique and how much better it is than other brands.
- The involvement model: seeking to involve and engage the viewer, perhaps using emotion or other creative techniques to draw in the audience, or inviting them to create content or seek further information.
- The salience model: adverts that aim to stand out by virtue of the nature of the campaign itself, which creates a point of difference; they promote sharing and discussion, which may become the talking point rather than the product or brand.
- The sales model: messages are created purely to provoke sales through attractive prices, discounts, rewards and other sales-based incentives.

Of the four frameworks listed, it is the involvement framework that resonates the most with the changing role of involving and engaging consumers within marketing in general. Theorists believe that the use of creativity in advertising can be one of the most important ways both to gain attention and to engage viewers.

THE TRANSMISSION MODEL OF MASS COMMUNICATION

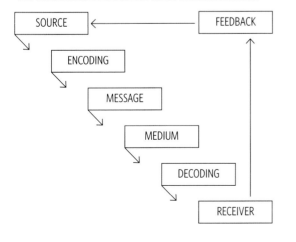

THE AIDA MODEL OF ADVERTISING PERSUASION

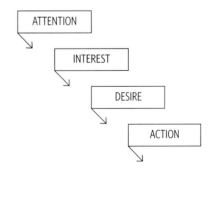

WHAT ADVERTISERS DO TO REACH CONSUMERS

These are some of the common creative techniques used in advertising (and other communications) to inspire a deeper level of involvement, and ultimately interest and desire, in viewers.

- **Colour** Human beings are attracted to intense stimuli conveyed using colour. (See p. 39 for a discussion of the use of colour in the development of branded logos.)
- **Scale and contrast** When viewers see a large, prominent object it is perceived as important, powerful and authoritative. Similarly, black-and-white photography can win attention in a colour-saturated environment.
- **Provocation** The use of nudity, sexually charged material or political, socio-cultural, religious or racial issues can be used to gain attention.
- **Semiotics** This takes into account the fact that receivers do not just mindlessly process messages. Viewers attach meanings relevant to the message's place in contemporary society among other culturally significant brands. See figure 7 opposite.
- **Polysemy** Similarly to semiotics, polysemy recognizes that viewers will scan an advert for socio-cultural factors they recognize and seek to formulate connections with what they already know.
- **Sensory and emotion** Include images that trigger basic instincts, such as attraction, affection, comfort, warmth, anger and fear, that are common globally.

1 Diesel, 'We Are Connected #Diesel ReBoot' ad campaign (2014), photographed by Inez Van Lamsweerde and Vinoodh Matadin. In its campaigns, Diesel often uses broad swathes of red, a colour that conveys a sense of danger, heat, passion and impulsive action.

2 Natan Dvir's 'Coming Soon' project (2013) on the *Reel Foto* blog depicts giant-scale fashion billboards dominating New York City.

3 IRO, Spring/Summer 2016 campaign, shot in black and white by Collier Schorr and featuring the model Anja Rubik.

4 In answer to demands for more diverse body types in its campaigns, Agent Provocateur cast Atlanta de Cadenet Taylor to model its diffusion line L'Agent, seen here shot by Liz Collins for the Spring/Summer 2016 campaign. The brand often refers to 1950s pin-up or burlesque themes to add a nostalgic element to its decadent image.

5

6

5 & Other Stories' Autumn/Winter 2015-16 campaign featured the transgender models Valentijn de Hingh and Hari Nef shot by a transgender crew of photographer Amos Mac, stylist Love Bailey and make-up artist Nina Poon.

6 Benetton's 'White, Black, Yellow Hearts' ad campaign (1996). Benetton often takes an anti-racist stance in campaign material. The simple message here is that we are all the same under the skin.

7 Semiotics explained: the sign, the signified, the signifier, denotation and connotation. This draws on the work of Malcolm Barnard (2002), who summarizes the work of the Swiss linguist Ferdinand de Saussure in defining the key terms of semiotics.

8 Diesel, Spring/Summer 2010, 'Sex Sells: Unfortunately We Sell Jeans' campaign, photographed by Miko Lim. Diesel often uses polysemy to draw the viewer in and to make links between the models and the message, thus prolonging the viewer's attention.

9 The Kooples, 'Sasha and Milos', Spring/Summer 2016. The Kooples is part of a new wave of young French brands using emotional connections to great effect. The simple concept of using striking couples, stating how long they have been together, produced a universal and recession-proof message.

The Sign: 'signifier' + 'signified' = the sounds and shapes of the word.

Signified Is the meaning of the signifier 'a pair of jeans'.

Signifier A blue fabric workman's garment.

The signified 'jeans' in written or spoken form does not look like or sound like the signifier but is used to signify/stand for or represent a pair of jeans.

Denotation The formal factual information we associate with a style such as line, cut or fit: A blue denim, five-pocket western style jean.

Connotation What the image or word makes a person think or feel: Young, free, rebellious, cowboy, comfortable, worker, reliable, classic or sexy depending on our individual perception of the signified.

7

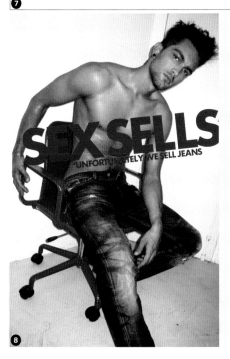

8

9

CELEBRITY IN ADVERTISING

The use of celebrity in advertising, and indeed in all promotion, has been hugely successful for the fashion industry. Celebrity endorsement is explored in the next chapter, but here we examine the impact of using a celebrity as part of a traditional advertising campaign.

Angela Carroll (2009) discusses the effectiveness of celebrities at evoking a viewer's *ideal self*. Self-concept is the construction of a consumer's self through brands and other purchases that reflect their notion of who they are in the eyes of others. We naturally have different roles in life, and so construct actual selves, ideal selves and social selves. The fashion brands consumers buy are a huge part of the outward-facing signals of group membership. Carroll refers to Grant McCracken's (2005) three-stage Meaning Transfer model as coming the closest to representing the role celebrities play in endorsement, here using the example of Rihanna's collaboration with Puma.

- **Stage 1** The viewer is familiar with Rihanna from her significant contribution to the music industry and involvement as a creative director, brand ambassador and collaborator in fashion projects. Unafraid to tackle different genres, she is photographed constantly for her cool, confident style of dressing. Her style works for both street-fashion brands and red-carpet luxury labels. These meanings and associations are attached to Rihanna, and the recall and recognition of these meanings are very quick.
- **Stage 2** The viewer transfers these meanings to Puma on viewing the campaign.
- **Stage 3** The consumer decides if Rihanna in Puma matches their own notions of their personal selves in the world. They may decide to wear Puma to project their own sense of cutting-edge street cool, or to feel part of ongoing hip-hop artist trainer design, including Kanye West's successful Yeezy range for Adidas as well as Rihanna's range. In this way Rihanna has conveyed a new sense of Puma to the consumer. Rihanna's confident style is in keeping with Puma's brand image, and to some of us she will represent how we would ideally like to be perceived.

Right Rihanna is a brand ambassador and advertising force for Puma. She has a role as creative director and achieved a successful collaboration with Fenty x Puma trainers.

The message to the consumer is clear: the use of celebrities such as Elle Fanning for Miu Miu and Lady Gaga and Madonna for Versace creates a perfect, rich, beautiful ultimate self to aspire to. The esteemed status they have achieved in society could be ours, too, if we buy into the brands they recommend.

The next section examines how, in an age of tighter budgets and demand for tools that provide interactivity and greater measurable return on investment, brands are using advertising in innovative ways.

TV ADVERTISING

Television's large and untargeted audiences have traditionally meant that fashion brands restricted TV advertising to entry-level products, such as fragrance and cosmetics, that a wider audience could afford. TV advertising is also expensive; the wide publicity surrounding the Christmas adverts of larger retailers shows that budgets of £1 million are not unusual. According to *The Guardian*, John Lewis' total Christmas campaign in 2014, 'Monty the Penguin', cost the UK retailer £7 million. The campaign included:

- The ad itself.
- A custom app.
- A story book.
- Monty the Penguin soft toys.
- A series of unbranded teaser idents on Channel 4.
- #Montythepenguin to fuel the campaign on social media.
- The lighting up of Twitter followers' homepages as the John Lewis-sponsored Christmas lights were turned on in London's Oxford Street.
- In-store events such as the use of augmented reality to enable children to see their own toys brought to life.

The campaign is a great example of spending money on other communication tools to add interactivity to a TV advert. It also works as an example of synergy between different channels of communication, as discussed in Chapter 3 (see p. 54). All these experiences worked individually to provoke delight, yet all worked together towards a common aim of creating joy in the Christmas experience.

Cable channels can provide a cheaper and more locally targeted option than prime-time terrestrial channels for the time slots in which an advert is broadcast. One brand that has advertised fashion rather than fragrance on TV is Louis Vuitton. The ad 'L'Invitation au Voyage' was aired on the US premium cable channel Showtime during an episode of the political thriller series *Homeland* in November 2012. Produced by the prestigious fashion photographers Inez Van Lamsweerde and Vinoodh Matadin, the ad featured the model Arizona Muse clad in Vuitton and visiting the Louvre in Paris, pursued by a mystery admirer.

TV sponsorship

Sponsorship is a way of using television advertising to make a more targeted statement by affiliating a brand to the aesthetics of a particular TV programme. Sponsorship has been found to be more effective than spot advertising, as viewers translate their positive associations with the TV programme to the brand. The brand also benefits from associations viewers make on social media as they become engaged and involved in the programme's plot. TV sponsorship allows the creation of a moving film showing the brand in association with the TV programme. These are known as TV idents or bumpers, and have the advantage of being the identity point at which to start viewing if the viewer is fast-forwarding the commercials. In 2012 Ralph Lauren became a corporate sponsor of

Left UK-based online retailer Missguided uses TV ads as an effective medium for colourful, effervescent, youth-orientated film. They have acted as sponsors for series 22 of *America's Next Top Model* and rolled out further advertising in the US on billboards.

RALPH LAUREN *Collection*

Above Ralph Lauren, Autumn 2012 collection inspired by *Downton Abbey.*

Masterpiece Classic aired by the US cable channel PBS, a series that broadcasts British historical TV dramas such as *Downton Abbey*, *Sherlock* and *Upstairs Downstairs*. Ralph Lauren's Autumn 2012 catwalk show demonstrated the direct influence of *Downton Abbey*, and the sponsorship was publicized as mutually beneficial. *Downton Abbey* was a surprise hit in the US; its second season attracted some 17 million viewers, and Masterpiece enjoyed a 27 per cent increase in viewers.

Fashion film

A major advantage of TV advertising is that it creates a film, and fashion film by celebrated photographers and directors is becoming a required part of a high-profile campaign. Throughout this book we feature examples of fashion film used in different contexts.

- Film as advertising narrative. Chapter 3 (p. 47) gives the example of Lacoste's *The Big Leap*, which was released to accompany a print and billboard campaign and to underpin the narrative of taking a leap of faith.
- Film as conversational tool. Chapter 5 (p. 88) looks at how vloggers increase intimacy by presenting films as style influencers. Chapter 6 (p. 121) explains how

Missguided has worked to inspire its followers to contribute footage of their own Missguided 'hauls'.

- Film as immersive promotion. Chapter 2 (pp. 36–37) gives the example of Alice's Pig, which actively uses YouTube to release short, fun, impulsive film clips that reflect the identity of the brand.
- Film as catwalk livestreaming. Chapter 10 (p. 179) examines how the livestreaming of catwalk shows has both democratized the fashion show and accelerated the fashion cycle.
- Film as unedited footage. Chapter 6 (pp. 120–121) also looks at the rise of 'behind-the-scenes' access, via tools such as Periscope and Snapchat that are intended to broadcast the moment rather than the posed situation.

PRINT ADVERTISING

Although it is reported to be on the wane, the glossy print campaign is still a part of fashion advertising. Devora Neikova (2014) comments on US *Vogue*'s legendary September 2007 issue, which contained 727 pages of print ads, an industry record. The September issues are the most bought-into of the year, as readers look for the new autumn styles available in the shops and preview designers' catwalk collections for the forthcoming spring. The September and March issues provide the most sought-after opportunities for fashion print advertising. Magazines make information about their readers and their rates available to potential advertisers through media packs, helping advertisers to match their consumer with the magazine reader.

Advertising space varies in price according to the readership and prestige of the magazine, the position in the magazine itself and the size of the ad (full or single page). The inside front cover is the most expensive position, followed by the outside back cover. Fashion magazines are usually subdivided; the first third of the magazine is more expensive than the other sections, at about £10,000–30,000 for a single page, depending on the prestige of the magazine. Brands may pay a premium to appear in certain popular features, next to sections (such as the contents page) where the reader may pause, or on the slightly favoured right-hand side of the magazine.

The prices indicated, for one appearance in one edition of a magazine, explain why full- and double-page ads – particularly at the front of fashion magazines – are generally the domain of luxury brands. The prices are, of course, negotiable, and factors such as booking the ad to run in a few editions can bring prices down. Even when this budget is spent, there is a risk that the adverts will be flicked past, so they must make an impression quickly. Readers, aware that this is paid-for advertising, are prone to head for more informative content, such as style tips from fashion editors to whom they afford more credibility. The lack of interaction with a static printed image also remains a problem.

Magazine advertising reach

The circulation figures – the number of copies in circulation per edition – of printed magazines are becoming less available as sales of print editions fall. Traditionally, this information was important to advertisers because it generated an idea of the potential reach of a magazine advert. Magazines have an extended life, being well-produced and generally read, reread or even passed on. According to Lea-Greenwood (2012), it has been estimated that a fashion magazine is read 2.5 times, increasing the reach 2.5 times beyond the circulation figures themselves; this is also known as the magazine's readership figure.

With the launch internationally of the Italian magazine *Grazia* from 2004 onwards, the traditional formula of a monthly hit of fashion changed to weekly. *Grazia* came up with a formula of delivering fashion content, features and news under the slogan 'The weekly who, what, wear'. It remains the weekly market leader, selling print editions in 22 countries and remaining the only weekly to have attracted luxury brand advertising from the likes of Prada, Gucci and Dolce & Gabbana.

Advertorials

Advertorials are adverts designed to appear as though they are part of a fashion shoot by the magazine itself. They benefit from some of the positive advantages of PR, such as enhanced credibility and third-party endorsement, discussed in the next chapter. These paid-for campaigns by brands and retailers include a contribution from the magazine's fashion team, a guest blogger or a celebrity, in the form of third-party copy that endorses the brand's range. They may resemble fashion shoots or style tips

Left Havaianas print advertising campaign, featured in UK *Vogue*, July 2017.

pages, but will always be accompanied by the magazine's name and the word 'promotion' or 'advertisement', usually in the top right-hand corner. These can be very subtle and sometimes overlooked by readers, who may mistake the content for magazine-generated coverage. This type of advertising can cost 20–40 per cent more than a traditional full- or double-page ad.

Small ads

For companies with a smaller budget, there is also the opportunity to buy smaller chunks of advertising space at the back of fashion magazines. These are sold by panel size, with a single panel measuring about 75 x 60 mm (3 x 2³⁄₈ in), and offer a very small space in which to make an impression. This back section of advertising is often presented as a directory, split into sections such as Boutiques and Collections or Health and Beauty. For about £300 per edition, the advertiser benefits from the same reach generated by the readership of the magazine, but stands an even greater chance of being flicked past at the back of the magazine.

Leaflet inserts

Leaflet inserts are the cheapest possible way of attempting to gain attention via the circulation figures of a magazine, and cost about £50–200 per thousand, depending on the magazine. These are the flyers that fall out when a magazine is opened. They are included here because the magazine is paid to include them at the point of distribution. If they are loose, they are likely to be disposed of at first read; the advertiser can pay more to have them bound into the magazine itself. It is fair to note that there have been developments in this area to make such inserts more attention-grabbing. In 2010 the Italian fashion house

Dolce & Gabbana created a new drink, Martini Gold, in collaboration with Bacardi. Using technology similar to the audio chips found in greetings cards, the American company Americhip produced an embedded LCD video screen known as video in print (VIP) technology. The insert with the embedded video was placed in the December edition of Russian *Vogue* to great interest from the press.

Newspapers

Newspapers offer advertising space at a lower cost than magazines. If they are felt to be suitable for a campaign, they have the advantage of being available at national or local level. Locally, they can be used to notify shoppers of an event, store opening or local discounts. They can be available daily and so stand more of a chance of reaching different markets, such as captive commuters on their way to work. As with small ads, they are available in smaller units of space than fashion glossies, and so provide more options at a particular budget. Taking out a quarter-page black-and-white advert in a local newspaper can cost about £250; the cost rises to £1,000–10,000 for a full-page colour ad in a national newspaper. The disadvantages of such advertising are that newspapers are discarded more quickly than magazines and are not perceived to be of such high quality. Weekend newspaper supplements, however, have formed a reputation for fashion coverage that is as accomplished as that of monthly or weekly fashion magazines. In particular, *The Times 'Style'* and the *New York Times Magazine* Sunday supplements and the *Financial Times 'How To Spend It'* supplement offer brands covetable editorial and advertising opportunities.

Right Magazine insert with VIP embedded video screen created by Americhip for Dolce & Gabbana and Bacardi, 2010.

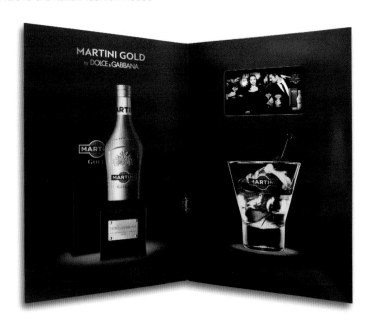

BILLBOARDS

Billboard advertising is the most common type of what is known as outdoor or ambient marketing. The term covers bus shelters, kiosks, railway stations and advertising on transport itself. Billboard space is sold by size, importance of location and whether it is standard or digital. Very roughly, a large 98-sheet standard billboard costs about £500 a week, and up to £2,500 for a digital or interactive version. Billboards have the advantage over TV advertising of being displayed 24 hours a day, and they can be placed where viewers may be prompted to shop. On the other hand, exposure time may be brief. Research conducted in 2006 by Charles Taylor, George Franke and Hae-Kyong Bang highlighted how to use billboards for best effect.

- Ensure the image is clear and distinct from its background and consistent with promotional messages on other media channels.
- Use no more than seven or eight words of type, and ensure that the typeface is clear and visible from a distance and reinforces one well-made point; this could be product, performance or price.
- Clever use of slogans promotes humour, or use other creative tools such as colour to grab attention.
- Locate close to premium or edgy shopping districts, or use to promote visibility in areas where there may be less competition for attention.
- Statements made on a giant scale grab attention and assume importance.

Brands can find that billboards attract the attention of out-and-about young urbanites who are in general watching less television. The decision whether to advertise on a billboard or on TV highlights the need to understand the customers' interests: are they watching speciality TV channels in conjunction with surfing the net? Or are they leading a more active urban life?

A fashion company that has recorded success from both TV *and* billboard advertising is the British online retailer Boohoo.com. In an interview with *Marketing Magazine* in 2014, its joint CEO Carol Kane acknowledged the speed and reach of traditional channels in building awareness of the brand quickly:

People might have expected us to start with digital advertising [Boohoo's target customer is a 15–25-year-old seeker of fast fashion], but we took the opposite approach. That fast-tracked us because we got our brand awareness up really quickly, even without having a presence on the high street. We started off with press and billboards, then in September 2011 we advertised on TV and haven't looked back.

Below David Bitton's ad for Buffalo Jeans (2014) on a billboard in Los Angeles, spotted on the blog *Jason in Hollywood* (jasoninhollywood.blogspot.co.uk).

Centre Boohoo.com billboard, Los Angeles, spotted on *Jason in Hollywood*, 2015. This example demonstrates many of the points discussed by Taylor, Franke and Bang. Boohoo.com concentrates on keenly priced fashion, and this is conveyed clearly. The text is large and the colours pick up those in the dress shown. It is a simple hit of information, framed perfectly by the blue Los Angeles sky.

Bottom Sportsgirl, Melbourne, interactive 'window shop', 2012 (see p. 72).

Left and above Kenneth Cole campaign for Mankind fragrance (2015): subway ad and forum.

Interactive billboards

Interactive billboards are used to integrate more closely with other promotional messages. A QR (Quick Response) code used on static advertising can be scanned by the viewer using a smartphone with a QR reader app, allowing them to go straight to the sales environment without having to use the company's website address. QR codes can be used on billboards more effectively than in print, since their large scale absorbs their clunky appearance. In 2012, when the Melbourne shop of the Australian retailer Sportsgirl was closed for renovation, the windows were covered in giant changing billboards with QR codes through which shoppers could purchase items at the click of a button, changing the notion of window shopping forever. Sportsgirl rolled this project out in its shops around the country. An early adopter of trendwatching. com's 'No Interface' trend (see p. 25), Net-a-Porter also used this thinking for the Fashion's Night Out celebrations in London and New York in 2011. It used an augmented-reality app, which – on holding a mobile phone or tablet over a garment on a billboard – activated catwalk videos, 360-degree views on a model and purchase information. Interactive billboards solve the problem of impact at a glance and allow 24-hour purchasing for people who are out and about, making every moment potentially about shopping.

Integrated billboards

Kenneth Cole's 'Be the Evolution' campaign (2015) to support the launch of its men's fragrance Mankind was named Best Street Furniture/Transit/Alternative Campaign that year by the Outdoor Advertising Association of America. The campaign proved outdoor media's ability to drive interaction on social media. Developed by the US agency Ready Set Rocket, it asked viewers to contribute to 'Experience Now', a series of 21 good deeds in 21 days. Viewers uploaded their pictorial evidence of having done a good deed to a #manupformankind social forum. Images were then compiled into a collage and posted on the main website, enabling a consumer vision of a better society compiled in real time on social media. Existing consumers were enticed via an email to get involved, and billboards on the subway suggested the type of deed that would be suitable, such as 'Donate old clothes to a local shelter' or 'Offer to take a photo for a tourist'. Praised for its integration of technology, consumer interaction and traditional and digital channels, the campaign also demonstrated synergy between the channels used.

GUERRILLA ADVERTISING

Guerrilla campaigns, which take on the appearance of a PR stunt or event or a piece of street art, have a greater potential to go viral on social media or achieve news coverage as an event rather than a piece of advertising. Here, they are still classed as advertising, since they are commissioned by advertising agencies and paid for by the brand, but attention is grabbed by the appearance of an impromptu happening or event. Two such stunts were created by the agency TBWA\Japan for Adidas in 2003 and 2004. In 'Vertical Football', a football performance in the air, two players suspended on bungee cords attempted to kick the ball back and forth against a giant green

Below left 'Impossible Sprint', TBWA\Japan for Adidas, 2004.

Below right 'Vertical Football', TBWA\Japan for Adidas, 2003.

Bottom Paul 'Moose' Curtis, clean or reverse graffiti for Puma, Manchester, photographed in 2007.

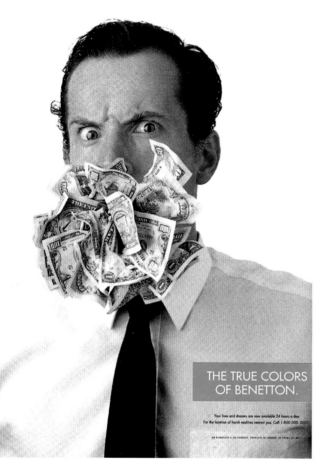

THE TRUE COLORS
OF BENETTON.

Your lives and dreams are now available 24 hours a day.
For the location of harsh realities nearest you, Call 1-800-000- 0000

AN ADBUSTERS.D AD PARODY. PRINTED IN LONDON. DEFINES £3. W/I

backdrop. The act stopped the Tokyo traffic – literally disruption in action – and gained coverage on local and international news channels. This was followed by 'Impossible Sprint' (2004), in which a 100-metre running track was placed up the sides of skyscrapers in Hong Kong and Osaka. Racers winched their way up ropes, one per track as in a normal race, with the incentive of a US$10,000 prize for the fastest time. The idea enabled heats, quarterfinals, semifinals and a grand final, leading to an increased interest in Asia for the forthcoming Olympic Games (for which Adidas had provided kit for 26 of the 28 sports) and repeated exposure of the event. CNN reporters even tried hanging down from the buildings alongside the competitors to generate the adrenaline rush of the challenge itself.

More recently street art has been used to advertise fashion in a more covert way. Techniques such as clean or reverse graffiti as pioneered by Paul 'Moose' Curtis have the advantage of being legal, and have been used by brands such as Puma, Adidas and Cheap Monday. Not everyone will 'get' or even notice these messages, but they promote a great sense of inclusivity for those who do.

Advertising is not always perceived positively. Adbusters is an organization that subverts advertising messages, which they believe contribute to an unsustainable consumer culture. They advocate 'culture jamming' or culture hacking, such as 'Buy Nothing Day'. Jammers, also called subvertisers, will alter corporate logos or paste over words to alter the original meaning and debrand or politicize the message.

Having examined how some traditional advertising methods are being integrated with online tools to encourage consumer interaction, we now move on to discuss how brands can use online opportunities directly for advertising.

ONLINE ADVERTISING

Advertising online has the advantage of immediate publication, and no time or geographical restrictions. In addition, it can be targeted more efficiently than TV, outdoor or print advertising to areas of interest or a particular type of viewer. The creation of online fashion magazines – which can be viewed at a time that suits the reader, on a desktop computer, tablet or mobile – has produced the most obvious online advertising environment for fashion brands. In common with traditional print media, the space is sold by unit size and position or location on the web page.

Banner advertising

The rectangular spaces at the top and down the side(s) of magazine web pages, where it is possible to advertise online, will be part of the magazine's media pack and are referred to as banners or tiles. They carry a hyperlink to the advertising brand's website, and a viewer who clicks on the banner is taken straight to the home page of the brand.

The cost of banner advertising is additionally calculated on a 1,000 impression basis, with one impression signalling one page view by a web user; this is often referred to as CPM or cost per mille. Banners in online magazines are available at the top of the website, referred to as the leader board, or as mid-page units

(MPU) or the larger half-page units (HPU). A prestigious magazine would charge in the region of £65 for 1,000 impressions of a HPU banner. It is crucial that banners catch the eye. It is possible to design animated versions, but the context must be considered, and on image-heavy sites such as magazines, news, blogs and newsletters, static banners can be less visually chaotic than those featuring flash animation. Banner advertising is also available on the websites of large online retailers and on social media platforms.

Google AdWords

In the fashion industry, advertising on Google remains by far and away the most effective method of driving traffic through to sales. An article by Rachel Strugatz (2014) cites data from eMarketer that puts global digital adspend at over US$140 billion, of which Google commands nearly a third. In Chapter 7 we discuss paying Google for an appearance in its visual shopping lists as part of a search engine optimization strategy (see p. 139), and it is also possible to pay for Google AdWords to appear right at the top of Google's results page from a consumer search. Such results feature an 'Ad' icon next to them. Although Google is not paid until a viewer clicks on the suggested link, as with all forms of advertising the viewer may recognize that these are paid for and be tempted to scroll down the list to find results that they feel are closer to their search requirements.

Adwords can be targeted to appear in certain locations or to certain types of consumer, and the click-throughs and even the sales generated are measureable. The brand or other customer provides Google with the company name and website address, and creates a short description based on the search terms with which the brand would like to be associated. Google.com (2015) recommends a budget of around £10–20 per day to see a sustained increase in traffic.

SERGIO BORZILLO OF NETBOOSTER

NetBooster offers digital solutions for companies looking to increase sales, market share, consumer engagement and retention, based on an optimized mix of search-engine optimization (SEO), pay-per-click advertising (PPC), affiliate marketing, display advertising and social media marketing. Analysis of user behaviour and data ensure that this is carried out in an efficient and measurable manner. The company has 25 offices worldwide, employs over 500 experts and can produce results in more than 30 languages. It has created digital campaigns for companies including Emirates, AccorHotels.com, Europcar and Hertz. Sergio Borzillo began his career in 2012 as a senior account manager at NetBooster UK. He is now Director of Paid Media and London Operations, responsible for managing, developing and delivering NetBooster's paid-media strategy for both UK and international clients. Here he discusses the role of digital advertising within the wider field of digital marketing and the advantages of placing advertising spend across a mix of consumer touchpoints, dictated by consumer behaviour.

Q: *Could you explain how your company uses digital tools to gain customers and boost sales?*
A: We put the decision-making process at the heart of what we do; at each stage the

NETBOOSTER PERFORMANCE STRATEGY SOLUTIONS

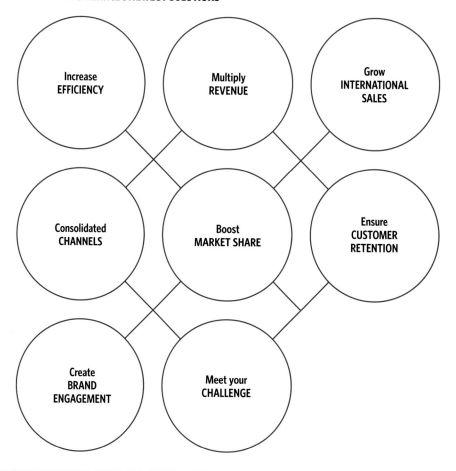

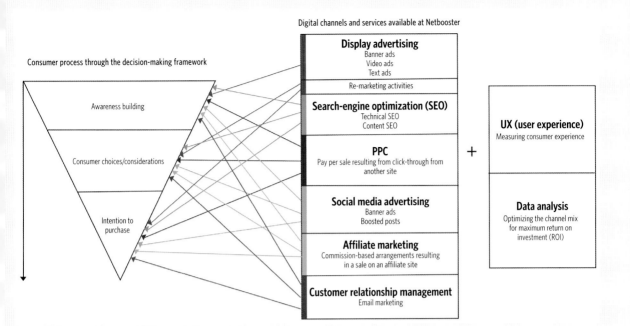

Digital channels and services available at Netbooster

Consumer process through the decision-making framework

Display advertising
Banner ads
Video ads
Text ads

Re-marketing activities

Search-engine optimization (SEO)
Technical SEO
Content SEO

PPC
Pay per sale resulting from click-through from another site

Social media advertising
Banner ads
Boosted posts

Affiliate marketing
Commission-based arrangements resulting in a sale on an affiliate site

Customer relationship management
Email marketing

Awareness building

Consumer choices/considerations

Intention to purchase

+

UX (user experience)
Measuring consumer experience

Data analysis
Optimizing the channel mix for maximum return on investment (ROI)

Above Digital marketing mix, showing how nearly all elements can be used to target consumers at different stages of the decision-making process.

consumer moves closer to the actual purchase. In digital marketing we create a mix of all the channels: SEO including content marketing, the paid search activities of PPC that can work using both text and image [see Chapter 7, p.139], social media, display advertising including readvertising and retargeting, which includes banners, videos or text ads. Then you have affiliate marketing and customer relationship management (CRM), which involve email marketing [see Chapter 9, p. 166], then our consultancy services UX (user experience) and data analytics that we apply to these channels to make sure this mix works in the best possible way. We can analyse data and customer behaviour when they land on a certain web page; with that information we might modify the position of an image to be more attractive on the page, for example. We use this expertise to be able to feed the digital mix and optimize all activities.

Traditionally, display ads in the digital world were compared to TV ads – you are not actively searching but you are passively getting the message, and it may stimulate you and cause some interest and awareness. SEO, PPC, affiliate marketing and CRM are said to be more performance related than display ads, as they influence choice and purchase. In reality this is not true; at each stage of the process you can use nearly all these channels in different ways. Display can also be used for remarketing, which

is about retargeting people who have already shown an interest in a brand's website. We are trying to convince them to come back and purchase, and therefore trying to influence them in their decision-making and intention to purchase.

The same thing is true of paid search; if a shopper is looking for trainers and they search for 'Nike trainers', very likely they will buy the brand because they know it and have bought it before. Someone searching using the term 'trainers', however, will not necessarily want just Nike; they may want the best available deal. Here our job is to ensure that we have compelling ads and compelling landing pages, so that after the consumer has looked at all the options they absolutely want a certain brand. There are additional tools; if a consumer has a Gmail account, you can create Gmail-sponsored ads that target people who receive emails from specific competitors, so that an ad will pop up in their inbox. For example, Nike would probably target people who receive emails from Puma, Adidas, and so on. Also people who have specific keywords in their emails, such as 'sports equipment' or 'sports', or specific demographic characteristics – again, these people are not actively searching, but you are creating awareness. So PPC and SEO can serve as awareness channels as well as performance channels aimed at generating revenue.

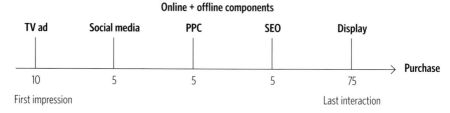

EVALUATING THE ROLE OF EACH CHANNEL FROM FIRST IMPRESSION TO LAST INTERACTION

Online + offline components

TV ad	Social media	PPC	SEO	Display	→ Purchase
10	5	5	5	75	

First impression   Last interaction

A rateable value can be attributed to each element to optimize channel mix.

The same thing can be done from a CRM perspective. You can buy a list of email addresses from a company. You have never heard of these people before, but you can contact them with a promotional message to create awareness. You can also use your internal list of customers who have bought before, contacting them again with regard to purchase. Social media can play a strong part in each stage of the process by using precise targeting and retargeting. It is possible, for example, to use something called custom audiences, where you take the email database you have and enter it into Facebook. Facebook will map the email addresses to people who use them to log into Facebook, and when there is a match you can target those people via Facebook with specific messages that might reward a frequent buyer or reactivate an older one.

Q: Do you recommend that a fashion brand should prioritize some channels over others?
A: For fashion companies, social media is essential. If you think about the millennial generation, these are people who have grown up in a world where digital is big. They are much less receptive to traditional advertising – TV, print – and much more receptive to a digital ad. Younger means more hours spent online, and you have to be where your audience is.

Some channels are more expensive than others. So if you have just launched a brand and you want to reach millions, but have budget limitations, I would suggest less PPC and more display. PPC is much more expensive than display, because the searcher's intent to purchase is much higher than that of those who are just viewing a display advert.

Having said that, it is not really advisable to use just one or two channels, because the customer is acting across channels, across devices, online and offline. The environment has

never been so complicated. If you think about the customer, they are trying to solve a problem in their purchasing. They do not care if the solution comes on social media, via display advertising or via an SEO or affiliate or TV or a billboard. It is a brand's objective to anticipate that need, to be in the right place with the right message, targeted at the right people, who are ready to purchase. Advertisers want to spend more money where they see they will get a sale. That is the objective of an agency: spend when customers are ready to purchase, and the return on investment (ROI) will be higher.

To create a future, you must also keep investing in creating awareness: it is possible to lose a previously successful brand message with a new generation of consumers. A lot of fashion brands, because of the margin they make, concentrate too much on purchase, rather than building a way-of-life culture around the brand; successful brands create a balance of both.

Q: What do you see as the major advantages of digital over traditional advertising?
A: With digital marketing, everything can be accounted for. If you are spending money on something, you know what you are getting back. This gives you the grounds to go to your management and say you want another £1 million to spend. On the other hand, it can be so accurate that it puts a lot of pressure on people working in digital because clients know about every penny spent.

The vast amounts spent on TV advertising, especially by brands targeting a younger generation, are wasted. That is why a lot of advertisers are switching budget from traditional to digital channels. TV is now moving into real-time bidding (RTB). Media buying used to be: if a brand wants to get this spot, at this time, this is the price. Soon it will work according to the demand there is for the slot, and the price for that space will go up or down accordingly. That is what digital is about. RTB takes advantage of not having to buy at a broadcaster or publisher's set rates. It raises the question of who is watching TV now. Viewers are on social media or watching TV over the internet, so the line is already blurred. We act across channels and across devices. That is not to say that TV advertising is dead, but to recommend spreading the budget to cover multiple touchpoints: TV, blogs, Tube billboards, radio in the car – wherever your customer is.

Now the journey from first impression to purchase is much longer and more complicated. A viewer may see a TV ad first, then a social media ad, read a blog or some reviews, do a Google search and see a PPC ad; then a friend might show them another search, they look at the website, they are retargeted with a display ad. Post-purchase now also feeds back into the first impression through product reviews. It is hard to say what did the job. It is important to have the technology to understand the role of each touchpoint and rate it for its contribution to the process (see diagram opposite).

When a brand makes an allocation of budget, I will use this information to put the right amount into PPC, etc., so that I choose the right mix and finance it in the right way. We optimize a brand's budget. There are still people who do not believe in digital, believing it's all about TV and ads on the street, but they need to recognize consumer behaviour. It is not the channel, it is the mix, and with the right technology I can measure what I see, not what I think.

A final advantage worth mentioning is the fact that ROI can be measured for specific categories within the product line. Multi-brand e-tailers (such as Net-a-Porter) sell a range of brands that will in part dictate the selling price, or their operational costs may go up for other reasons. You cannot spend on PPC for a product that is delivering a margin of 10 per cent compared to one that is delivering 30–40 per cent. It is not wise to spend £2 for a click for a product that you are selling at £5, but you can pay up to £50 per click for a product that is returning you £2,000–3,000. Insurance and finance products can see £50 paid for a click. Fashion products may be worth 50p a click because they are different in terms of value and lifespan. To spend £500–600 on acquiring a customer is not important, as long as the money is made back. With low-value products, you should be careful not to exceed your revenue target, otherwise that revenue becomes unprofitable.

Different elements of the mix may fall in and out of favour over the next few years, but that is not a worry, since digital companies are very used to being responsive.

ADVERTISING ON SOCIAL MEDIA

Social media, especially Facebook, is fast turning into a pay-to-play platform. Chapter 6 discusses how brands are using campaign material to create content for business social media profiles. Including advertising initiatives here, however, is intended to show the divide between a content strategy and an advertising strategy on social media. Of course, in campaign planning these are likely to be considered together as part of the company's digital or online strategy.

Advertising on Facebook

Facebook is the most important and currently the most progressive platform on which to advertise, and has made significant developments, especially in producing advertising to display effectively on mobile phones. Facebook was expected to command around 8 per cent of global digital ad revenues by the end of 2014 (Strugatz, 2014), and according to Adweek.com (2016) it has reached 1.59 billion monthly active users (MAU).

The first type of advertising Facebook offered was banner advertising down the side columns of Facebook pages (which remain free for any individual or company to set up). The appeal of these was that the huge audience could be targeted more specifically by demographic factors such as age, gender or location, or by interests,

behaviour or connections. Facebook has been incredibly good at data capture of their users, making targeting an effective exercise. The measurability of the advertising response data provided by Facebook directly helps brands to see the results, justify budgets and plan actively. Such rigorous targeting tackled advertising's disadvantage of not delivering a personal message, by ensuring that viewers saw only adverts relevant to them. Facebook has since introduced the ability to create a lookalike audience to target followers similar to the ones a brand may already have, and has incorporated data from third-party providers to allow targeting by the audience's offline interests.

Facebook offers the widest variety of advert formats or types, including:

- Boosted posts, whereby advertisers pay a flat rate for a single post or a short series of posts that will appear higher up the rankings in the newsfeed of the selected audience.
- Ads in the form of video, image slideshows and carousel ads, which allow multiple content to be included in one hit.
- Dynamic ads, which target audiences with ads for products they have viewed on the host website or app.

Facebook uses Atlas software, which can track user interest across browsing platforms and across different devices. Atlas can match a purchaser's email address given in a physical store to their Facebook ID. This supplies a previously unknown link to show when a consumer may have seen an ad on social media and then purchased the item physically rather than online.

Facebook has changed the way advertising is paid for by allowing advertisers to set their own budgets, either daily or for the required lifetime of the ad. This means that companies can decide to spend thousands a month and have social advertising as their only advertising tool, but also that much smaller budgets will also see results. Advertising on Facebook essentially works as a bidding process, since, depending on budget, Facebook will place the ad in the optimum position to reach the target audience. When setting the budget, it is also possible to optimize the bidding process by specifying the amount the advertiser will pay to have the required audience view the ad.

Left A Facebook page with targeted adverts appearing in the newsfeed. The word 'sponsored' at the top left indicates that this is a paid-for advert.

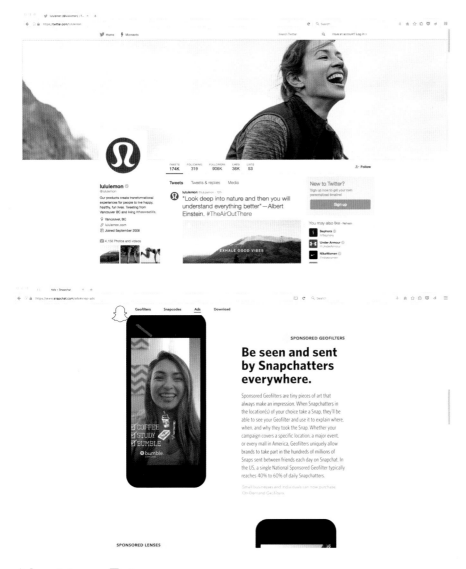

Advertising on Twitter

Advertising options are not quite as sophisticated on Twitter, and the platform has fewer users than Facebook, with 320 million MAUs. The platform has created a lot of interest through its ability to provoke user comment, in particular to hashtagged words and phrases, which invite all users to take part in trending topics and current opinion. As on Facebook, audiences on Twitter can be targeted by demographics, interest or device, or by identifying users similar to existing followers. In addition, Twitter can be used to identify keywords in the tweets of desired followers. Twitter offers:

- A promoted tweet, which reaches more users' timelines, profile pages and 'who to follow' recommendations.
- Website cards containing images and a call-to-action link to the host website.

Brands can set their own budgets, and are charged only once a follower is gained or a post replied to or retweeted. Twitter also provides advertisers with data sets that show the number of impressions (reads or scroll-overs), engagement rates, retweets and those users who have made a post a favourite.

Platform	No. of MAU	Types of advertising	Advantages	What the viewer sees
Instagram	400 million	Photo ads 60-second video ads Carousel ads that swipe to other images and link to website	Can be used with Facebook's self-service ad manager interface, which allows the setting of ad objectives, target audience and budget Ad works on Facebook and Instagram Facebook's Advert Reporting software tracks views and engagement	The word 'sponsored' to indicate an ad
Snapchat	Over 100 million per day	Snap ads, ten-second full-screen ads with additional swipe feature to further content Location-based sponsored Geofilters can be added when Snapchatters add a filter to an image in a certain location Sponsored lenses, which allow fun user interaction by pressing and holding the image to add a sponsored animation or image layer	Fun, shareable content is less invasive than other platforms Interaction times are immediately measureable	The word 'ad' on snap ads and 'sponsored' for Geofilters and sponsored lenses
Pinterest	100 million	Promoted Pins	The content merges seamlessly with other collectable images Audiences can be targeted by areas of interest Promoted (and organic) Pins drive traffic directly to the brand's website Brands can choose to pay for engagement or for visits to the host site Pinterest Analytics gives trackable results	The words 'promoted Pin' under the image
Tumblr	Over 80 million posts on blog accounts per day	Sponsored posts Sponsored video posts on a continuous loop Sponsor a day by placing a logo and tagline on the Tumblr dashboard; this links to content created on a tab in the Explore page	Users are targetable through gender, location and interest Advertiser Analytics measures interaction and engagement	A subtle dollar sign in the upper right-hand corner of sponsored posts A tab on the main dashboard for a sponsored day
YouTube	1 billion	Video ads that can play before, alongside or in search results	A daily budget can be set; there is no payment if an ad is skipped within 30 seconds Viewers can be targeted by age, interests, gender and location Built-in analytics measure performance	A small black banner with the option to skip the ad

Advertising on other platforms

This table opposite shows advertising possibilities on other platforms. All posts that are sponsored, boosted or promoted must be made obvious to the viewer as indicated.

Advertising online has addressed many of the disadvantages of traditional offline advertising, providing the viewer with a direct chance to interact with a message that should in some way be connected to their age, their area of interest or their web behaviour. For brands, the results are measurable, meaning that advertising can be placed closer to users, in spaces they have developed themselves as credible forums in which to share their opinions.

However, it is credibility that seems most at risk for brands, with extended use of advertising messages that must be made obvious as such. In the near future, will viewers simply start to weed these out in the way they do with print campaigns, and scroll quickly to more engaging and organic content? Or will they admire sites that withstand the pressure to create revenue through advertising? Brands will have to work hard to remain innovative to provoke actual engagement.

REFERENCES

Adweek.com, 'Here's How Many People Are on Facebook, Instagram, Twitter and Other Big Social Networks', *Social Times*, 4 April 2016, www.adweek.com/socialtimes/heres-how-many-people-are-on-facebook-instagram-twitter-other-big-social-networks/637205

Barnard, Malcolm, *Fashion as Communication*, 2nd ed., Routledge 2002

Carroll, Angela, 'Brand Communications in Fashion Categories Using Celebrity Endorsement', *Brand Management*, 17/2 (October 2009), pp. 146–58

Dahlén, Micael, Fredrik Lange and Terry Smith, *Marketing Communications: A Brand Narrative Approach*, Wiley 2010

Emarketer.com, 'Worldwide Ad Spending Growth Revised Downward', 21 April 2016, www.emarketer.com/Article/Worldwide-Ad-Spending-Growth-Revised-Downward/1013858

Euromonitor International, 'Emerging Markets Now Taking a Bigger Piece of the Advertising Pie', 16 March 2014

Fill, Chris, *Marketing Communications: Brands, Experiences and Participation*, 6th ed., Pearson 2013

Google.com, 'AdWords', accessed 2 June 2016, www.google.com/adwords/costs

TheGuardian.com, 'John Lewis unveils Christmas ad starring Monty the Penguin', 6.11.2014, www.theguardian.com/business/2014/nov/06/john-lewis-unveils-christmas-ad-starring-monty-the-penguin

Hackley, Chris, *Advertising and Promotion: An Integrated Marketing Approach to Communications*, Sage 2010

Lea-Greenwood, Gaynor, *Fashion Marketing Communications*, Wiley 2012

Marketingtechnews.net, 'Global digital ad spend to hit $285 bn by 2020', 21 June 2016, www.marketingtechnews.net/news/2016/jun/21/global-digital-ad-spend-hit-285-billion-2020/

Neikova, Devora, 'The Fashion Advertising Campaign: Big Business and Brand Identity', 24 September 2014, www.notjustalabel.com/editorial/fashion-advertising-campaign-big-business-brand-identity

Strugatz, Rachel, 'Google's Lead Shrinks as Brands Go Social', *WWD: Women's Wear Daily*, 208/76 (October 2014), p. 1

Taylor, Charles, George Franke and Hae-Kyong Bang, 'Use and Effectiveness of Billboards: Perspectives from Selective-Perception Theory and Retail-Gravity Models', *Journal of Advertising*, 35/4 (December 2006), pp. 21–34

Tesseras, Lucy, 'Q+A: Boohoo.com's Joint Chief Executive Carol Kane', *Marketing Week*, 29 January 2014, www.marketing week.com/2014/01/29/qa-boohoo-coms-joint-chief-executive-carol-kane

FURTHER READING

Ries, Al, and Laura Ries, *The Fall of Advertising and the Rise of PR*, HarperBusiness 2004

Springer, Paul, *Ads to Icons: How Advertising Succeeds in a Multimedia Age*, Kogan Page 2009

DISCUSSION

Do traditional theories of advertising, such as AIDA, and O'Malley and Hall's four frameworks, encompass all the possibilities of advertising via social media? Would you add a new model?

Look at a celebrity-led campaign and consider how it illustrates McCracken's Meaning Transfer model.

Consider the most original advertising message you have seen lately. Do you think we are seeing an end to traditional print and TV ads?

Chapter 5
PR, ENDORSEMENT AND SPONSORSHIP

How do public relations (PR) work in the fashion industry? Find out how to:

- Gain and maintain online and offline editorial publicity
- Raise the profile and enhance the credibility of new and existing brands among fashion journalists and influencers
- Implement third-party endorsement techniques such as product placement, the use of celebrities and sponsorship, to place brands in natural, desirable settings that are more credible to the consumer than traditional advertising
- Manage bad publicity

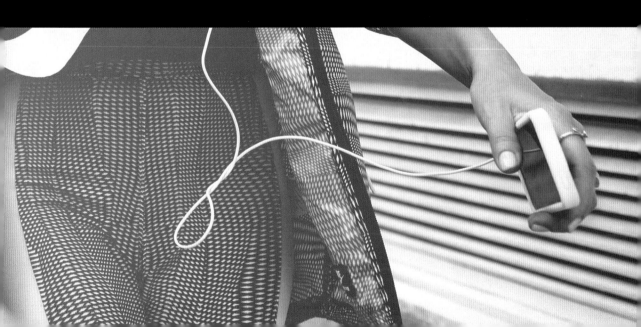

PR FOR FASHION: AN OVERVIEW

PR has become an essential component of the promotional mix. For new brands and start-ups, achieving external recognition should be the first point of consideration. Prospective stockists, interested investors and potential consumers will search for confirmation of third-party interest before committing to brands. Most companies engage in PR not just for its effectiveness in raising awareness and enhancing brand image and brand reputation, but also because for budget holders PR is one of the cheapest tools in the communications mix. It does not carry the media costs associated with advertising, and some forms of PR such as unpaid celebrity endorsements or featuring in a magazine fashion shoot result in free but highly credible exposure. Well-considered PR can also act as a way of extending the newsworthy longevity of more expensive tools such as advertising or sales promotions.

Definitions of PR

Most authors on the subject, such as Chris Fill (2013), Gaynor Lea-Greenwood (2012) and John Egan (2015), cite all or part of the definition by the Chartered Institute of Public Relations:

The discipline that looks after reputation, with the aim of earning understanding and support and influencing opinion and behaviour. It is the planned and sustained effort to establish and maintain good will and mutual understanding between an organization and its publics.

In fashion, PR is used to raise or maintain awareness of designer labels, brands and retailers using newsworthy items such as new concepts and directions, new collections, events, collaborations or celebrity involvement, via coverage written by a respected third party in consumer and trade magazines, newspapers, influencers' social media feeds, blogs and other information forums.

The first part of this chapter concentrates on the tactics and effectiveness of, and issues involved in, raising and maintaining awareness of a label and ultimately creating demand.

The tools of PR

PR is the most diverse of the communication tools, and the number of different tactics that come under its umbrella is a surprise to many. These tactics are sometimes referred to as the PR mix. This list includes the tools that will be addressed and expanded on later in this chapter.

- Online and offline editorial coverage.
- A basic level of product placement.
- Celebrity seeding via gifting.
- Event management including press days.
- Publicity stunts and buzz marketing.
- Seeding brands with third-party influencers and bloggers.

PR people can be either in-house (a small team or individual employed directly by a brand) or an outsourced company that represents a complementary mix of designers, retailers, corporate clients and brands on a monthly retainer fee. The fees charged by PR companies are subject to negotiation depending on the client and the services needed, although budget holders should estimate around £1,200 per month. The PR team will be involved in realizing aspects of the list above, but also organizing the material needed to carry out those tasks and tracking the success of each choice. Supporting materials and tasks include:

- Developing close relationships with the editors of fashion and lifestyle publications.

THE
HOT LIST
Our edit of the new high-street drops

COMPILED BY GRACE SMITHAM · PHOTOGRAPHS BY NOVALISDIGITAL.COM

Left *Marie Claire* 'Hot List' page from October 2016, featuring recommended brands and products. Fashion editors are extremely powerful and respected forces in the fashion industry, and their recommendations resonate strongly with readers.

86 PR, endorsement and sponsorship

- Arranging press releases and branded lookbooks, and advising on which models and photographers are desirable.
- Writing and proofreading copy.
- Researching and advising on which celebrities to gift to.
- Organizing events, including venue, invitations, drinks, food and guest lists.
- Organizing the guest lists for trade fairs and/or catwalk shows.
- Organizing days on which press can view collections.
- Tracking and delivering styles to magazines or stylists for use in shoots.
- Updating and monitoring press coverage, compiling press clippings and the results of online traffic.
- Researching which influencers and third-party bloggers may be suitable to tie up with, and advising on the running of the brand's own blog.

PR CREDIBILITY: THE ADVANTAGES AND DISADVANTAGES OF PR

A return to Fill's (2013) rating scale of effectiveness for communications, shown in the diagram below, focuses on the ratings for PR and enables an analysis of the advantages and disadvantages of PR as a communication tool.

Advantages of PR
- The level of credibility afforded by the audience is high. The nature of PR coverage is that approval comes via a respected third party who endorses the brand to readers.
- Costs can be low. Editorial coverage in magazines and blogs is essentially free. Events, gifting or publicity stunts can be carried out at a controlled or low cost to the brand, yet the resulting coverage does a huge job of raising awareness.
- Although the ratings for personalization and interaction are given as low, online coverage does allow for reader comment.

Disadvantages of PR
- The level of control for the brand is low. PR material such as press releases, lookbooks and samples are issued to a third party to publish, or require a third party to endorse them. This may be targeted as much as possible, but the external media source then dictates the interpretation of the piece.
- Third parties such as celebrities fall in and out of favour.
- Wastage can be high. Tactics such as gifting to a celebrity do not necessarily result in the desired press coverage and can be expensive to organize. Editorial publicity is notoriously hard to achieve, and editors do have commitments to brands that advertise with them.

- Monitoring and time spent tracking the success of PR can be high. Journalists do not advise brands of all editorial inclusion or styles spotted on a celebrity. The monitoring of fashion magazines, blogs, online forums and newspapers is labour-intensive.

KEY CHARACTERISTICS OF PR AS A COMMUNICATION TOOL

Communications	Public relations
Ability to deliver a personal message	Low
Ability to reach a large audience	Medium
Level of interaction	Low
Credibility	
Given by the target audience	High
Cost	
Absolute costs	Low
Cost per contact	Low
Wastage	High
Size of investment	Low
Control	
Ability to target particular audiences	Low
Management's ability to adjust the deployment of the tool as circumstances change	Low

EDITORIAL COVERAGE

Editorial coverage is defined as published coverage where a journalist has added their own copy or used their designated space seemingly to endorse, promote or discover a brand or designer. Sometimes the terms 'publicity' or 'editorial publicity' will also be used.

Offline or print editorial coverage

In fashion magazines, offline editorial can be achieved in two ways: first, by inclusion in a style-spotting or similar page given over to the discovery of new designers (see the *Marie Claire* 'Hot List' on page 86), new products or ranges and new stores. Second, magazines can include a brand or designer in their own stylized photo shoots, featuring named photographers and models, that are centred on fashion trends and presented as essential buying for their readers.

In the case of printed magazines, photo shoots are shot well in advance of publication, and garments, shoes or accessories will typically have been sent to the editor four to six months in advance for monthly magazines and four to six weeks in advance for weeklies. PR companies must constantly keep in touch with fashion editors to see which themes they are planning for future publications so that they can send in suitable garments from the labels they represent. Generally, when products are featured in magazines, the press clarifies the retail price and availability of the items featured; magazines are careful to include labels that it is possible for their readers to buy.

Online editorial coverage

The term 'editorial' also applies to coverage in online magazines, third-party blogs, influencer feeds, online news forums and style aggregators.

Influencers

Key influencers will be targeted with press information in the hope that they will provide vital online support. Research into, and the identification of, credible third-party blogs and influencers to endorse and publish their opinions of brands (a process known as 'seeding') has become a key part of the role of a PR. The fashion industry has seen a huge boom of respected influencers reporting on fashion shows, brands and products, recommending them and even collaborating with brands – either as part of the design process or by being the new face or ambassador of the brand.

The term 'influencer' is used for a top tier of bloggers, vloggers and profiles on social media that are noted for their audience reach, the credibility they have built with audiences and their levels of engagement. This method of working has coined its own term: influencer marketing.

Vloggers

Video blogging and posting the results on YouTube has grown from its origin as an effective medium to convey peer-to-peer make-up tutorials, to cover short films of recent buys, style tips and beauty advice from personable, popular vloggers. Film allows a much more intimate view of the presenter; followers are involved in their lives, seeing their houses, their pets and their friends, and are able to appreciate down-to-earth honest views from a real voice.

Viscose top £585 and viscose shorts £450 both Miu Miu; satin and wood platforms £812.36 Rochas; pearl, gold and enamel lip ring (right hand) £335 Delfina Delettrez at Matches Fashion; metallic leather bag £840 Pierre Hardy; cotton socks £10 Falke

Left Top and shorts by Miu Miu, platform shoes by Rochas, Falke socks and a Pierre Hardy bag feature in this story, 'Hands Up for Glamour' from *Glamour* magazine, 2017. The photographer is Ben Rayner, with styling by Jaime Kay Waxman and model Sasha Melnychuk.

Right Cosmopolitan.co.uk offers advice on key trends for Autumn/Winter 2016. The online version of *Cosmopolitan* magazine, the site's effective tone of voice and use of competitions strike a chord with younger audiences.

Centre *Love Aesthetics* blog, 2015 (Love-Aesthetics.nl). *Love Aesthetics* was founded in 2008 by Ivania Carpio, whose eye for colour and texture has led to collaborations with fashion photographer Nick Knight and Dutch *Vogue*. Her coverage of labels is as respected by her followers as that of a fashion editor.

Below right US-based Chiara Ferragni's blog *The Blonde Salad* has, according to *Fashionista.com* (2015), the broadest reach of any blogger, with more than 3 million Instagram followers. Items she recommends on Instagram sell out almost immediately. Brands that pay for advertising space on her site have seen conversions to sales.

Below left Vlogger Tanya Burr is a regular at London Fashion Week and has been part of the judging panel for the *Elle* magazine beauty awards. She is pictured here with fellow vlogger and brand ambassador Jim Chapman.

HOW BRANDS AND RETAILERS ACHIEVE EDITORIAL COVERAGE

Because this type of exposure is so valuable, brands invest a great deal of effort in order to attract attention. They communicate their main seasonal ranges by compiling press packs of information.

Press packs

A typical press pack contains a press release and the latest product photo shoot compiled into a folder or booklet known as a lookbook. The press pack should provide written and visual information that conveys news about the brand, in a concise and engaging hit of information. Fashion editors, journalists and bloggers extract from it the material they need to formulate a small editorial piece, a news item, a post or a coveted place in a fashion shoot. Press packs were traditionally physical items that would often also contain a gift incentive for the media. In order to meet the need for the increased speed of digital publication, the press release and the lookbook are now often produced digitally to be sent via email, thus reducing the need for a 'holder' of the information. Brands may, however, decide that a one-off use of the unexpected might create a more immediate visual impact with editors, and will work to decide how best to present their ideas.

Media lists

Before sending out press packs, brands draw up a comprehensive list of magazines, newspapers, online channels and social media platforms to target. The list will primarily contain published magazines and newspapers with a similar readership to the brand's own profiled consumer, together with blogs and other forums that are key to shaping online opinion. The turnover of staff on fashion magazines is incredibly high (apart from the editors at the very top), and a common problem is sending a pack to a person who is no longer at the magazine. The best way to avoid this is to take names from the list of staff and management printed in the latest editions. Fashion assistants, assistant editors and stylists may be targeted less frequently and therefore may be more receptive to press-pack information.

Press releases

Press releases contain the key descriptive and informative details of the product. In them, brands may also wish to inform fashion editors and journalists of new collection inspirations, new lines, seasonal ranges, store openings, the appointment of new creative directors and any other newsworthy information that will keep them in the minds of readers and potential consumers. Press releases are

Left Sephora press pack, 2013. The San Francisco agency Hub Strategy & Communication worked with Sephora to create a personalized invitation to a new loyalty programme. Editors received a lipstick, an iPhone case and a set of limited-edition signed prints, with a welcome letter to the scheme. In lieu of a hard-copy press release, a digital copy was supplied on a glossy black key-shaped memory stick.

prepared in the hope of being eye-catching and attention-grabbing to the fashion media. They are written in the third person, as if someone else has already written about the brand. This is an important courtesy to busy journalists, who can then extract straight from them.

Writing press releases

When writing a press release, it is important to avoid jargon and to use descriptive, concise and factual language instead. The press release is an important point of origin for descriptive words and phrases about ranges and products that can inform product copy on the brand's website and be used as part of an SEO strategy (see p.139). It is recommended that the text of a press release should be no longer than one A4- or US letter-sized page. The language should inspire the reader to view the range immediately, so releases are often accompanied by a few key photos of the range. Increasingly, press releases are sent via email. It is, therefore, good practice to set up digital press releases as two-up page display PDFs with the text on one page and images on the other, so that journalists get an immediate impression. Below is a useful checklist of what should be included in a press release.

- The brand's logo or the designer's name should be included at the top and on all subsequent pages, to reinforce the brand's name. If a page does go astray, the logo will clarify to the journalist who it is from.
- A catchy or provocative title can draw in the reader.
- The first paragraph should be a summary of the range or product; often this is all that will be read. It must grab attention and entice further reading. Increasingly, opportunities for editorial are found on social media or blogs, which are by nature bite-sized, engaging hits of information for followers. They may use content from the first paragraph of a press release.
- The second paragraph should expand on influences, fabrics, prints, textures and colours. Sightings on celebrities and other press coverage can be included here, as can practical information, such as prices and stores that stock the range already.
- Quotations regarding the designer's or other creatives' inspiration or stories about the founder work well, and suggest that interviews have already taken place with interested media.
- The release should conclude with where and when the range will be available, and include the brand's own website for e-commerce or further information.
- Press contacts should be given for high-resolution photos (for magazine publication), further images and details. Smaller brands and start-ups without a PR department can use a press@...... address to give the impression that they are larger than they are.

Laundry Maid Jeans

LMTJ 013 Super Skinny jean   LMTJ 001 Tailored Jean   LMTJ 002 High Rise Skinny Jean

LMTJ 008 Slim Carrot Jean   LMTJ 009 Peg Top Chino   LMTJ 007 Wide Leg Jean

Above A typical fashion press release, here for Laundry Maid Jeans, features a visual overview of the collection. The model is Rachel Rutt.

- Spelling, grammar and general writing style should be thoroughly checked before the press release is issued. The fashion media are experts in this field and can be expected to have a low tolerance for mistakes.

Lookbooks

Lookbooks are a compilation of photographs that show the theme of the new collection or product range. In the fashion industry, these are undertaken two to four times a year in line with the major selling seasons. The photo shoots a brand carries out with a view to achieving editorial coverage should also be linked to and convey its identity. Lookbooks are the most immediate visual impression of what the brand is about, for editors and ultimately consumers as well. For smaller brands, one photo shoot may have to cover the lookbook and the product shots used on the website, as well as the pictures used on the brand's own blog, social media and wider communication material such as retail point of sale (see p. 200). For new brands, translating identity into the choice of a model and

Left Lookbook shot of Tatiana Shamratova taken by the photographer Willem Jaspert and styled by Cheryl Leung for Laundry Maid Jeans. The model is set against a minimal, non-distracting background. The hair and make-up are simple and natural. The styling complements the product; there are small touches of the work ethic that is central to the brand's identity, but these do not overwhelm the fit and silhouette of the jeans.

- **Minimal pose photography** Models pose with straight shoulders, hips and back, with their arms straight by their sides and their feet pointing straight ahead (see Cos image on p. 42). The effect is direct and commanding and throws focus on to the shape of the garments.
- **Flat lays** These are shot on a white or neutral background and show the garment as if it is lying on a flat surface. Such photographs are typically requested for shot pieces of editorial such as the *Marie Claire* coverage (see p. 86).
- **Ghost or invisible mannequin photography** Garments appear three-dimensional, as if they have a bust or hips in them. This is achieved by shooting the garments on a mannequin, then removing the mannequin using digital editing software.

Today, lookbooks and photographs are usually supplied to the press digitally and may be just for online use. It is still, however, good practice for brands to store shoot photographs in three different resolutions and physical sizes: small size and low resolution for online use; medium size and high resolution for small editorial use; and large size and high resolution for large reproduction. Although lookbooks may need to be available on a memory stick or in emailable form, brands usually have some printed editions for physical press packs, for giveaways to retailers and for use at trade fairs.

Gifts as part of press packs

Incentives, gifts and freebies are an extremely important part of PR. Despite digital formats reducing the opportunities to convey gifts, they are still expected by the press. The more creative brands can be, the more they are likely to pique the interest of the media and gain exposure. The gift might be the product that the brand is trying to promote, but it can also be any other creative, pampering or amusing gift.

The importance of attracting the attention of gatekeepers to fashion exposure should not be underestimated. Positive coverage can result in demand as effectively as that raised by an advertising campaign, so much so that demand may exceed supply (this is thought to be a good problem to have in fashion PR!). Editorial coverage can kick-start the constant stream of exciting newsfeed that consumers need to keep the brand at the front of their minds. Coverage can also springboard quickly into personal selling and other communication, or even financial opportunities such as the interest of investors.

a series of poses can be a challenge, and may require test shoots and advice. Fashion media personnel, especially those who work for upmarket publications, have an extremely sophisticated eye, and if brands use friends or real people as models, or an unknown photographer, the result must be extremely edgy or polished to avoid being quickly binned or identified as a low-budget concern.

Lookbooks should communicate what the garments or accessories look like within the identity of the brand. It is important that the styling does not detract from the garments and obscure the possibilities for an editor to use the clothes in their own photo shoots and stories. It is the role of the fashion editor rather than the brand to place the products in directional, highly stylized stories. This is sometimes referred to by photographers as the difference between commercial and fashion photography.

Lookbook and website photography styles

In recent years, and in tune with the rise of e-commerce, more formulaic photography styles have become popular. Provided they fit the brand's identity, they have made life easier for brand managers.

- **Non-recognition photography** For online retailers with hundreds of items to shoot, photographing a model without a head saves money on hair and make-up and solves a continuity problem with models; if the viewer cannot see a face, they cannot see how many different models have been used.

Left Net-a-Porter product shots feature models cropped at the chin. This means viewers do not attach the relationship of a face to the brand.

Centre Acne models line up.

Below left Another favoured technique of Net-a-Porter is achieving a 3D effect using invisible mannequin photography.

Below right Mulberry gave this elegant espresso cup to the press for Spring/ Summer 2014 London Fashion Week, reflecting its collaboration with the English china company Wedgwood.

EVENTS MANAGEMENT

Event marketing – such as events hosted by the fashion brands and companies themselves or those for which they are seen as organizers or sponsors – is growing in importance in the fashion industry as part of tactical PR strategies. Brands can invite loyal followers or target potential new customers with specific events such as store openings, range launches or sales previews that provide customers with a chance to interact with designers, celebrities or other speakers of interest. PRs will be expected to provide contacts from their networks, catering and drinks, DJs and even suggest a guest list of the right people, which may include celebrities. Newsworthy events can attract editorial coverage in their own right.

Press days

Press days can be held in the brand's own showroom or the showroom of its PR company. They usually take place twice a year, after the new season's collections have been shown either on the catwalk or at a trade fair, and they act as an invitation to fashion journalists and key influencers to view the collection. The aim is to encourage supportive press coverage to tempt buyers to place an order. PR people or agencies need all the relevant product information for these events, such as forthcoming campaign material, lookbooks, press releases, retail prices and availability dates.

Events surrounding fashion shows and trade fairs

The role of catwalk and trade shows as a vehicle to promote fashion labels and brands is examined in Chapter 10. In this section, we examine where a PR person will seek to be involved in fashion industry events that are not usually open to the public.

PR people will certainly want to oversee who is invited to fashion shows, whether they take place on a catwalk or as part of a static trade exhibition. Both events are open by invitation only to buyers, press, influencers and other relevant members of the fashion industry. The invitation itself may be generated in-house, and can give the PR department a chance to innovate and be creative, especially when the event is a designer show.

Goodie bags are a feature for guests at all catwalk fashion shows, and small giveaways are a good idea for trade shows. Again, the PR person will be asked to see who in their networks might be prepared to contribute items. Gifts range from the practical (sleep masks, hits of caffeine, teeth whiteners) to the reviving (shots of alcohol, hot drinks, sugary food) to the pampering (make-up, skin brighteners, nail polishes, and so on).

Above A Superdry press event at the Ham Yard Hotel, London.

Below Giles created this large foam claw-shaped invitation as an introduction to its Spring/Summer 2015 show, which began with animal cries and tropically coloured lighting.

Above The Noon By Noor Autumn/ Winter 2014-15 runway show goodie bag, as part of New York Fashion Week, included Smythson of Bond Street stationery and Zoya nail polish.

After-show parties are a feature of all the international fashion weeks, and can be relied on to attract press coverage of off-duty models, designers and media representatives. Trade-show events will include seminar speakers, trend presentations and catwalk shows featuring brands that are showing at the exhibition. Parties and evening events afterwards also provide a valuable opportunity for designers, sales people and buyers to mix in an informal setting.

Interactive events

Now becoming much more important are events that involve an activity, demonstration or motivational talk organized by brands to increase awareness, but also to allow members of the public to participate. These promote the lifestyle the brand wishes to project to consumers, and thereby get potentially interested people involved. In October 2015 the UK's premium department store Harrods gave over the month of October to the promotion of menswear. It hosted a series of in-store events under the title 'Cover to Cover', which featured an evening in conversation with the brand ambassador and vlogger Jim Chapman, who gave his thoughts on the exclusive collection Burberry had produced for Harrods. Other brand collaborations were featured in the store's menswear magazine and window displays, including exclusive contributions from Louis Vuitton, Zegna, Brioni, Gucci, Paul Smith and Tom Ford.

Fashion's Night Out was an initiative that began in New York in 2009 and was originally intended to help boost recession-hit fashion stores. Participating stores along Fifth Avenue and Lower Broadway and in the Meatpacking District stayed open until 11 PM for one night in September, treating all comers to VIP-style drinks, goodie bags, DJ sets and the opportunity to meet designers, celebrities and fashion editors. This inclusive event was sponsored by *Vogue* and CFDA (Council of Fashion Designers of America). The idea spread to other cities, including most notably London and Milan, but also Amsterdam, Tokyo, Mexico City, Paris and other US cities such as Los Angeles and Philadelphia.

Above Kenzo's after-show parties have become some of the most sought-after events at Paris Fashion Week. Here, the actress Scarlett Johansson attends an event organized by creative directors Carol Lim and Humberto Leon on board the *Louisiane Belle*, following the designers' aquatic-themed Spring/Summer 2014 show.

Below Burberry and Brioni covers shot by the photographer Ishi for Harrods menswear magazine *Cover to Cover*, October 2015.

Bottom A T-shirt and tote bag designed by the artist Takashi Murakami for Fashion's Night Out in Tokyo, 2010, in association with *Vogue* Japan.

PUBLICITY STUNTS AND BUZZ MARKETING

Stunts created or suggested as PR activity are designed to provoke editorial coverage for the brand in the same way an event would. They can be used to create a buzz around brands entering the market, or as a subtle tactic to keep established brands in the news. These are different from the tactics of guerrilla advertising discussed in Chapter 4 (see p. 73), in which an advertising or communications agency is paid to create a stunt that generates PR coverage. Publicity stunts can be created by brands on very little budget to charm, provoke thought and – preferably – encourage people to buy, and news of the stunt can be spread further by blogging or on social media channels. One such stunt was the pre-launch campaign for Marc Jacobs Daisy perfume in Copenhagen in the summer of 2015, when the fountain on Strøget, the main shopping street in Copenhagen, was decorated with daisies while young women distributed giant daisy flowers to passing shoppers. This was both a charming act in itself and an incentive to visit the city's department stores where the product could be sampled.

We now turn to the tools of celebrity endorsement and sponsorship that relate to PR – in that they seek credibility through third-party endorsement – but (because of the fees involved at some levels) will not be expected to come from the PR budget.

Above A plan for a Laundry Maid Jeans publicity stunt. Astroturf was to be cut with holes filled with potted geraniums in the shape of the name of the brand. This was to be rolled out in green spaces, reminiscent of the use of plants to spell out the name of a town. A tactic like this borrows from street art: some people may not even notice, others may think it amusing and spread the word. The whole thing could be rolled up and removed should it cause offence.

Below Distributing daisies in Copenhagen to promote Marc Jacobs' Daisy perfume, 2015.

PRODUCT PLACEMENT

Product placement is a contrived way of placing a brand in a natural setting, making the brand appear to have been chosen by the character played by a TV or a film star. The rise of reality TV has led to opportunities for 'real' people to be apparently using real products, and is a popular choice for product placement. Product placement has a similar objective to editorial coverage: the brand appears to be endorsed by an admired character, and therefore gains credibility in the minds of the audience.

Product placement was originally thought to be an effective antidote to the cluttered and transparent messages of advertising. If viewers were fast-forwarding through TV advertising, then an effective strategy would be to place products, brands and labels more covertly within TV programmes or films themselves.

In general, in the UK and Europe, the US, Canada and Australia, paid-for product placement – where money has exchanged hands between brands and TV channels, programmers or individual presenters or actors – is allowed as long as prohibited items such as cigarettes and alcohol are not used, the audience is not underage and the viewer is made aware that product placement has taken place. In China, South America and India, product placement is relatively new and regulations have not yet been formed. In the UK and Europe, broadcasters must display a logo that informs viewers that programmes include product placement. Some types of product placement cross over and integrate with types of sponsorship and endorsement and other tools, especially advertising.

Basic placement may be achieved for free, but enhanced and integrated product placement can be handled by specialist product placement agencies which, in return for a fee, can seek opportunities and guarantee placements in programmes suitable to the brand. There are various types of placement.

- **Basic placement** The seemingly inadvertent use of a brand or product, or a brand's campaign, in a film or TV programme.
- **Enhanced placement** The product is featured or named in the plot of a TV show or film, or a brand puts itself forward to offer a prize as part of a competition on a show. In this situation the programmers will have been paid for the placement, and the brand can be said to be sponsoring the show.
- **Integrated placement** The product is integral or central to the plot. A featured actor may pose for the brand's campaign shoot and appear in TV advertising. Brands may take it one step further and decide both to be featured, using product placement, and to sponsor the advertising for the TV show. Since this involves revenue to the TV network, this is effectively advertising, and is discussed as TV sponsorship in Chapter 4 (see p. 67).
- **Programming** The brand is at the centre of the plot.

Below left The US TV series *Stylista* follows entrants competing for a job at *Elle* magazine under editorial director Anne Slowey, pictured. One competitor is fired each week until the winner gets the job, a prize of US$100,000, a lease on a Manhattan apartment and a year's clothing allowance at H&M. *Elle* magazine is central to the plot and so is an example of programming, whereas H&M is named as part of the prize and so could be said to sponsor the show.

Below right *Mary's Bottom Line* (2012), set in the Headen & Quarmby factory in Manchester, is an example of programming. After many trials, Mary Portas' brand Kinky Knickers went on to be stocked across the UK and available via the brand's own e-commerce site.

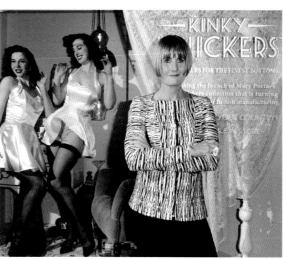

CELEBRITY GIFTING AND ENDORSEMENT

According to Lea-Greenwood (2012), a celebrity can be defined as 'someone who is known in the public domain'. This covers an increasingly wide remit: sportspeople, models, actors, musicians, reality TV stars, bloggers and those with self-generated fame alone. Celebrities are generally known for their ability to attract publicity, however fleeting this may be. Most consumers are interested in what celebrities are working on, who they are seeing romantically, where they have been and what they were wearing on all these occasions. As far as the brand is concerned, its involvement in this type of imagery takes place in one of two ways.

- By celebrity gifting that can be researched and undertaken as part of PR.
- By celebrity endorsement, which, because a contract and fees are required, will come from the wider marketing budget.

Celebrity gifting or unpaid endorsement

This occurs when a celebrity is photographed in an item that appears to have been chosen by them because they like it. This can occur naturally; in the UK, the 'Kate Middleton effect' has benefited many retailers. Premium high-street chain Reiss saw its profits double in 2013 after awareness of the brand rocketed following the global distribution of photographs of the Duchess of Cambridge wearing its clothes. In 2016 Reiss commenced an ambitious international expansion programme focused on North America, Asia and Australia.

This type of luck can also be engineered, and may be the result of a gifting strategy to an individual or target list of celebrities, on which a PR can advise. This can incur the cost of the garment for the brand, but the demand and credibility that are created is deemed to be worth it. Crucially, in press releases or statements the brand can say that the celebrity wears or likes its product, but cannot imply that they bought it.

Far left Demand for the nude bandage-style dress worn by Kate, Duchess of Cambridge, to meet Michelle Obama in 2011 caused the Reiss website to crash.

Left The Los Angeles-based brand Rails has had an enviable increase of awareness in the buying public, typical of many LA labels. With no advertising campaigns or celebrity endorsement deals, the brand's signature check shirts have become an essential normcore piece for off-duty celebrities, such as Gisele Bündchen, seen here at the Superbowl in 2015.

Right The Kosovo-born British singer, TV presenter and actor Rita Ora has signed an organized portfolio of eight fashion-related endorsement deals, with brands including Calvin Klein, Superga, Roberto Cavalli, Rimmel, DKNY, and Madonna and her daughter Lourdes Ciccone Leon's Material Girl range for Macy's.

Celebrity endorsement

Celebrity endorsement is a contractual agreement between a label or brand and a celebrity or their management, for them to appear publicly wearing the brand. A brand chooses celebrities who personify it, and may sign that person to appear in a traditional fashion advertising campaign or make appearances wearing its products. The agreement will place the desired celebrity under certain restrictions, the most typical being that they cannot appear in competing brands. The image-transference effect of the use of celebrities in advertising, which also applies to endorsement, is discussed in the next section. Endorsement deals can also encompass one-off payments to appear in a brand, to speak publicly about it or to appear at events as a representative of the brand.

Some celebrities notch up an impressive number of complementary endorsements and, as an added attraction, can be signed to assist in the design of ranges for the brand, so that their style may be made fully available to consumers. Such celebrities are also known as brand ambassadors. Since around 2012, when the term 'influencer' came into popular use, an increasing number of style influencers have adopted this role for brands.

INDUSTRY PROFILE
MATTHEW ZORPAS OF
THE GENTLEMAN BLOGGER

Matthew Zorpas created his blog *The Gentleman Blogger* in 2012 after being repeatedly photographed by friends who were intrigued by the tailored suits he wore to teach at Istituto Marangoni in London. He was quickly noticed by the fashion industry, and attracted the interest of Armani after his first blog post went live. Shortly afterwards he was approached by Tommy Hilfiger, and became the online face of its made-to-measure tailoring range. Business-minded from the start, his organization today comprises a team of four; among other ambassador roles, he is the UK ambassador for Coach, for the car company Mini and for IWC luxury watches. He also works as a digital creative consultant, continues to lecture and is the author of *London 100: A Gentleman's Guide Book* (2013). He has an enviable, organically built total reach of 500,000 followers across the blog and other media, including 60,000 unique readers of the blog and 115,000 followers on Instagram.

Below Matthew Zorpas is prepared for his global online and offline campaign for Gianfranco Ferré L'Uomo fragrance. Gianfranco Ferré are the first luxury brand to use a digital influencer for a full campaign.

Q: How does the blog happen? Do you work with the same photographer and have a stylist?
A: When I started, I did not have the money to invest in a photographer. I invested in a good camera and my friends were shooting me, I was guiding everyone creatively and it really worked. Then in 2014 I started working full-time with one photographer, who is always with me at the shows, etc. He has a passion for photography and by working with me gets good exposure. The styling still comes from my own creative side. I am the whole package, plus luck and timing. I enjoyed dressing up to teach at Marangoni, putting on a tailored suit. This was in the days before *The Gentleman* was a commercial proposition, before the likes of Topman had a suit line and everyone was in chinos and tees. A young guy in a tailored suit and tie every day was a big story for everyone. I was in the right place at the right time.

Q: How do you get noticed as a blogger?
A: Actually people like me are now influencers. In terms of bloggers, we have a clear distinction between female and male fashion bloggers. There is also a clear distinction between the tiers, so you have the top-tier bloggers, such as Chiara Ferragni (theblondesalad.com) and Kristina Bazan (kayture.com), who are two of the biggest female bloggers in terms of their following, perception and also the budgets with which they are requested to work. There are fewer top male bloggers, so it is more a question of quality. We all have similar audiences in terms of numbers, so brands are looking at the most suitable influencer for the activity, range or size of project they wish to promote.

Q: Why did brands start to work more closely with bloggers?
A: Bloggers understand and work with the specific periods and occasions, such as Christmas or Father's Day, and these can be tied up with a specific product the marketing department wants to promote. From my side, I will create a blog post that includes nine images

Above Matthew Zorpas partners with Hugo Boss to recommend stylish essentials for Autumn.

and two paragraphs. That story is then linked back to a specific product and I take care of the whole production. The marketing department gives me the budget and the product, and I take care of that organic engagement with the audience. When working with a brand digitally, everything can be specified in the contract – how many Instagram posts, how many Tweets, how many shares I am going to make – everything is actually down to a bullet point and that decides the price I charge. I can measure the success of my input into sales on a specific product if it is linked from my blog, and I think my status is stronger as a result. Chiara and Kristina, for example, can show one product on their Instagram and that product will sell out. So the concept works very well as a return on marketing budgets.

Q: Tell us more about being a brand ambassador.
A: My aim since 2014 has been to get ambassadorships. I decided that I needed to secure a six-month plan with individual clients. Before, everything was very haphazard, with people coming to me with short individual briefs or projects and no long-term associations. That might mean that I would be working on ten brands every single week, but the way I work is designed to look organic. The first brand we managed to convince to work in this way was Coach. I was its UK ambassador for a year, Mini followed, and I became the UK ambassador for IWC from January 2016. We are breaking into all these different revenue streams through these exclusive relationships. It helps me to be a more stable business.

Q: What other things do you have to undertake as an ambassador?
A: I'm required to attend events and boutique openings. These could be anywhere in the world. Or, with the UK launch of the Mini Clubman, for example, I appeared in online promotion material, such as on the company website and social media, but also offline in print ads. I am doing the job of a model and a celebrity who it is credible for them to mention. But the key is that I am a celebrity with a connection to the consumer.

DBA [Digital Brand Architects], the biggest blogger agency in the US, is already putting bloggers it represents forward for offline fashion campaigns. Soon two or three bloggers will definitely appear in a luxury fashion ad; the first brand to do it will be the innovator and everything else will follow, and that will change the whole game. [Since achieved by Gianfranco Ferré in 2016.] Events-wise, I can do more offline. I would like brands to think 'Let's get Matthew in store and see how many people he can bring in'; 'Let's get Matthew to DJ and see how many people we can reach'; 'Let's get Matthew to host a dinner for us with all the executives, chief designers, etc.'

Q: Is it like being a celebrity?
A: You get the same craziness as a celebrity, the same passion and energy of those who follow you. To meet and greet is a new thing for bloggers. You travel to another city and you find these global audiences, and that, for me, is a surprise every single time; as soon as it is announced that I am there I get five or six messages from the most random countries and cities. Chiara, for example, will find 500 people waiting outside her hotel, eager to take a selfie with her. I'm sure we will turn into proper celebrities.

Q: Do you feel you will remain credible to your audiences?
A: I noticed that one of the most popular pictures I posted was as soon as I announced the Coach ambassadorship, so there is a huge audience that is not thinking I am becoming commercial and getting paid to say this; they see it as credible – that as an individual who started from zero I have been able to become an ambassador. I am in two minds. What is the biggest audience out there? Do they prefer the

organic message that does not bring you any money, status or activities, or do they prefer the message where they see a commercial activity as a bond between a brand, the blogger and the audience? I think that as bloggers we always present the commercial relationship as a bond – I am proud to be working with Mini, I am delighted to do that and that they are working with me – but we are still into this relationship-building that I think is very delicate.

Q: *Do you see yourself going down the advertising route to generate revenue?*
A: I don't do it – I'm not a believer. Usually advertisers pay you per click-through. A typical brand would only pay me if a transaction has come through from my blog, despite the presence of its brand or advert on my blog page daily. If I go to a blog I am looking for inspiration; it is unlikely that I will have £1,000 to click on a banner and buy a wallet at that particular moment. Instead, I will see the wallet, be influenced by the presentation and perhaps go out five days later to buy it elsewhere. As a blogger I will have placed the message, but that message will not translate directly to me in terms of a sale. If a brand asks, I could give it spaces paid for maybe monthly, but it doesn't look great. If it works and translates into sales, fine, but overuse of advertising can look aggressive.

Q: *How do you see your future – will it be a challenge to remain relevant?*
A: There is a challenge in that the platforms are shifting, so, for example, Snapchat is gaining in importance. This happens because the audience is getting tired. If you are a visionary you will be able to see that everyone is shifting towards something that is instant, but as soon as that proposition becomes commercialized people move away from it. Instagram, for example, is launching sponsored posts and already people are getting tired of it. Snapchat is the new thing.

The audience I have acquired since 2012 – which is continuing to grow – is getting older as I do. Why IWC now? Because my audience is reaching 30, the time when they will invest in their first watch. Why has Mini linked up with me now? Because my 30-something audience wants a Mini, not a Rolls-Royce. I may try to be relevant with a younger audience by using Snapchat, but it is a new audience even for me. All brands try to remain relevant to younger audiences, but mine is Facebook and Instagram, and realistically it will probably stay that way.

Right *The Gentleman Blogger* site.

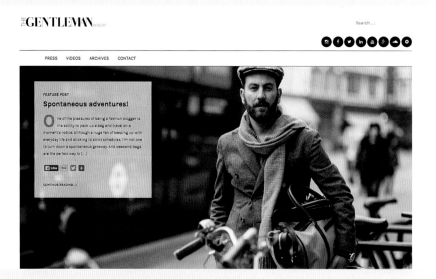

Celebrity seeding

Just as with the identification of important influencers, it is good practice to keep an eye out for up-and-coming models, musicians and actors that may fit the brand identity. This can be a beneficial tactic for both parties. As Lea-Greenwood (2010) points out, the brand will hope that, as the celebrity's fame grows, he or she will constantly be named as the 'face' of the brand, and that each other's achievements will transfer, maintaining a positive association.

The question remains whether the use of celebrity is the way forward for new and existing fashion brands. Despite many who say it may be on the wane, surprising new associations keep springing up.

When it comes to product placement and the use of celebrity, there continues to be a trend for the use of more 'real' personalities, such as reality TV stars or influencers, who help to weave brands into the fabric of viewers' or readers' everyday lives. The concept and use of celebrity may become new, different or surprising, but it does not yet seem to be on the decrease.

Below Olivier Rousteing, the creative director of Balmain, has cited Kim Kardashian as a muse. The association has enhanced his real interest in celebrity culture and afforded her a credible, couture glamour.

Right When the designer Henry Holland named his long-time friend Agyness Deyn as his muse, the two were hardly photographed apart. They gained column inches for appearing at events and awards together, and cemented each other's credibility.

SPONSORSHIP

Micael Dahlén et al. (2010), for whom 'sponsorship is about building long-term relationships which last and create mutual value,' draw an important distinction between sponsorship and hosting events. The brand signing a sponsorship agreement is not responsible for the events themselves; it is signing to invest in an event or series of events, in the hope of reaching a wider but desirable target audience over a period of time, to gain much wider exposure from the association. Dahlén et al cite Nike's 13-year sponsorship of Manchester United to provide sportswear and apparel for the team (ending in 2014), a deal that amounted to a US$500 million investment in the club by Nike. Sponsorship works in the same way as celebrity endorsement: there is an image-transfer process between the two organizations, and they are expected to be compatible in terms of image. Nike's strapline 'Just Do It' became associated with Manchester United's consistency of approach, encouragement of young players and winning formula based on respect for the manager at the time, Sir Alex Ferguson. Sponsorship deals are always between two organizations; for a brand to sign one person is an endorsement arrangement. Large sportswear companies will have both sponsorship and endorsement deals.

Although Egan (2015) cites growth in the use of sponsorship (global spend according to sponsorship.com was US$53.3 billion in 2014 – a steady 4 per cent year-on-year growth rate since 2011), sponsorship, apart from that already discussed as part of product placement or TV advertising, is not a massive part of the communications mix for fashion brands. The exception is LVMH, discussed

in Chapter 11, which runs the LVMH Prize, a competition for young designers (see p. 197). LVMH also sponsors the Hyères International Festival of Fashion and Photography, an annual award that has been responsible for the discovery of the designers Viktor & Rolf and Felipe Oliveira Baptista, both of whom now run their own labels. LVMH, which provides members of the judging panel, benefits from the exposure to young talent and the philanthropy associated with supporting young design.

Fashion brands – most commonly hair products, cosmetics and high-street chains such as Topshop – also sponsor events such as the international fashion weeks or graduate fashion shows. Brands are signed up to sponsor and to provide hair and make-up or accessories for the shows, in return for coverage on the looks and products used, or to mentor young designers.

Left Benetton placed an advert featuring five coloured condoms arranged as the Olympic rings in several Spanish newspapers to coincide with the opening of the 1992 Barcelona Olympics. Benetton angered the Olympic Committee by implying that it was sponsoring the games.

UNITED COLORS OF BENETTON.

Left Dutch beer brand Bavaria is a notorious ambush marketer. During the 2010 World Cup in South Africa, attention was drawn to 36 good-looking female supporters wearing bright orange dresses. Despite the dresses being unbranded, eagle-eyed organizer FIFA spotted an ambush attempt and threatened to throw out what transpired to be hired models. Yet more coverage was gained when some of the women were questioned by police, because ambush marketing is illegal in South Africa.

STEALTH AND AMBUSH MARKETING

Perhaps more possible on a smaller budget and with the ability to provoke publicity from sheer daring, acts of ambush marketing attempt to attract some of the attention that surrounds big events. Ambush marketing is when a company tries to derive the same value as sponsorship out of events, without being actual sponsors. For example, a company may try to associate itself with an event and perhaps benefit from the confusion of multiple events and sponsors, with the result that people believe that it is a sponsor.

Ambush marketing is common among competing brands for major events. The ethics are somewhat questionable if the money involved in sponsorship deals is considered, not to mention the time it takes to draw up such deals in the first place. It is not perhaps very fair for

competitor brands to move in to deflect attention on to themselves.

Perhaps because of the large fees involved, or the lengthy organization required, sponsorship tends to remain the domain of larger, more established companies. Sponsorship opportunities with the widest audiences occur mostly when the brand values align with the positive sides of sporting events. Future opportunities for sponsorship and ambush marketing might exist in the less cluttered area of music festivals. In the UK, dressing for the summer festival season has become a major boost to high summer sales of clothing, yet for now festival sponsorship remains largely the domain of mobile-phone networks and finance, food, drink and media companies.

IS ANY PUBLICITY GOOD PUBLICITY?

For a brand, one of the challenges associated with seeking these forms of third-party endorsement is dealing with lack of control. Celebrities can misbehave or fall from favour; films and TV series can flop; and the misuse of PR material can result in negative publicity or unexpected interpretations. The use of fur in fashion, for instance, is controversial: one side of the fashion industry fiercely endorses its use and the other condemns it in emotive newsworthy protests. A fashion journalist can take either stance when reporting on fur garments.

Can negative publicity be good PR? In most circumstances, any publicity is considered good publicity, because it secures media coverage and gets consumers talking about the brand. If a brand is negatively affected, it may need to engage in reactive PR and plan a clear crisis-management strategy.

Crisis management: reactive PR

So far, all the ways to achieve third-party endorsement have been presented as techniques brands use to achieve positive editorial coverage – termed proactive PR. If, however, negative publicity does arise, brands must seek

Top The luxury Italian fashion brand Fendi faced debate and press in the up-and-coming city of fashion Seoul in 2011 over its use of fur on the catwalk. Fearing protests from animal-rights movements, the organizers threatened to cancel a widely anticipated and elaborately planned fashion show. Fendi eventually did not show the fur garments in its Autumn 2011 collection, despite claiming that fur was part of the 'Fendi DNA'.

Above left A typical anti-fur protest organized by PETA (People for the Ethical Treatment of Animals) as part of Paris Fashion Week, 2007.

Above right Following the collapse of the Rana Plaza building in Bangladesh in April 2013, Primark (one of many brands that used the clothing factories in the complex) was quick to provide a package of financial support, emergency relief and enhanced building safety to the affected workers, their families and the site. This appeared on the company's website and was widely reported.

reactive PR. A crisis beyond the brand's control must be dealt with as soon as it occurs, since it could harm the brand's reputation. Preparing crisis management is, therefore, also important for those involved with publicity for the brand. Typical negative publicity in the fashion industry can be generated by:

- The use of undersized models.
- The use of controversial manufacturing sources, such as sweatshop labour or child labour.
- The use of controversial fabrics such as fur, endangered hide or feathers.
- A celebrity or high-profile individual associated with the brand falls from grace.

One of the most important factors in crisis management is the way companies deal with and treat problems. In common with many industries, there are two main strategies.

- To cite the impeccable heritage of the brand or label, distance itself from the incident and seek to replace what has happened with more positive press.
- To apologize, be completely honest and transparent, refer to corporate values and seek to improve performance in the eyes of the public.

Generally speaking, the increased amount of consumer comment – especially opinions on celebrities – that occurs after incidents has benefited brands by the use of other channels of expression. Followers can override traditional media and take to blogs, social media and news forums to debate both the positive and negative viewpoints raised.

Without doubt, the importance of obtaining publicity for fashion brands will remain, and, budget depending, the techniques of product placement, celebrity endorsements and sponsorship are extremely effective at building credibility and provoking the further publicity that is needed to keep the brand in the mind of the buying public. However, the widening scope of the term 'brand ambassador' has been a key development in recent years. Particularly interesting is Matthew Zorpas' role as an ambassador that could potentially achieve leaner, more efficient results than product placement, endorsements and sponsorship. By increasing its work in this arena a brand could consider one external agency, the influencer, who in theory could handle everything from managing budgets and measuring results, to modelling in TV and billboard advertising, to PR, endorsement activities and driving social media. It would be an agency that, most importantly, is already directly connected to a large, loyal and receptive audience. It will be a phenomenon worth watching over the next few years.

REFERENCES

'Au Revoir Fashion's Night Out', *Business of Fashion*, 27 February 2013, www.businessoffashion.com/articles/bof-comment/au-revoir-fashions-night-out

Dahlén, Micael, Fredrik Lange and Terry Smith, *Marketing Communications: A Brand Narrative Approach*, Wiley 2010

Egan, John, *Marketing Communications*, 2nd ed., Sage 2015

Fill, Chris, *Marketing Communications: Brands, Experiences and Participation*, 6th ed., Pearson 2013

Lea-Greenwood, Gaynor, *Fashion Marketing Communications*, Wiley 2012

Sponsorship.com (2015) Sponsorship Spending Report, www.sponsorship.com/IEG/files/4e/4e525456-b2b1-4049-bd51-03d9c35ac507.pdf

FURTHER READING

Adweek.com, '10 Reasons Why Influencer Marketing Is the Next Big Thing', *Social Times*, 14 July 2015, www.adweek.com/socialtimes/10-reasons-why-influencer-marketing-is-the-next-big-thing/623407

Considine, Austin, 'Invasion of the Head Snatchers', *New York Times*, 16 December 2011, www.nytimes.com/2011/12/18/fashion/hm-puts-real-heads-on-digital-bodies.html

Dostalova, Zuzana, and Sandra Merkel, 'Standard of Regulation for Product Placement Research Work for Advertising and Media', 5 April 2012, www.prezi.com/vvbbpnlisy0a/standards-of-regulations-for-product-placement

Goldfingle, Gemma, 'Bloggers vs "Influencers": Who Rules Fashion's Social Universe?', *Drapers*, 18 May 2016, www.drapersonline.com/retail/bloggers-vs-influencers-who-rules-fashions-social-universe/7007352.article

Mathews, Angie, *Placed! A Foundational Guide to Being a Fashion PR Badass*, CreateSpace Independent Publishing Platform 2016

Smith, Paul R., and Ze Zook, *Marketing Communications: Integrating Offline and Online with Social Media*, 5th ed., Kogan Page 2011

DISCUSSION

Think of a brand you admire. Who would you approach to gain editorial coverage for this brand?

What tools from the PR mix does your chosen brand use? How would your chosen celebrity or influencer improve the PR mix?

Do you think overt sponsorship is more effective than stealth or ambush marketing? Why?

Chapter 6
SOCIAL MEDIA

How can social media be used to promote fashion? Find out how to:

- Gain an overview of the social media landscape and its rapid adoption as an effective part of a communication strategy for brands
- Use social media to broadcast campaign material that inspires and benefits a brand's target markets
- Foster a reciprocal relationship with a brand's followers in this ever more transparent and democratic environment
- Blend social media into promotional campaigns, online and offline
- Create targeted and coherent content, including e-commerce possibilities, within this fast-moving medium

SOCIAL MEDIA: AN OVERVIEW

The term 'social media' refers to the various online communications channels that are dedicated to community-based input, interaction, content-sharing and collaboration. The aim of any brand is to inform and engage a follower to create better interaction between the two. According to Paul R. Smith and Ze Zook (2011), social media focuses on the consumer as being at the centre of the company, and allows marketers a new medium through which to listen to consumers, communicate with them and engage them in the brand.

In this chapter we will examine some of the more popular sites used by fashion brands. For the purposes of this book, we define Facebook as a social curation site, Twitter as a microblogging site, Pinterest as a social curation site, Instagram as an image-based social networking app, Snapchat as a photo and video messaging app and Tinder as a dating site – all social networks or platforms within the larger field of social media.

Brands and designers have launched profiles in the name of the company or label on platforms such as Facebook, Twitter and Instagram, often appearing across all channels and working with the nature of each platform. They have placed their brands in this consumer-centric forum that has created an opportunity for followers to comment on, contribute to and create content with the brands in which they are interested.

Social media has worked more than any other tool to push the demand for instant access to the latest fashions. Followers can access livestreaming of catwalk show content and images of influencers and celebrities in gifted items from the latest collections. Customers no longer want to wait the six months between the catwalk shows and the appearance of the looks in the shops or online; they want those items now, straight from the catwalk. For brands that rely on using catwalk images to fuel social media profiles, the pressure is intense. This only adds to the traditional timing worries in fashion. Unpredictable weather patterns are beginning to render the traditional Autumn/Winter and Spring/Summer seasons obsolete. The pressure to produce pre-collections, which fare better in terms of timing but add to workload, is causing new and existing labels to wonder how fashion will be produced and sold in this exhaustive cycle.

Moreover, the more familiar networks of Facebook and Instagram currently being used in the fashion industry are changing, as new tools and mediums such as Snapchat and Periscope seek to allow unedited access to the previously exclusive, polished world of fashion. These newer platforms are enabling the predictions of an open and inclusive fashion world made by Victoria Loomes of trendwatching.com (see p. 22) to become reality.

Right Ralph Lauren on Facebook. The label uses the various headers within Facebook effectively to provide a short history, a timeline of events, a purely visual record through photos and a place to watch videos.

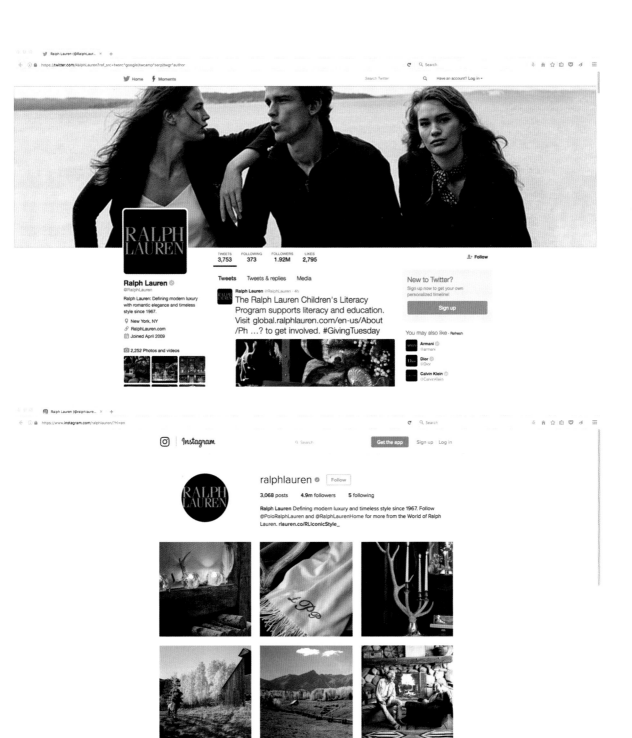

Top Ralph Lauren on Twitter. The more conversational nature of Twitter allows a more individual focus on news events, celebrity sightings and community projects as well as new product lines.

Above Ralph Lauren on Instagram. Instagram provides a stream of visual information through the use of picture tiles that can be clicked on to obtain short blocks of information.

SOCIAL MEDIA IN COMMUNICATIONS

In this version of Chris Fill's (2013) four Cs framework (below left), the effectiveness of social media has been added to Fill's original chart to assess its advantages and disadvantages as a communication tool.

Advantages of social media

- Social media's position among its interested followers allows a high level of personal communication, interaction and credibility with an audience.
- In order to build an effective and profitable brand presence on social media, it has become more necessary to pay for advertising or to boost the presence. This, however, is still cheaper than offline advertising.
- Owing to the efficient targeting of audiences by most social media platforms, especially Facebook, people can be matched to brands by their existing interests and behaviour on social media.
- Run effectively, or outsourced to a specialist agency, social media can integrate easily with other aspects of campaigns, or even work as an effective hub for promotional activities carried out by the brand.
- Analytics, especially on Facebook and Twitter, measure aspects such as reach, engagement and number of likes and shares achieved.

Disadvantages of social media

- There is a low rating for management control; followers may love a post, take exception to it or even be provoked by it to post negative comments.
- Social media profiles are easy to set up, but it is harder to maintain the brand tone of voice, consistency of content, and quantity of posts needed for the audience.
- Creating content for social media can be cheap or even free, but is incredibly time-consuming.

Key to the growth of social media in the promotion of fashion is that the advantages far outweigh the disadvantages, and most of the disadvantages can be overcome by outsourcing or by dedicating a team of staff to the role. Social media has already become firmly integrated into the communications mixes of many brands.

THE FOUR Cs OF COMMUNICATION TOOLS, WITH REFERENCE TO SOCIAL MEDIA

Communications	Social media
Ability to deliver a personal message	High
Ability to reach a large audience	Medium
Level of interaction	High
Credibility	
Given by the target audience	High
Cost	
Absolute costs	Low
Cost per contact	Low
Wastage	Low
Size of investment	Low
Control	
Ability to target particular audiences	High
Management's ability to adjust the deployment of the tool as circumstances change	Low

KEY CONSIDERATIONS WHEN USING SOCIAL MEDIA

Throughout this book are examples of campaigns that have used social media in an innovative and integrated way, notably Barbour's 'Heritage of Adventure' campaign of 2015 (see p. 49), which was developed as a social element to sit alongside a wider campaign. Followers were invited to submit their own photos and video clips of outdoor experiences, inspired by the adventurer Sean Conway. Similarly, Kenneth Cole's 'Be the Evolution' campaign that same year (see p. 72) worked alongside billboards to encourage viewers to contribute to a forum of good deeds on social media.

Such activities highlight the importance of disruption to the passive way campaigns are normally viewed by audiences, by making followers actively part of building and contributing campaign material. Two further themes are in evidence.

- The blending of online and offline. Both campaigns are aimed at the follower, wherever they may be. Brands are moving towards more immersive communication, where the consumer no longer distinguishes between the online and the offline but creates a constant dialogue.
- Offering an incentive to contribute. Barbour offered contributors who used @Barbour or #HeritageOfAdventure the chance to win £500 to spend on Barbour products. Cole used a more subtle technique, building the status of followers who were seen to do something good for society.

Social media and e-commerce

In order fully to engage younger, centennial-age audiences, and to meet audience demand to buy immediately, it is expected that initiatives to make social media more directly shoppable will emerge over the coming years. Direct attempts to set up storefronts within Facebook, initially dubbed 'f-commerce', did not work so well, and Gap, J.C. Penney and Nordstrom closed their Facebook storefronts. Burberry, however, was the first fashion brand to try Twitter's 'buy' button during a fashion 'Tweetwalk', a livestreamed catwalk show. This crucial link from engagement to sales attracted more brands keen to track ROI (return on investment).

The interview with Daniele D'Orazi on p. 122 highlights the importance of integrating a content strategy with advertising on social media. Instagram's use of 'shop now' buttons on sponsored posts suggests that this will be relevant for shopping functions as well. Chapter 4 discusses advertising on social media in more depth, but in the next sections we will highlight campaigns that have used organic content to the best effect, and the shoppable features of each social media platform.

It may be some time before brands address the management and stock risks involved in selling directly from the catwalk (see p. 179 for more on Burberry, which did so from its show at London Fashion Week in September 2016). Until then, a more centralized approach to social media could be part of the solution to demand for immediate availability. Brands can advertise, place PR material such as news, lookbooks and film clips, and build a database of users. If more shoppable features are added, social media could work as a hub for fashion brands to communicate quickly and directly with audiences.

Left Missguided announces that all its snaps on Snapchat are shoppable.

FOLLOWERS OF SOCIAL MEDIA

Social media grew from a desire among people to connect socially, and the success of any brand in this non-commercial environment depends on how it adjusts to forming a reciprocal relationship among its followers. The practitioners Tim Cameron-Kitchen and Yvonne Ivanescu (2016) emphasize how important it is for brands to use the correct tone of voice. They also make the point that establishing a brand with human qualities (see Chapter 2) will help its online personality to attract friends and followers.

Also important is the realization that these are no longer passive audiences, but sophisticated communities acting out of a strong sense of self-interest. Association with certain fashion labels gives a powerful sense of online social identity to other like-minded followers. The British TV programme *Rich Kids of Instagram* gives a compelling insight into the materialistic world of the super-wealthy, who are totally absorbed in maximizing their own brands or profiles on social media through the consumption of luxury goods.

There is also a more altruistic desire to show generosity, evidence of knowledge gained and good environmental behaviour, hence the success of the Kenneth Cole campaign (see p. 72). Followers want brands to help them be the best they can be in the way that matters to them. Followers need engaging and consistent content, and activities that will boost their own profiles. Content such as style tips, fun campaigns the audience can get involved with, and incentives to contribute should take priority over sales and self-promotion. Making clear the incentives and benefits associated with contributing can provide a reason for followers to form a like-minded community around brands they admire. However, the major disadvantage of social media is lack of control. Contributors may choose to be contrary, savage, witty or adoring, and this is out of the hands of the brand.

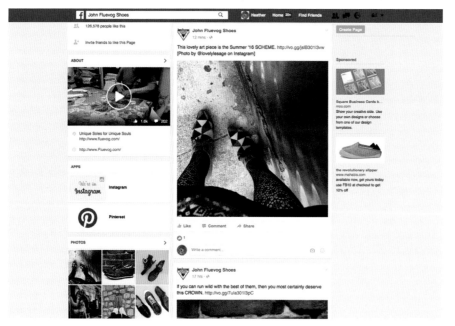

Above *The Rich Kids of Instagram* has grown from an elite set of wealthy young people who posted images of glamorous holidays, supercars, fabulous amounts of money spent on designer labels and flights on private jets, to become a reality TV show and a novel published in 2014. Bastian and Maria Yotta, pictured, caused a stir after Instagram images of their decadent US$100,000-a-month lifestyle emerged. Their online persona proved to be no exaggeration.

Left The Facebook page for John Fluevog, a brand that is credited in Chapter 7 for maintaining an excellent relationship with visitors via its e-commerce site, demonstrates the company's distinctive tone of voice.

Left The John Fluevog profile. The content feed is under 'Timeline', a brief company history under 'About', an Instagram-style photo feed under 'Photos' and a transparent page of analytics under 'Likes' (this would not usually be shared). The apps to connect quickly to other social networks are displayed in the image opposite. The landing page is alive with video, image and audience interaction.

Left By targeting a problem with online adverts and not women, Dove enabled users to tackle problems with self-esteem and surround themselves with positive messages.

FACEBOOK

Since February 2004, when the first college students joined Facebook, the network has grown rapidly to become the largest in the world. In August 2015 its founder, Mark Zuckerberg, announced that one in every seven people on the planet had logged on to Facebook in a single day (BBC News, 2015). See pp. 80–82 for user figures on all networks.

Facebook offers a well-structured business-page template that allows brands to put in a header photo, a short description, a company history, some more facts about the company and their content feed. Fashion brands have made good use of this: most labels have a Facebook page to communicate with their consumers about product launches, campaigns, store openings and any other newsworthy information they want the consumer to have.

Facebook also allows apps to be embedded in business pages, which help it to operate as a central hub. These, according to Cameron-Kitchen and Ivanescu

(2016), include the ability to link quickly to other social media platforms or to the brand's e-commerce site, or to generate a lead capture form to assist with building a database of users.

The Australian arm of the skincare brand Dove, as part of the global brand's long-running campaign for real beauty, used the idea of audience involvement by developing a specially created Facebook app as part of its 'The Ad Makeover' campaign. This app allowed users to replace niggling banner ads on their Facebook pages about rolls of body fat and 'muffin tops' with positive messages such as 'The perfect bum is the one you're sitting on.' The brand contributed its media buy of banner ads to facilitate this.

TWITTER

Twitter, which was launched in 2006, is a free microblogging service that allows only 140 characters for each message or 'tweet'. These can comprise opinions on news or trending topics, new products in stock, thoughts for the day or simply promotional messages. The registered members can broadcast tweets and follow those of others by adopting an @ handle. Interaction is the vital component of Twitter, and according to Cameron-Kitchen and Ivanescu (2016) some 68 per cent of all tweets are replies to other tweets. For brand users, this gives the extra advantage of being able to reply directly to comments from other followers and to retweet positive contributions. Using a hashtag (#) in a tweet opens up any conversation to a wider audience of users who may be interested in the same subject. Twitter has become very popular within the fashion industry, particularly since it became possible to embed images and videos in tweets. The fast-moving nature of the platform suits the industry: old tweets are quickly made invisible by new material, and fashion brands are constantly tweeting news. Sound bites from creative directors such as Marc Jacobs and Olivier Rousteing have done much to make the previously elite world of designer fashion more open, approachable and accessible.

Burberry has been pioneering in its use of Twitter, having trialled its 'buy now' feature. Also worthy of mention is the brand's catwalk show on 23 February 2015, in which it involved a larger audience by encouraging its

Below Burberry's Autumn/Winter 2015-16 personalized tweet to followers. **Bottom** Topshop, digital billboard at London Fashion Week, 2015.

#mycalvins
calvinklein.com

Calvin Klein Jeans

1510
OUTFRONT

followers to tweet using the hashtag #tweetcam to @BurberryTwitter, which activated a camera within the show. Each resulting image was labelled with the follower's Twitter handle and a timestamp, thus personalizing a snapshot of the show.

Both Calvin Klein and Topshop have experimented with integrating Twitter handles and hashtags created for a campaign in print or even billboard advertising campaigns. Topshop used a digital billboard at London Fashion Week in 2015 to broadcast a combination of the next season's trends, using photographs taken from the front row of the shows, and to listen in to what industry influencers were talking about on Twitter. Some of the trends that emerged quickly appeared on the billboards as hashtags, such as #colourblocking, #pleats and #utility. Followers were then invited to tweet a trend of their choice to @Topshop and receive a curated shopping list from similar available stock lines. The campaign is a great example of the consistency of Topshop's intention to democratize the fashion show, of an exclusive reciprocal benefit for followers to contribute, and of embedding online media to complement the offline campaign. Of course, more subtly it suggested how ahead of the game Topshop is in producing trend-led fashion, available straight off the catwalk.

Above Calvin Klein, Spring/Summer 2016 campaign featuring Justin Bieber and other celebrities. The campaign provoked followers to contribute their own thoughts and experiences to #mycalvins.

INSTAGRAM

This image-based social networking app was launched in 2010 for the sharing of photos and videos. It is similar to Facebook or Twitter in that everyone who creates an account has a profile and a visual newsfeed. However, Instagram was designed to be used primarily on a smartphone. Cameron-Kitchen and Ivanescu (2016) cite research carried out in 2015 by Iconosquare (a complementary app that helps to manage Instagram accounts) that showed that 75 per cent of Instagram users are aged between 15 and 35, of which 43 per cent are students and 48 per cent young professionals. For fashion brands interested in this target market, and which produce visual campaign material, lookbook shots or commentary on street style, Instagram has proved very effective. For users, the additional creative benefits such as photo filters and editing options have allowed another dimension of interaction. Brands can have more than one account, including fun and entertaining feeds, such as @choupettesdiary, a profile apparently run by Karl Lagerfeld's pampered cat, who acts as the perfect manifestation of Chanel in cat form.

Instagram has added a 'shop now' button to sponsored posts, but a third-party app, LIKEtoKNOW.it – as run on *Vogue*'s Instagram feed – also provides a way for followers to buy what they see on Instagram. If a follower 'likes' an item in *Vogue*'s feed that has a 'liketk.it' link, they will be emailed links to where they can buy the product.

Instagram also works with hashtags, so brands can use them to tap into the general mood of followers on the network, or create their own campaign-specific hashtags. Michael Kors, for instance, used Instagram as part of its #JetSetSelma campaign. Followers were asked to upload photos of their Selma bags either with iconic international landmarks or in everyday settings to reflect the versatility of the owner and the bag. As an incentive, the brand offered a free bag per week for a month between October and November 2013. An event at the Tokyo National Museum in Japan brought the campaign into the physical by projecting over 5,000 images, including user-generated content (UGC) uploaded using the hashtag #MKTokyo. The photographs were printed and used to form a living wall in the museum, with the intention of provoking further conversation and engagement in an upscale offline setting.

LIKE*to*KNOW.*it*

I SIGN UP FOR LIKETOKNOW.IT

2 LIKE AN INSTAGRAM PHOTO WITH A WWW.LIKETK.IT LINK

3 RECEIVE READY-TO-SHOP PRODUCT LINKS TO YOUR INBOX

Top *Vogue* runs the LIKEtoKNOW.it app on its Instagram feed to provide links to buy featured products with a liketk.it tag.

Above Michael Kors' #JetSetSelma campaign depicted the brand's Selma bag in locations all over the US, Europe and the Far East.

PINTEREST

Pinterest is a web and mobile application for the collection and curation of online images. It allows users to bookmark and save images that appeal to them according to themes, preferences and interests, and to arrange them on a board that can be shared and liked by followers. The action of pinning an image to a board maintains a link to its original source on the internet. Fashion brands can tell a wider visual story about a product by including inspirational images, for example, or by providing followers with more helpful information than is possible via Instagram. Previously only a platform for viewing, Pinterest later launched buyable pins, whereby followers see blue price tags on Pinned items. Tapping the tags takes the viewer to further product information and the option to buy using a credit card or Apple Pay. The retailer then receives and ships the order directly, and no fee is payable to Pinterest.

Brides storyboarding items of interest to share with friends are big users of Pinterest. Oscar de la Renta made interesting and experimental use of this in a 'live Pinning' before its bridal catwalk show in April 2012. Followers watched as show preparations were Pinned, models went through hair and make-up and final pieces were shot ready for the catwalk. This experience created a wider audience for previously exclusive techniques that could be added to the brides' own boards.

Pinterest users can also add a hashtag to Pinned content, by way of a board header or in a product description. This can act as a useful tool for followers who may search for niche topics they are curating by using the hashtag; in this way, brands may gain exposure to new audiences.

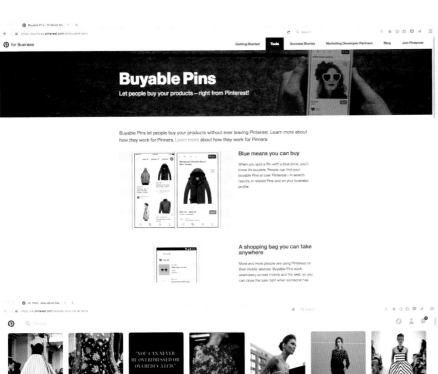

Left A price written in blue text alongside a Pinterest 'Pin' indicates that the featured product can be bought through the platform.

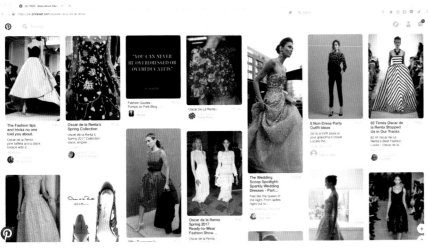

Left Oscar de la Renta's live broadcast of its 2012 bridal catwalk show depicted a storyboard of show preparations, hair and make-up, and product shots.

SNAPCHAT

Snapchat is a photo and video messaging application, launched in 2011, that allows users to take a photo or short video and add a caption. Users can set the time in which images disappear from Snapchat to between one and ten seconds; this is part of the network's appeal, and is represented by the ghost logo. Users and brands also have the option to create a 'story' that can be added to progressively throughout a day and will be visible to followers for 24 hours. Fun editing tools such as the ability to draw on or add animations to images make Snapchat content customizable, creative and less serious for users. Snapchat's audience, mainly aged between 13 and 24, is of interest to relevant fashion brands. The network is intended to show raw, unedited and unpolished footage that is about capturing the moment.

Burberry was the first in the fashion industry to embrace this shift to a more candid environment, having used Snapchat in the past to post stories about a new store opening in Los Angeles accompanied by a clever customization of the ghost logo. In 2016 Burberry previewed its runway collection on Snapchat and then went a step further by offering followers a live, real-time glimpse of the shooting of its Spring/Summer 2016 campaign. The photographer, Mario Testino, posted live content on Snapchat during the shoot, an example of making the previously inaccessible more transparent and available. Snapchat has enabled shopping via a third-party app that works from screenshots saved by users. Once they are saved, users can link directly to the products featured by influencers on Snapchat.

Above For Burberry's #SnapchatCampaign for Spring/Summer 2016, the top fashion photographer Mario Testino posted live, real-time content on Snapchat throughout the shoot. This was followed by a showing of the finished campaign.

FASHION ON TINDER

Diesel created a storm of publicity by being the first fashion brand to place its Autumn/Winter 2015-16 ad campaign on the location-based dating site Tinder, among ads for dating and porn sites. Launched in 2012, Tinder is easy, simple and fun, allowing users to decide if they like a fellow user first by image, then by tapping through to a profile. It uses GPS to identify where its users are through the integration of Facebook details, allowing users to select on the basis of location. The app allows users to swipe right and left depending on their opinion of a photo and/or profile. If both users like each other, the site matches them and they can contact each other. Diesel and its agency, Spring Studios, showed creative thinking by making playful, tongue-in-cheek 15-second videos that suggested the models used could be possible matches for each other. The campaign was consistent with Diesel's irreverent image, and ran across traditional and online media, including this less expected channel.

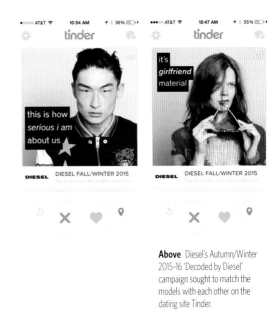

Above Diesel's Autumn/Winter 2015-16 'Decoded by Diesel' campaign sought to match the models with each other on the dating site Tinder.

FASHION FILM AND PERISCOPE

Film has become a staple element of the fashion campaign in recent years, and its uses are summarized on p. 68. It helps to bring the product to life and is a perfect medium for the immediate, inclusive nature of social media; it can also be used to add moving images to e-commerce landing pages. Cameron-Kitchen and Ivanescu (2016) cite the British brand Missguided as a good example of encouraging followers to submit their own video clips to YouTube, by using vloggers and followers to talk about and comment on Missguided 'hauls', finds of great value and fashion interest they have secured from the site.

Missguided is also another example of a successful tone of voice on social media.

Larger designer labels have also experimented with livestreaming content such as catwalk shows, behind-the-scenes coverage and interviews with designers and endorsers, and new technology such as Periscope has made this more effective.

Continued on page 125.

Left A Missguided 'haul' of winter sun holiday pieces. There are scores of similar videos on YouTube.

INDUSTRY PROFILE
DANIELE D'ORAZI OF APPNOVA

Appnova was founded in 2006 as an independent digital agency. Based in Rome and London, its flexible 16-strong team creates e-commerce solutions, web design, social media and digital strategies for luxury and lifestyle brands in sectors such as fashion, beauty, accounting, finance and healthcare. Appnova has worked on various projects for fashion brands including Joseph, the Cambridge Satchel Company and the Woolmark Company. Daniele D'Orazi has MA degrees in both Sociology and Media, Communications and Critical Practice, and worked in creative photography and film-making before becoming a social media strategist in 2006. He has been Head of Digital Marketing at Appnova since 2010, and is one of the senior creative

strategists at the company. He also lectures in digital marketing and branding at Istituto Marangoni in London.

Q: How do you begin to work with clients?
A: We work with all kinds of brands. We sit down with the client, we go through the pen portraits [customer profiles] and workshops about the brand scenario, discuss competitors and what kind of KPIs (key performance indicators) they are expecting. Then we create a strategy, and sometimes we take care of the content as well. These strategies must then be applied. Sometimes this doesn't go to plan; things such as priorities or the company's management can change. It is at least six months before you start to see results if you start from nowhere or if you want to reposition a brand online via social media channels. Brands may think that if they have some history, if they are cool or if a couple of influencers are sporting their bags, they will get a million followers tomorrow, but it just doesn't happen. The second thing is ROI (return on investment): how can you measure if a number of branded bags sold in Japan because of a video that went online? It is not directly possible.

Q: What would you consider to be the benefits of each of the social media platforms?
A: Key to success is the ability to advertise on these platforms. We do not do anything with Snapchat at the moment – the best way is for brands to use influencers on Snapchat. They did a good job with Disney. A takeover is when the brand lets an influencer take over the account and create content. If you have the budget as a brand, you can delegate the content to a key influencer on Snapchat. Really, it is 12-year-old kids who are into co-creation and do not want to see anything directly from your brand (unless you are focused on creating youth content, such as a company like Vice Media). The classic fashion video of models shot in black and white, smoking in Paris, does not work on Snapchat. Twitter, too, has its limits; it is good for customer service and online PR, and it's also

Below Laurel Pantin is an example of an influencer on Snapchat. She was Senior Fashion Editor of *Sweet*, the first fashion publication to launch on Hearst's Snapchat Discover platform. She later moved to *Coveteur*.

good if you are witty. Marc Jacobs is doing a good job because the DNA of the brand is about being witty, but if you do not get it, or the copy is horrible or off-brand, or there is confusion over branding, it does not work.

The most realistic way for brands to use social media is to use Instagram, because that is the hottest thing, and Facebook, because of the way you can advertise – you are sure you can buy visibility. You pay and you reach people. If you use Facebook in a smart way, it is like a hub from which you promote your Instagram account, Twitter and e-commerce. Advertising on Instagram is more complicated than it was; now that kids are mixing streetwear with high fashion and even porn on channels such as Tumblr, it becomes difficult to target people in a surgical way. Not many influential people follow many brands on Instagram. They are active at looking, but not really in following or leaving comments, so it is more difficult to gather data. What they are doing now is gathering information about you on Instagram and then targeting you with advertising on Facebook; it is the same company. What I like on Instagram I get targeted with on Facebook, so it does work.

Diesel has also appeared on Grindr, Tinder and porn sites. Behind these ideas is Nicola Formichetti, who is ahead of the game, and a genius at communication. He has changed the way we perceive Diesel online: everybody is thinking about millennials; he is thinking about what motivates the next generation on, his sense of community fostering, always digital [media] first. The latest campaign using emojis is smart. The only thing is that you appear on Tinder and it works only once. You disguise the brand as a stunt and everyone is talking about you, but people see that it has been done once, and that's it.

Q: Can it be difficult to decide a brand's tone of voice on social media?
A: Marc Jacobs is the best example of how to establish this. They use Instagram a lot. They have three main accounts. One is corporate – this is the brand, these are the products, the copy is very corporate but cool; they have another that is Marc Jabobs, very witty, very cool, him hanging out with his friends (they replicate a scene from [the film] *Zoolander*, for example); and the third is Neville Jacobs, which is the perspective from Marc Jacobs' dog. There is the corporate brand on Instagram – our values, our DNA – then the

witty, more punkish side – almost backstage, behind the scenes – then another side featuring the dog. Using three accounts, you have a very good idea of the brand, and the whole thing comes together. Apple does not use Twitter as a brand, for instance, but through the CEO; he is active on Twitter, on behalf of the brand but also as a person.

You have to be consistent. We manage content for some brands, but not all. I prefer not to do it any more. Everything should be produced or at least curated in-house, especially for brands whose brand guidelines are not so specific. A brand can be serious and understated; if you are not part of the brand, then before you understand the tone of voice, you will be back and forward by email, questioning if the word 'awesome' is right or on-brand.

Q: For fashion brands, do you find certain content gets more viewer feedback than others?
A: It can be dangerous to adjust your campaigns, social media strategy or digital strategy too much in reaction to follower feedback. The likes and positive or negative comments you get may not be from your existing customers; they may be from someone who hopes to afford the brand, or from someone who is responding to a post that is not relevant. Using a more personal voice could mean dilution. It could dilute a luxury brand to talk about how sad we are to lose the dog. Céline does not have social media accounts, but it does use influencers to post items on their own social media, so it is using social media indirectly. Karl Lagerfeld's Karl.com is a great example of how to do content, e-commerce and branding; it includes a section called Karlism, which are statements from him on how to look at life.

Q: How often do you suggest that a fashion brand update its social posts?
A: It depends on the platform. If you post 25 times a day on Facebook, you are going to have a problem with overloading followers. If you post on Instagram the target audience is more flexible because younger kids consume more content. It depends, but you must be consistent in approach. The bottom line is that if you start a Twitter account, you need to use it.

Right Diesel's Spring/
Summer 2016 follow-up
campaign to 'Decoded',
also developed by Spring
Studios, features emojis
developed by the brand
(here 'holy denim'), and
the androgynous model
Stav Strashko.

diesel.com

holy
denim

DIESEL

Right Karlism by Karl
Lagerfeld, Karl.com.

Q: *Do you think social media will continue to be a driving force in helping brands reach out to followers in the next five years? Have you noticed any other trends emerging?*

A: I don't think we can now disconnect people who are connected 14 hours a day. We have to become smarter. The future is niche – look at dating sites. They have become more niche; it used to be one big site but now there are sites for cyclists or rock climbers. The future is brands like Supreme or Palace or Adidas with Yeezy; they use social media to create a buzz, expectation and desirability, but the actual volume of product is quite low. We are still exploring. I think you have to look at niche streetwear brands, the mix of high

and low fashion. On Tumblr, kids are mixing skateboards, Givenchy and pornography – the younger target audience has a complex psychology. The future is this mix of everything. We have to understand science, but content is the most important. Post cool content and people will like your brand; post irrelevant content and people will not want to follow you. Content is the future.

Periscope

Periscope, a live video-streaming app for iOS and Android, was bought in January 2015 by Twitter before it went public and then launched on 26 March 2015. As with Snapchat, Periscope is designed to broadcast impulsive, raw and unscripted content, and allows even more real, unedited access. Because of the link to Twitter, broadcasts can be viewed through Twitter share, and real-time dialogue with followers can be initiated. Labels such as Marc Jacobs, Burberry and Topshop have already embraced Periscope during fashion weeks. Topshop – in its broadcast of GoPro footage of the photographer Nick Knight shooting the brand's 'Unique' Autumn 2016 catwalk collection – has probably come closest to the true ethos of Periscope.

Social media can be used to advertise, to publicize, to run promotions or competitions, to analyse users' behaviour and even to shop directly. It can be used at the heart of a campaign or as a key driver of interest to particular areas of a campaign, and is an essential way to gauge reaction to brands among an engaged, if self-interested, audience. Key points to bear in mind are:

- Be prepared to pay for exposure, but do so innovatively, in keeping with the platform.
- Reciprocate by providing benefits or incentives.
- Blend online with offline experiences.
- Be democratic with previously exclusive material.

Whether or not social media can be used as a direct route to sales is still a matter for debate. Innovations such as Facebook's app to embed a quick route to a brand's e-commerce site, or Pinterest's buyable Pins, seem for the moment to be proving a more popular and less direct invasion of social media's true environment. It is, however, almost bound to happen, given the increased audience demand to buy fashion immediately. Burberry's groundbreaking collection sold from the catwalks will surely be emulated via a social media platform. It is bound to ensure that both the brand and its buyers gain maximum enjoyment, additional insights and benefits from the transaction.

REFERENCES

BBC News, 'Facebook has a Billion Users in a Single Day, Says Mark Zuckerberg', 28 August 2015, www.bbc.co.uk/news/world-us-canada-34082393

Cameron-Kitchen, Tim, and Yvonne Ivanescu, *Profitable Social Media Marketing: How to Grow your Business Using Facebook, Twitter, Instagram, LinkedIn and More*, Exposure Ninja 2016

Smith, Paul R., and Ze Zook, *Marketing Communications: Integrating Offline and Online with Social Media*, 5th ed., Kogan Page 2011

FURTHER READING

Chaffey, David, and David Mill, *Content Is King*, Routledge 2012

Fill, Chris, *Marketing Communications: Brands, Experiences and Participation*, 6th ed., Pearson 2013

i-D magazine, Fashion issue, no. 341 (Spring 2016)

Spybey, Kat, 'Socialising with Generation Z', *Drapers*, 17 March 2016, www.drapersonline.com/business-operations/socialising-with-generation-z/7005108.article

Sutherland, Emily, 'The Sharing Economy', *Drapers*, 11 July 2016, www.drapersonline.com/business-operations/the-sharing-economy-turning-social-media-posts-into-sales/7008832.article

DISCUSSION

What are the challenges faced by brands using informal platforms such as Snapchat, Periscope and Tinder? What are the risks?

Daniele D'Orazi says that the future of social media is niche – you have to know your audience very well to stay desirable. This means fewer, but more engaged followers. Do you agree?

Consider the idea of narcissism on social media. What pressures do you feel as a generation of social media users? How do you think fashion brands utilize or encourage narcissism?

Chapter 7
THE DIGITAL ARENA: E-COMMERCE AND ONLINE FASHION PROMOTION

How can viewers be persuaded to buy online? Find out how to:

- Persuade consumers to interact with a brand using high-quality, engaging editorial content
- Use responsive design to make e-commerce sites that are effective across all devices
- Entice browsers to stay and purchase
- Chart, measure and respond to consumer behaviour online by using tracking techniques to gain knowledge about a brand's customer base

THE GLOBAL SIZE AND VALUE OF FASHION E-COMMERCE

Despite initial concerns regarding deliveries, fit, returns and security of payments, there is now a buoyant global picture of an online fashion retail market estimated to be worth US$414 billion by 2019 (industryreportstore.com, 2015). Euromonitor's report *Shopping for fashion: Bricks, clicks and in-betweeners* of 2016 placed apparel and footwear as the largest internet category, accounting for nearly a fifth of global internet sales. Mintel's report *Clothing Retailing* (UK, 2015) estimates that 73 per cent of fashion stores with an online presence are multichannel retailers that also have physical stores, with 27 per cent being pure play (online retail only). Outsider Amazon.com successfully claimed the largest share of the pure play market by achieving 9.1 per cent of online sales of clothing and footwear following a 2015 campaign featuring model Suki Waterhouse.

WEBSITE DESIGN AND EASE OF NAVIGATION

As the key gateway to a brand's e-commerce presence, successful website design is crucial not only to representing the identity of the brand, but also increasingly to offering an easy-to-navigate, interactive interface for the consumer. As part of an integrated communications plan, the website should reflect the ethos of the brand through its layout, its use of logo, product shots and colours, and the mood it conveys. For all digital promoters of fashion, there is also increased pressure to maintain creative and interactive copy across the brand narrative, product descriptions, blogs and social media linked from the main website.

The appearance of the landing or home page and the content 'above the fold' (the immediate visual space the viewer sees before having to scroll) is vital to attracting viewers. Once this is in place, the site should then aim to lead the consumer into an environment where they can purchase securely and like, comment or share in as few clicks as possible. It is also important to provide clear links to the conversational aspects of the site by making blogs and social media links evident.

Astonishingly, the average bounce rate – the time in which consumers become bored or frustrated, or simply leave the site – is only about 3.8 seconds, and 75 per cent of viewers abandon pages after 5 seconds. It is, therefore, ever more essential that sites be visually engaging and easy to navigate. Techniques such as the opportunity for consumers to personalize, review or creatively contribute are proving successful at converting browsers into buyers.

Landing page layout

Simon Bell, managing director of the creative agency Diligent Commerce, argues the case for filling a website landing page with a full-width image, based on a wider trend for fully responsive layouts (see p. 130). In a second type of successful layout, image tiles or sales banners advertising special offers, how to wear new trends or newly arrived items can link straight to an opportunity to buy. The online magazine style of the Net-a-Porter site has prompted a trend for more magazine-based web layouts among other fashion sites and online retailers. In 2013 its success resulted in the publication of a monthly magazine, *Porter*, which is released both in print and online.

Whichever format your site takes, however, website designers suggest that certain elements – such as 'add to basket' buttons, checkout details, blogs and social media links – are kept in similar places to those of other successful fashion sites, to avoid confusion. To enhance the consumer experience and recall, personalization of items such as greetings messages or shopping-basket icons can prove effective.

In a highly competitive industry, product photographs can be the most important aspect of a brand's online identity. The role of these high-definition shots should not be underestimated, and they should be retouched if necessary to show the product at its best. Accompanying copy such as product descriptions should be original, descriptive and creative, with a view to including the search terms shoppers are likely to enter if they search by product rather than by retailer.

Most brands include an 'About us' or 'About the company' link in the top menu. This type of information can be used to reinforce brand narrative and can assert the founder's credibility as creator of the brand. Larger online retailers do not generally make this so evident.

Above Net-a-Porter landing page.

Below left Original photo from Laundry Maid Jeans shoot, 2010.

Below right The same photo retouched to remove excess creasing at the top of the legs and smooth out the knees.

INDUSTRY PROFILE
SIMON BELL OF DILIGENT COMMERCE

Simon Bell is Managing Director and co-founder of Diligent Commerce, a company that specializes in creative e-commerce solutions for luxury and premium fashion and lifestyle brands. Set up in 2011, Diligent now consists of a 20-strong team of account and project managers, expert web designers and developers and e-commerce marketing specialists, and also uses outsourced expertise.

Diligent aims to create highly attractive and immersive e-commerce sites for brands that are passionate about reflecting their ethos of creativity in their websites, and that seek to convert highly engaging content into sales. Fundamental to the work Diligent produces is the desire to create a superior online environment that matches the expectations of an in-store luxury experience. Among other prestigious accounts in the field of fashion, Diligent has created sites for the upmarket swimwear label Melissa Odabash, the pure-play online beachwear brand Maison du Maillot, the Berlin-based denim specialist 14 oz., the heritage tailor Crombie and the royalty-endorsed luxury label Amanda Wakeley. At the time of writing it had won new accounts with a coloured diamond specialist, a premium chocolate brand and a wedding outfitter.

Q: *Would you say the full-screen image, with lots of content above the fold, is a signature of the Diligent look?*
A: The full screen is a signature. Fixed-width now looks dated. Using the full-screen width in a way that is fully responsive across different devices and in high definition gives a much more modern, immersive experience. Above the fold does not have so much significance now the consumer has more experience and is more used to swiping, pinching, flicking, and so on.

Q: *In your experience, has the use of video in fashion sites been a good thing?*
A: Video as used by the likes of Burberry – which works when you hover with the mouse – rather than video that you have to start and stop or which plays regardless, works well as moving imagery when stitched in with fixed imagery. More and more video will be used; it might possibly be in shorter form, but it is here to stay. It definitely improves conversion to sales on product detail pages, since it is possible to see how the clothing moves and how it sits on the model. It brings the garment to life.

Q: *In your experience, is any other type of image or technique working on fashion home pages?*
A: Apart from the movement towards sites that are optimized for all devices, more personalization and the use of technology that recognizes prior behaviour and merchandises the buyer's selection have worked well. Most clients emphasize conversion rates, and premium fashion has only a 1 per cent conversion rate. Trying to improve that does drive a bit of an obsession with conversion rate. There tends to be a gravitational pull towards the same constructs that work even in the premium market: the norms, such as always having a shopping basket at the top right, and a prominent 'add to basket' button. It is, therefore, difficult to be genuinely creative; there is a classic user journey through most, if not all, sites. Viewers are trained to expect a certain journey, and to be avant-garde is a risk that brands take at their own peril. The importance of search, for example, has been governed by Google because certain components of content on landing and listing pages are recognized by Google. Over time customers will become more confident. As we maximize sales we create the norm. In store we have accepted changes to the norm; online, at the moment, we need a certain amount of hand-holding.

Q: *How important is the role of brand narrative in developing a site?*
A: It will come more to the fore. There are several influences. Google, for example, picks up content and is all about beating the cheats and reflecting genuine dialogue. Google rewards you by increasing your search rankings

Below Diligent
e-commerce brief for the
Melissa Odabash website.

Bottom Fully responsive
solution by Diligent for
Melissa Odabash.

if you promote conversation around original content, such as blogs and a brand story. Individual brand retailers have to work hard to beat the multi-brand players that act as online department stores. A mono-brand has to make the online experience worthwhile; it must be more engaging, rewarding and interesting than a visit to a department store. It's a challenge, but retailers should put more time and effort into branding their e-commerce sites, to entertain and engage consumers with their brand story. It may be years before a window shopper returns to make an actual purchase; the brand story, therefore, must be strong enough to remain in their minds.

Q: Do obvious links to social media remain important for a fashion website?
A: Just as blogs are an important part of raising credibility, social media links also must be evident on sites. Brands and retailers need to think about a bigger journey than just a visit through to the checkout. In terms of experience, customers visit to see who the brand is, then sometimes again to window shop, often long before purchasing. Social media helps to build how the brand can communicate with consumers and visualize how they could use the product in different situations by offering information and advice, such as what to wear for a forthcoming event. Social media can also help Google rankings, because it is classed as a genuine online conversation. A social media profile adds logic and a different dimension to a brand: Twitter helps with its newsworthy aspect; Facebook adds a friendly social element.

Q: How important is the ease of navigation through a site?
A: Sales through mobile sites are starting to predominate. Responsive websites must work across all machines, but m-commerce is a major driver of online shopping. The product must be easy to find, easy to search for and easy to buy. If the payment pages or the checkout process look too hideous or scary, or the shopper is diverted to another site, he or she is likely to abandon the purchase. Payment problems are the biggest cause of abandoned sales on fashion sites.

Q: What else is working in fashion to encourage browsers to stay, shop and buy?
A: It is important to consider the marketing content that goes with an e-commerce site. People don't come just to buy. Editorial content such as magazine-style tips works well. This is the material that says who you are, what you stand for, that gives the back story and the image you want to convey. Provenance, genuineness and authenticity – information previously available from advertising – are important to readers. People need to buy in to the brand in order to justify the purchase. Friends can advise through social media, but style tips from people who know what they are talking about add context. Brands that can combine the magazine content of discovery with the social element and the actual purchase are really making the most of the online opportunity.

Q: What would you say is the future for e-commerce?
A: In 20 years' time it will be amusing that we once used keyboards; it will be possible to interact directly with voice commands right through the process, including the final sale. This scenario will drive more creativity. More video will come into play. It will be tougher for smaller brands to compete, but people will start to gravitate towards the more creative. E-commerce will be saturated, but it will have lots of momentum behind it – it will be interesting and exciting!

M-COMMERCE, RESPONSIVE DESIGN AND FASHION APPS

The interview with Simon Bell raises the issue of the importance of m-commerce and what he terms 'fully responsive design'. These points are discussed further in this section.

M-commerce and responsive design

According to a 2016 Euromonitor report, *Fast Fashion in 2016: Digital opportunities and agile threats part 2*, global purchases made via a mobile phone are expected to surpass those made via a computer in 2019. The success of m-commerce is attributed to its connectivity with consumers' everyday lives and its ability to provide immediate location data. According to Kat Spybey writing in *Drapers* (2014), in the first quarter of 2014 alone 34 per cent of online traffic to UK retail sites came from mobile phones. In 2013 fashion accounted for 42 per cent of UK mobile traffic and was second only to books in terms of visits to sites.

A visit to an m-commerce-enabled site lasts three minutes longer than a visit to a site without m-commerce, and the bounce rate can be reduced by 20 per cent on such sites. Online fashion retailers are strongly advised not to ignore responsive design – when a website automatically adjusts to work equally well on a desktop computer, tablet or smartphone. A site with this ability is said to be 'fully responsive'.

Below Milan Style is a curation of fashion content from various sites, created by Tom Walsh Design. It is designed to be fully responsive, an experience of equal quality whether viewed on a desktop computer, a tablet or a mobile phone.

Fashion apps

Fashion apps, with their ability to be closer and more targeted to the consumer, convert browsing to sales twice as much as ordinary websites, and can increase sales by 10 per cent. There can also be as much as a 50 per cent reduction in bounce. Apps can be 'native' (developed to run on a specific platform that can be customized by the retail brand) or, more commonly, custom-built by third-party developers to suit the needs of the brand. App features can work with GPS to provide location-based information and rewards and/or the chance to save, share through social media and gain access to exclusive content. Push notifications (targeted messages) generated by the app engage the user directly with content, news or special offers specific to their interests.

Software such as Cortexica's 'find similar' function is revolutionizing the way apps can offer innovative and engaging service ideas. Using this software, apps such as Snap Fashion allow users to take a photo or even a colour sample of something they like; the app then scours the inventory databases of contributing retailers to find a similar item. The software works by mimicking the processes the brain follows in spotting similarities between objects. Contributing retailers gain increased traffic to their sites, and pay commission to the developer of the app.

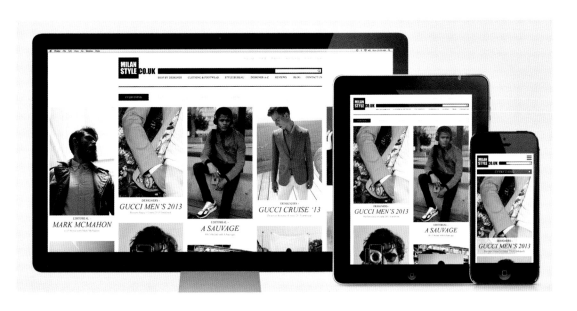

WEBSITES AND
CONTENT MARKETING

Most brands and retailers use their websites as a hub to put out online content to shoppers. In this case content comprises the blogs they write, the social media feeds they generate and any immersive editorial copy they use on their sites.

Brands use their blogs to optimize the use of their own editorial copy, to encourage a valuable two-way dialogue directly with the consumer via interesting and provocative posts. Blogs help to nurture relationships with target audiences, and a content strategy based on sharing insider knowledge, style tips and great creative photography that consumers want to share further is working well for fashion brands.

The need to improve the quality and quantity of editorial content published by fashion brands and retailers is currently under much debate. According to James Carson's best practice guide of 2014, published on the *Econsultancy* blog, many fashion brands were not using their editorial feed for much more than product and competition news. His research into 20 fashion websites revealed:

- Editorial that was poorly integrated into the site; a lack of a clear link to the brand's blog.
- Low publishing frequency: many sites were publishing less than one story a day.
- Little advisory content: only a few examples of style advice or style tips were given.

Right The US brand J.Crew uses its blog, hello.jcrew.com, to post inclusive items for followers, such as how key pieces and finishes were created by designers, how the designers' sketches were developed, how to achieve the beauty looks used in catwalk shows and style tips from the brand's head stylist.

Below The retail brand Anthropologie uses its blog to give advice on interiors, recipes, city guides, short interviews and other aspects of lifestyle interest to its readers.

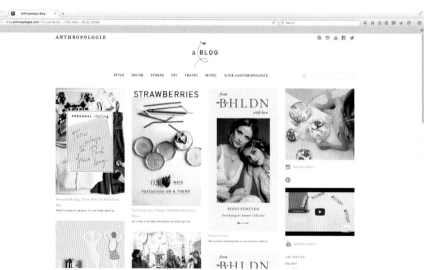

- Poor headlining: story headlines were not indicative of content, or were not optimized so they could be found by readers searching for a similar term.

That online fashion retailers must be as effective at editorial as traditional published fashion sources is a huge challenge, but one that Diligent Commerce's Simon Bell (see p. 130) cites as a winning formula. According to Bell, the larger players – such as ASOS and Net-a-Porter – are currently achieving the best results.

JOHN FLUEVOG

The quirky, individual Canadian premium shoe brand John Fluevog is a great example of how to present an organic balance of brand message and consumer voice on a website. There are several features that exemplify successful practice in encouraging consumer involvement through reviews and by rewarding creative contributions.

- Large-format, clear, scrollable product shots, usually accompanied by a consumer testimonial.
- A lively and enthusiastic description that sets the brand's tone of voice. John Fluevog shoes or 'Vogs' are designed in product 'families' and have a clear unique selling point (USP) of comfort as well as style. Most descriptions explain how the shoe fits into the existing range, or give insights from the designer into its development. Fit comments from a store, which could be construed as negative, are presented as helpful sales advice from experts.
- Consumer reviews tend to follow in the same spirit and language; even problems that are broadcast act as helpful tips for future purchasers.
- Consumers are invited to upload photos of themselves in the product. The website photos are grabbed in Instagram using the proper hashtags. These are useful for visualizing how the shoes will look with a certain type of clothing or a different sense of style.

Consumer contributions

Brands work hard to make the consumer's journey on their sites a pleasurable one and to create engaging and 'sticky' content, in the hope that consumers will in turn contribute positively to the site.

- The site hosts the brand's blog, the *Flueblog*, presented in a strongly visual, Instagram-style format, and the Fluemarket, an online marketplace for buying, selling or swapping 'previously loved' Vogs. It also hosts Open Source Footwear, a forum where members of the public can submit product designs and be credited for those that are selected.
- Fluevog Creative, another area of the site, gives the consumer an opportunity to design a marketing campaign for the brand.

Left A product page on the John Fluevog website.

Below Consumer photos used to accompany product reviews.

Centre Open Source Footwear, where viewers can upload their own shoe designs.

Bottom Fluevog Creative, where fans can offer ideas for adverts for the brand.

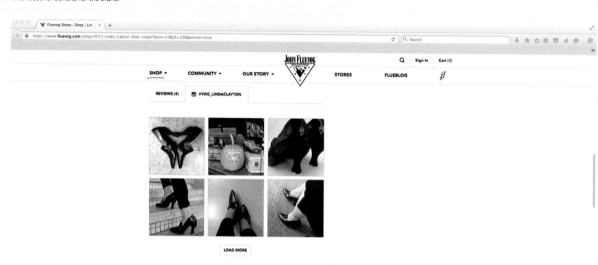

FURTHER TECHNIQUES TO CONVERT BROWSING INTO SALES

The following factors are further considerations for e-commerce developers. They are likely to help a viewer justify an online purchase and, through the use of improved online customer service, make them feel that their custom is valued.

Unique trading models

E-tailers are finding innovative ways of providing a visitor with a unique or different experience that is over and above what they would find in a shop.

The US-based site Cut On Your Bias (cutonyourbias.com), for example, allows consumers to collaborate with selected designers and create their own versions of styles from a template. Viewers then vote on the co-created ideas, and the most popular is put into production. Similarly, Trunk Club (trunkclub.com) has disrupted the conventional online retail model by providing a stylist upfront to select a 'trunk' of garments. Shoppers pay only for the styles they like, and the stylist uses this information to tailor future selections.

Smart merchandising

Retailer-controlled product prompts, such as 'We recommend' or 'Complete the look', are used with particular success by the premium e-tailer Net-a-Porter and the young fashion online retailer ASOS. These messages help to personalize the visitor journey and help them to make choices among the large ranges.

In 2011 ASOS, in conjunction with the online shopping experience specialists SDL Fredhopper, introduced personalized recommendations based on the browser's buying history and the similar purchases of others. According to Joris Beckers, CEO of Fredhopper, quoted in an article by Alison Clements in *Drapers* in 2011, the experience is as close to an in-store shopping experience as possible:

> It's just like being in a store, with a member of staff on hand to suggest products that will help complete an outfit, and present items that will suit an individual's size, style, interest, etc. A recommendation engine drives smart merchandising. It's a vital tool in giving the consumer more of what they want, and for the retailer that means higher sales.

The market leader Net-a-Porter provides suggestions of how to style items to achieve a total cutting-edge look, and offers the viewer a gallery of similar alternatives that they may prefer or be interested in as well.

Above The US online platform Nineteenth Amendment (nineteenthamendment.com) provides designers with a shoppable lookbook of their collections. Visitors to the site have access to exclusive pieces from global designers, available at special prices for 19 days. Styles are made on demand in the US and can be delivered in as little as four weeks. This allows designers to sell without traditional inventory costs, facilitates production and logistics, and provides them with merchandising data so that they can make smarter design decisions.

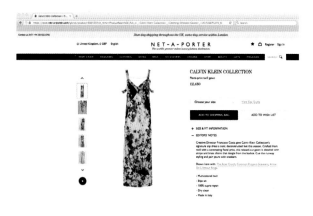

Above and right Net-a-Porter product page; 'How to wear it' and 'You may also like' product prompts.

E-commerce customer service

Aside from providing the consumer with an immersive experience through copy and image, it is also important to recognize the inroads into effective online customer service that have been made by the market leaders ASOS and Net-a-Porter. One of the ways in which retailers and brands can demonstrate good customer service is to answer email enquiries promptly and efficiently. Consumers also like to see the reassurance of a phone number that is prominent and provides a direct form of contact, alongside other forms of query answering, such as a 'Frequently Asked Questions' page. ASOS. com is using technology effectively to offer better online customer service. Innovations such as providing customer service representatives on Twitter, and the 'Follow My Parcel' function, which allows shoppers to track their purchases in real time, have been developed to meet the needs of the company's young, time-starved audience. In addition to 24/7 customer-care services, Net-a-Porter provides fashion consultants to give styling advice such as wardrobe updates or to help the shopper to pick gifts for friends and family.

Delivery and innovation in delivery services

Larger online retailers, such as Amazon, ASOS and Net-a-Porter, have set up excellent, fast delivery options that can be very hard for smaller brands to compete with. In some cases, an item from a label or brand purchased through a site like this can be delivered more quickly than through the brand's own site. The sustained rise in online shopping has been attributed to the introduction of services such as 'click and collect'. Mintel's 2016 report *Online Retailing* estimates that 59 per cent of online buyers had used click and collect, mostly to avoid postage charges and for the convenience of in-store pick-ups. It is anticipated that further innovations, such as more click-and-collect

hubs at convenient destinations such as railway stations, will stimulate future growth in this area. Other delivery initiatives from the larger online retailers, including 90-minute deliveries, next-day, evening and weekend deliveries and even delivery by drone are expected to fuel growth.

High delivery charges remain a significant reason for shoppers to abandon baskets at online checkouts. Deliveries must still be as affordable (preferably free) and fast as possible, but innovations such as ASOS's delivery to a staffed pod where goods can be tried on and returned immediately demonstrate the importance of progress in this area.

Online payments

The payment process was once thought to be a major barrier to the uptake of online shopping, and it is still the case that a considerable number of online sales are lost through over-complicated or apparently unsecure payment pages. Website designers currently suggest signing up to trusted secure payment systems such as PayPal to avoid cancelled sales, since they are a proven aid to converting browsers into paying customers. Secure Socket Layer (SSL) certificates, which usually appear in the form of a shield logo on payment pages, can be provided by a source such as GeoTrust. Information such as credit-card details transmitted between a browser and a web server is open to abuse if it remains in plain text. The use of SSL security encrypts this information and reassures the consumer by confirming that their connection to a web server is secure when they make a payment online.

SEARCH-ENGINE OPTIMIZATION (SEO)

It will help all promoters of fashion to have an awareness of the purpose and function of search-engine optimization as they write supporting copy for images or consider how blogs, social media and emails to customers can enhance online retail. There is agreement in the fashion industry that although there are other search engines to consider, it is Google – which is used for 80 per cent of online searches – with which many fashion companies strive to optimize their sites to perform.

Search algorithms

Search algorithms are computer programmes that scan our search queries for more than 200 signals or clues as to what we might actually want. Therefore, algorithms refine our searches and stop us from being bombarded with unwanted information. Google occasionally rolls out major changes to these programmes, giving the updates names such as Panda, Penguin and Pigeon. Many of the recent updates have been designed with the intention of rewarding brands and retailers that provide authentic copy, which, when matched with consumers' search terms, raises the ranking of that brand on Google's search page results. In August 2013 Google released Hummingbird, which scans internet-based chat for genuine conversation and comment about product. This spots online conversation about a particular brand or item, rather than the words entered into a search box.

Content SEO

All website developers encourage the use of distinctive copy, such as headings, that can be meta-tagged to help increase SEO when consumers search using the same or similar terms as the copy, for example 'locally made' or 'tailored jeans'. If these headings are made increasingly long tail or have more descriptive content they can work more effectively with Hummingbird, for example 'locally made, high-waisted jean with tailoring details'. Similarly, image titles can also be tagged in case consumers search directly for a product name. Maintaining the retailer's or brand's own blog and social media also provides an opportunity to reiterate these phrases and titles, and can help to create organic SEO. Another strategy to boost content SEO off-site is to contact external influencers to encourage a natural extension of editorial content; for example, by becoming recognized as a reliable source of accurate trend information.

Technical SEO

Technical SEO includes bidding directly with Google or other search engines for niche keywords and phrases that will raise the status of the brand in search ratings. These could take the form of unique descriptive terms about the brand, such as collection influences (for example 'folklore bohemian'), or even key seasonal words, such as 'glitter' or 'diamante'. This is usually carried out by in-house specialists in SEO, or by independent experts.

In comparison to the slower burn of a social media strategy (although one may support the other), SEO provides a proven route to greater return on investment (ROI), and the effects are measurable in terms of click-through rates. This makes it an attractive consideration even for those with small budgets.

AFFILIATE WEBSITES AND PAY-PER-CLICK

A pay-per-click (PPC) arrangement may be struck with an external website to pay a certain amount for a click-through from one site to another. As an example of what is termed 'search-engine PPC', Google began to charge online retailers per click to appear on its visual Shopping listings. A retailer can bid the price it is willing to pay per click to be included, and will pay only for clicks-through from the Shopping listings to its website. Since Google pulls these images right to the top of search results, especially if search terms feature a specific product or retailer name, this can be an effective method of driving traffic to the website.

A brand may also pay another brand commission as a result of generating a lead or a sale; this is called having an affiliate channel. Affiliates are effective at driving traffic between branded sites and forums of shared interest, such as locally made goods or celebrity coverage sites. A brand may have a network of PPC arrangements and affiliates that it believes will drive increased traffic to its site.

THE SEVEN Cs OF CONSUMER INTERFACE

In a summary of the aspects discussed so far, Chris Fill (2013) refers to Jeffrey Rayport and Bernard Jaworski's model of the seven Cs of consumer interface (2003), a useful checklist of necessary elements for good web presence. This list is an update of their findings:

1. *Context*

Even though consumers are becoming more confident online, consider what will appear above the fold: a full-screen image, possibly a video, or sales tiles and banners.

2. *Content*

Text must be creative and original and stimulate consumer conversation; images should be carefully retouched and constantly updated with the latest styles to arrive in-store. Using film on product detail pages can be worth the investment, since it has a higher conversion rate to sales than still images.

3. *Community*

Provide immediate or nearly immediate visible links to social media feeds and blog content. Consider opportunities for enhanced involvement, such as co-creation of product or campaigns.

4. *Customization*

Keep functional items, such as shopping baskets, in familiar places, but consider offering personalized greetings, icons and recommendations alongside the opportunity to review.

5. *Communication*

Regularly maintain and update social media platforms and blogs, and consider ways of involving the consumer with trends, product or even marketing developments.

6. *Commerce*

Keep clicks from product shot to shopping basket to payment page to a minimum and as uncomplicated as possible. Consider unique trading models.

7. *Connection*

Consider the ways in which the shopper can reach and communicate directly with the retailer or brand. Consider driving traffic via PPC or affiliate sites.

MEASURING ONLINE BEHAVIOUR

How do promoters check that the measures they take are effective? Google provides Google Universal Analytics, a set of tools that help online retailers track and trace consumer behaviour and interaction with any website. They can show monthly information in the form of:

- Site usage: number of visitors, number of page views, bounce rate, average time spent on the site, percentage of new visitors to the site.
- Visitors overview: the peaks and troughs throughout the month of consumer visits.
- Map overlay: a visual idea of where traffic comes from.
- Traffic source overview: a breakdown of clicks-through from search engines, affiliate or referral sites, or from direct hits to the website. This highlights the importance of SEO and gives an indication of which search terms were used.
- Content overview: a digest of the most popular pages.
- A technical profile showing types of browser and type of connection that generated hits.

Google recommends keeping the bounce rate to less than 45 per cent, so behaviour on the Laundry Maid Jeans site (see image opposite) suggests that there may have been a problem with site navigation or consumers leaving the site before purchasing.

Pure-play online fashion retailers have seen huge successes in offering 24-hour sales, improved delivery options and excellent customer service. It is, however, necessary to keep innovating and creating unique trading models, since bricks-and-mortar shops have seen these advantages and are seeking to merge them into their practices. The examples given in this chapter provide the online shopper with new designers unavailable elsewhere, or a service such as styling that goes beyond a standard online transaction. Ideas like these and the use of well-produced content that inspires and involves audiences will be key to the future of online promotion.

Laundry Maid Jeans
Dashboard

Jul 4, 2009 – Aug 3, 2009
Comparing to: Site

• Visits

Site Usage

192 Visits
635 Pageviews
3.31 Pages/Visit
48.96% Bounce Rate
00:02:39 Avg. Time on Site
77.08% % New Visits

Visitors Overview

• Visitors

Visitors
163

Map Overlay world

Traffic Sources Overview

Search Engines 84.00 (43.75%)
Referring Sites 64.00 (33.33%)
Direct Traffic 44.00 (22.92%)

Content Overview

Pages	Pageviews	% Pageviews
/index.php	171	26.93%
/jeans-c-1	148	23.31%
/skinny-jean-c-1_6/skinny-jean-	43	6.77%
/shopping_cart	37	5.83%
/tailored-jean-c-1_7/tailored-	36	5.67%

Laundry Maid Jeans
Map Overlay

Jul 4, 2009 – Aug 3, 2009
Comparing to: Site

Visits
1 ■■■■■ 64

192 visits came from 30 countries/territories

Site Usage					
Visits 192 % of Site Total: 100.00%	Pages/Visit 3.31 Site Avg: 3.31 (0.00%)	Avg. Time on Site 00:02:39 Site Avg: 00:02:39 (0.00%)	% New Visits 77.08% Site Avg: 77.08 (0.00%)	Bounce Rate 48.96% Site Avg: 48.96 (00.0%)	
Country/Territory	Visits	Pages/Visit	Avg. Time on Site	% New Visits	Bounce Rate
United Kingdom	64	4.53	00:04:48	59.38%	31.25%
United States	41	1.76	00:00:30	95.12%	68.29%
Australia	19	4.37	00:04:39	57.89%	36.84%
Germany	10	3.90	00:01:46	80.00%	50.00%
Canada	5	3.20	00:00:38	100.00%	60.00%
Argentina	4	2.00	00:00:21	75.00%	75.00%
China	4	3.00	00:01:02	100.00%	25.00%
France	4	4.50	00:00:52	100.00%	75.00%
Pakistan	4	2.75	00:02:06	50.00%	50.00%

Google Analytics

Above Google Universal Analytics of Laundry Maid Jeans: dashboard summary and map overlay, which here traces the effect of marketing activity in Australia.

REFERENCES

Carson, James, 'Four Key Trends from the Fashion Ecommerce and Content Marketing Report', 16 December 2014, www.econsultancy.com/blog/65906-four-key-trends-from-the-fashion-ecommerce-and-content-marketing-report

Clements, Alison, 'Turning Browsers into Buyers', *Drapers*, 20 May 2011, www.drapersonline.com/retail/ecommerce/turning-browsers-into-buyers/5025508.article

Euromonitor, *Fast Fashion in 2016: Digital opportunities and agile threats part 2*, 2016

——, *Shopping for fashion: Bricks, clicks and in-betweens*, 2016

Fill, Chris, *Marketing Communications: Brands, Experiences and Participation*, 6th ed., Pearson 2013

Industryreportstore.com, *Clothing and Footwear Continue to be the Fastest Growing Sector in Retail Space*, 2015

Mintel, *Clothing Retailing*, UK, 2015

——, *Online Retailing*, UK, 2016

Spybey, Kat, 'Ecommerce: The Rise of Image Recognition Technology', *Drapers*, 6 August 2014, www.drapersonline.com/business-operations/digital-/ecommerce-the-rise-of-image-recognition-technology/5062950.article

FURTHER READING

Hepton, Anna, 'Drapers Digital Awards: Startups Shortlist', *Drapers*, 12 March 2015, www.drapersonline.com/business-operations/drapers-digital-awards-startups-shortlist/5072800.article

Knowles, James, 'Style and Substance: Using Editorial Content to Drive Online Sales', *Drapers*, 28 June 2014, www.drapersonline.com/business-operations/digital-/style-and-substance-using-editorial-content-to-drive-online-sales/5061711.article

Kulmala, Marianne, Nina Mesiranta and Pekka Tuominen, 'Organic and Amplified eWOM in Consumer Fashion Blogs', *Journal of Fashion Marketing and Management: An International Journal*, 17/1 (2013), pp. 20–37

Rayport J.F. and Jaworski B.J., *Introduction to E-Commerce 2nd edition*, McGraw-Hill 2003

Sharma, Amen, *The Google Checklist: Marketing Edition 2016*, CreateSpace Independent Publishing Platform 2016

Smith, Nicola, 'Searching Times: Keeping up with Google', *Drapers*, 28 June 2014, www.drapersonline.com/business-operations/digital-/searching-times-keeping-up-with-google/5061710.article

DISCUSSION

Think of fashion sites on which you have stayed and browsed. How did they prevent you from 'bouncing' to another site?

Think of your last online fashion purchase and the stages from buying to delivery to return. What helped you decide to buy, and what else would have helped you?

Chapter 8

PERSONAL SELLING AND OFFLINE FASHION RETAIL

How can offline selling thrive in the digital world? Find out how to:

- Increase a brand's exposure through personal selling
- Maximize the much overlooked area, for smaller brands, of selling both business-to-business and direct to the consumer
- Make use of agents to get stocked in stores
- Appeal to consumers when they are shopping on the high street
- Provide a unique experience for shoppers using visual merchanising, store layout and decoration
- Blend online and offline into a seamless omni-channel experience for consumers

PERSONAL SELLING AS A COMMUNICATION TOOL

To return to Chris Fill's four Cs framework (see p. 61) to summarize the key characteristics of each communication tool, it is possible to analyse the advantages and disadvantages of personal selling (see the table below).

Advantages of personal selling

- It is a one-to-one transaction; it has the strongest ability of all the tools to deliver a personal message, and a high level of interaction can therefore occur between the sales staff and the end consumer or the business that is being sold to.
- Any perceived lack of credibility between the two parties can be worked on by good relationship skills.
- Successful personal selling can be measured directly against sales or orders. If return on investment is the focus, sales figures can be seen directly and managed by the brand.

Disadvantages of personal selling

- The costs can be high, as noted in Fill's chart, but this applies to all larger companies using commission-based sales-force selling or retailers employing sales staff. As the Trapstar example demonstrates (see p. 146), smaller companies can take action

themselves. In general, retailers and end consumers love to meet the creators of brands.
- It is not generally, by itself, a tool for raising awareness; without any demand or presence in the existing market, it is hard to achieve any sales.
- It can be prone to negative associations with selling and sales techniques such as aggressive behaviour to achieve results.

The defining feature of personal selling is that messages can be tailored to suit the selling situation. Sales staff become skilled at dealing with buyers on a one-to-one or dyadic (two-people interaction) basis. Tasks can be tailored to suit the individual account, and simple techniques can be employed, such as leaning in to engage a buyer, mirroring body language to help build a bond or simply talking enthusiastically with passion for, and knowledge of, the product.

Personal selling in the fashion industry

There are two main scenarios in which sales personnel are used in the fashion industry.
- B2B transactions, in which the brand or producer seeks to sell its garments into suitable retail outlets, and it deals with the necessary buyers or store owners to sell in the ranges as they are developed. This is also called wholesaling.
- B2C transactions, in which retail staff are employed by a company that has its own retail space to carry out the front-end sales directly with consumers.

Many larger brands, such as Tommy Hilfiger, have both types of staff. They have a wholesale operation, which sells into selected independent stores (single or small chains of independently owned stores) and larger department stores across the globe, and their own retail outlets. B2C selling also includes online selling (see Chapter 7) and the success of TV shopping channels in selling clothing and accessories, especially jewellery, directly to viewers.

THE FOUR Cs OF COMMUNICATION TOOLS, WITH REFERENCE TO PERSONAL SELLING

Communications	Personal selling
Ability to deliver a personal message	High
Ability to reach a large audience	Low
Level of interaction	High
Credibility	
Given by the target audience	Medium
Cost	
Absolute costs	High
Cost per contact	High
Wastage	Low
Size of investment	High
Control	
Ability to target particular audiences	Medium
Management's ability to adjust the deployment of the tool as circumstances change	Medium

colette

Above Colette on Rue Saint-Honoré, Paris, one of the world's top independent stores, was known for its mix of upper-end brands and exclusive collaborations with designers. Staff were expected to be at the forefront of fashion knowledge and sell from a wide range of labels.

Left Maison Margiela's MM6 flagship store in Seoul, South Korea, by the Korean architect Mass Studies. The store was originally designed for Martin Margiela's fellow Belgian deconstructionist Ann Demeulemeester. The incorporation of outside and inside reflects the questioning, intellectual nature of both labels. Staff working there would be expected to represent this ethos.

GETTING INTO STORES: TRAPSTAR

Mikey Trapstar, one of the founders of the streetwear brand Trapstar, learned the retail trade by selling Italian labels such as Dolce & Gabbana and Moschino in London. He and two childhood friends started to create clothes for themselves and a few other friends, reflecting their own love of street culture, and Trapstar was born in 2006. They faced a problem familiar to small start-up fashion brands the world over: how can you get stockists interested when you are up against larger organizations with significant marketing budgets that will help to drive footfall to retailers? Trapstar recognized the value of limited availability as a driving force; in a similar way to the early days of the Japanese brand A Bathing Ape, which released only a few pieces to very exclusive stores, demand for Trapstar grew quickly in the local community.

Retailers, however, were still resistant to stocking Trapstar; the brand was too young, too inexperienced, too small, too unknown to get attention and drive desire for its clothing. The brand did, however, find one shop on London's Portobello Road that was happy to take a more collaborative approach. If Trapstar created the necessary buzz in-store for one weekend, the shop would stock the brand. The right people were assembled, along with the right product, and the idea of a weekend-long store invasion was born.

In effect, Trapstar launched its own pop-up retail system within another store. A string of successful store invasions gave the brand the confidence to launch its own flagship store, and led to it being stocked by the likes of department store Harvey Nichols and being involved in several collaborative projects, including mentoring new creative talent.

Trapstar cites images of Jay-Z and Rihanna wearing the brand, seen globally on the internet, as fundamental to increasing its exposure, particularly in the US. However, with no actual training in fashion or marketing, no funding or budget for sophisticated communications, against all the odds Trapstar has launched from scratch a brand that has the potential to resonate with streetwear fans across the globe. Having created a grass-roots demand for its product, it pioneered a selling technique that incorporated an event as its primary strategy.

Right Mikey Trapstar in store-invasion mode.

BUSINESS-TO-BUSINESS SELLING

The size and scope of sales operations within fashion companies depends largely on the size of the brand or company in question. For smaller start-up brands, such as Trapstar, sales may be initially handled in-house. As the brand grows, it must decide how to handle all the new accounts opened, the new orders placed and the deliveries that must be made across larger regions or even countries. Most brands then need to work with sales agents to help them achieve effective growth.

Sales agents

Sales agents usually work on commission, and will cover sales to a designated territory or region within a country on behalf of the brand. They may carry ranges personally to show to stores within their regions, or invite buyers to a hired showroom space. They act as a vital link between the shop floor and the brand, and provide information about what is selling, competitor brands, sales promotions that are working well and forthcoming campaigns. The relationships they build with buyers are crucial in competitive businesses like fashion, where brands can easily be replaced if there are persistent problems with pricing, delivery dates or quality. Sales agents can also ensure that point-of-sale (POS) material coordinates with other campaign material, and help stores to meet the minimum quantities asked for by brands. Fashion is considered a risky business, and so agents can command higher commissions, in the region of 10–15 per cent of the wholesale price of the pieces in the range. The wholesale price comprises the landed price of the garment (fabric, price of manufacture, trims, labelling and delivery from the manufacturer to the brand) with an amount built in to cover profits and further costs to the brand, including sales commissions. As a very general rule, wholesale prices are double the landed price of the garment.

To attract new accounts and grow the business, brands and designer labels typically show as part of an international fashion week or at a trade fair, depending on their market sector (see Chapter 10 for a full discussion). Trade fairs act as a forum for the brand's sales agents to see as many new and established accounts as possible during the course of one event, to inform them of the new season's collections.

Below Sales agents accompanied by a model, working for the brand Geisha, place orders with interested buyers at Berlin's trade fair Premium.

The role of a distributor

When a brand grows even larger, or wishes to expand into another country, it will often use a distributor that is more familiar with desirable store destinations and logistics in the desired territory or country. The interview with Aine McCourt on p. 150 expands on the differences of working practices between agents and distributors. Distributors sell the brand's range from a showroom alongside other brands they distribute. They compile orders on behalf of the brand and take on the logistics of sorting and transporting those orders to each customer to meet the required delivery dates. The cost of distribution can be a shock to new brands unless it has been planned into the wholesale price from the start. Distribution cost is the main reason why brands are more expensive in foreign markets than in their home nation; a brand can mitigate this by offering its goods to other countries at a discounted wholesale price.

As the Trapstar example illustrates, there is room for creativity within these B2B trading models, and the benefits of personal selling should not immediately be overlooked in favour of the idea of trimming down some of the tasks and costs by selling online. Although personal selling is not traditionally a tool to create brand awareness, it works very well with a form of communication that does: PR. With some exposure somewhere, such as mentions on a blog, trade press coverage at a trade fair or news coverage of an event, integrated with the use of personal selling, it is possible to get a fashion brand up and running and start some cash flow coming in. If a new brand has no budget for anything else, PR and personal selling are the fastest ways to raise its exposure in the market.

BUSINESS-TO-CONSUMER SELLING

Sales staff who work for high-street retail chains or branded store outlets and are involved in retail selling on the shop floor have especially felt the impact of the rise of online selling. Consumers often now arrive in-store having made comparisons of the item they want, knowing the price they are willing to pay and having sought tempting sales promotions that are available online. The number of retailers owning websites and the increase in the use of technology have, according to Josh Leibowitz (2010), separated customers from sales associates. Shoppers now seek to use fashion stores as gallery spaces to browse and try on, but may not make the final purchase in-store. This behaviour is termed throughout the industry as:

- **Webrooming** Researching online, then buying in-store. Fashion performs better here than some sectors, since some shoppers still prefer to try garments on in-store.
- **Showrooming** Browsing in-store, then buying online. This is when tempting online promotions or increased shopping hours win out.
- **Boomerooming** Shoppers browse online, visit the stores to research or try on, then buy online.

Such behaviour has reduced the role of sales associates to that of handling the cash transaction and has, therefore, seen a reduction in the incentive to make a sale. Leibowitz (2010), however, cites research by management consultants McKinsey that found that 40 per cent of consumers remain open to persuasion on entering a store, and lists the right number of knowledgeable, well-trained, motivated sales staff as vital to creating the right environment for consumers to make decisions. Peter McGoldrick (2002) also reflects the importance of product knowledge in successful retail selling, and adds the case for personality traits, citing research findings that staff who exuded enthusiasm and warmth were more likely to offer a rewarding service experience for shoppers. Gaynor Lea-Greenwood (2012) adds that sales personnel are employed to reflect the target market, and it is certainly the case that fashion students often support themselves by part-time work in fashion retail. Fashion, accessories and footwear have a high rate of impulse purchasing, although this urge is strong across all industries. John Egan (2015) cites Global Association for Marketing at Retail figures from 2012, which demonstrated that 76 per cent of purchases were still made in-store and that 55 per cent of those were made on impulse. A salesperson with product knowledge and enthusiasm and who reflects the lifestyle and appearance of the customer may be a powerful persuasive force.

The Spanish retail chain Zara is one fashion company that has seen good relationships between management and shop-floor sales staff benefit shoppers. According to Graham Ruddick (2014), twice a week Zara's store managers send an order to the commercial team at Zara's HQ. These orders are based on data about what has sold out, but also anecdotal evidence from the shop floor of consumers' preferences. Zara uses this information to

Left The US casualwear giant Abercrombie & Fitch faced criticism in European markets for employing only slim, attractive sales staff. The brand sought to attract young, cool shoppers by employing sales staff with those qualities.

Above In 2015 Apple achieved news coverage when the brand retrained its usual tech-savvy staff with style-based knowledge. This was to help initiate conversations based on trust with potential consumers of the Apple Watch.

replenish the stores quickly and also to spot emerging trends that in turn inform the design team. Zara's shoppers then benefit from super-quick injections of product based on what they already like. As an added incentive, Zara's sales managers can receive up to 100 per cent of their salary in bonuses for hitting sales targets. For Zara's chief executive and chairman, this is about motivation as well as not losing the human touch.

TV selling

The selling of clothing and jewellery on cable TV shopping channels such as QVC (Quality Value Convenience) and HSN (Home Shopping Network) has been an unexpected success. In TV selling the dyadic nature of personal selling is reflected in a simulated setting where the viewer will be drawn into a dynamic conversation between, usually, two hosts who enthuse about the benefits of the product. Research conducted by Louise Fritchie and Kim Johnson in 2003 recognized the role of persuasion within this type of B2C selling. Of the six persuasion strategies they tested, the most successful were:

Social proof Looking to others to determine how we should behave. Viewers hear that many others are successfully buying and enjoying the featured product. Shopping channels often use trusted and much-liked presenters who build a loyal following.

Scarcity The implication that the item is scarce or that there is a limited time to purchase before the supply runs out. This is used to great effect on shopping channels through stock countdowns and calls from relieved purchasers.

Authority Experts such as journalists or fashion editors may present items. Celebrities often create ranges that may be exclusive to a channel, and they can be called on to add weight to presentations.

In many ways this relates to Trapstar's experience. Seeing people – including the creators – enjoying the clothing as part of a weekend store invasion is a powerful persuasive force that could be replicated in other events that involve the creators to add the element of authority. Trapstar has also used scarcity by manufacturing limited runs of merchandise. Zara can make smaller batches of more risky lines, employing and making public a 'once it's gone, it's gone' strategy, to keep shoppers coming in looking for the new.

INDUSTRY PROFILE
AINE McCOURT OF EMILY AND FIN

The Australian Aine McCourt began her career as Managing Director of the Sydney-based sales and distribution agency The Wardrobe, which represented up to 25 brands with a customer base of 300 independent retailers and all major Australian department stores and retailers. She then moved to One Teaspoon, a previous client, where she was Head of Sales globally, before becoming Brand Director at the premium Australian brand Shakuhachi. She is currently International Sales and Marketing Manager for the British brand Emily and Fin.

Emily and Fin was established in 2002 by Emily Whittle and Ffion Armour-Brown, and is known for its charming retro-inspired prints, thoughtful design and attention to fit and quality. With McCourt on board the brand has achieved an admirable list of stockists, including accounts throughout Europe, Australia, New Zealand, the US, Japan and Canada. It has a mix of sales agents and distributors in different markets. It uses specific agents in Ireland, northern UK, Belgium, Holland and Germany, and distributors in Australia and New Zealand.

Q: What can brands do to help themselves attract the initial interest of sales agents?
A: Invest in lookbooks and their imagery. Also make sure you have established your brand's story and unique selling point. A brand must be able to communicate its USP or it is in danger of being perceived as just a label. Brands should also aim to have an online presence – not necessarily e-commerce, but a central source of information and social media is essential.

To make themselves more attractive to potential agents and/or distributors, brands should attempt some sales themselves. A brand with an existing 5–10 stockists is a much more attractive proposition. It also gives an agent an idea of the type of store the brand can be stocked in. A brand wants a showroom that has the existing relationships with the retailers in the market within which they want to be positioned.

Brands should also be prepared to invest in trade shows. If agents and/or distributors see a brand exhibiting season after season, they will believe that brand is something they should know about. Trade shows involve a significant financial and long-term investment. Brands should exhibit at multiple tradeshows for at least three seasons in order to establish whether the trade show is a viable sales channel/territory.

Q: How important do you feel the role of some prior marketing is to attracting agents?
A: Any prior marketing or press coverage and/or placement in blogs, magazines, newspapers or online publications would be really advantageous for a brand seeking an agent or distributor. This gives the brand an immediate appearance of authority in the marketplace.

Q: How can brands meet sales representatives?
A: The best way is by attending fashion networking events and by being present at trade fairs. Building relationships with the trade-show organizers is key. The organizers will know the people in their industry well and can make introductions to agents and distributors. Brands can also take the route of paying a fee to a third-party agency, such as the Anton Dell Fashion Consultancy, that will connect a brand with its global network of agents and distributors. Globally, countries have trade bodies such as UKTI (UK Trade and Investment) that can help to connect interested brands with agents and distributors.

Q: How do most agents then work with brands?
A: Generally speaking, an agent who does not have a permanent showroom will still have to hire temporary showrooms in key areas. This might be a hotel room, for example, and there they will show a sample range to interested buyers. Most agents charge the same commission – between 10 and 15 per cent. Commission might vary depending on how established the brand is, whether the agent is introducing the brand to the territory, whether the brand is handing over existing business, and so on. As a general rule of thumb in the current climate, brands should expect to pay 15 per cent.

Right Emily and Fin, Spring/Summer 2016 lookbook, front cover.

emilyandfin
SPRING / SUMMER 2016

Q: *What is the difference between an agent and a distributor?*
A: Essentially, agents use the brand's sample collection to sell from, and give the resulting orders to the brand. The brand will have agreed to pay them around 10–15 per cent sales commission, which it does not pay until the orders have been delivered and the store has paid the brand.

Distributors purchase a brand's sample collection and then work to compile the orders they achieve into one bulk order for the brand, taking a discount of 25–40 per cent off the brand's wholesale price total. Distributors working on this model typically pay the brand a deposit with the order, which will be shipped to the distributor's head office when it is ready. The deposit acts as a financial safeguard for the brand and helps to ensure the orders will be met. It can help a small brand pay for the production where there is growth but a struggle for cash flow. It then distributes the order to the independent retailers and chases them for payment. The distributor model is good for bigger territories and territories you are not familiar with or where there is a language barrier.

Payment terms can vary, but initially distributors take on the risk of chasing payments and pay the brand before shipment of the orders. They will often ask for 30-day terms, but I would recommend this only after a solid financial history has been established between the brand and the distributor.

Q: How can brands build lasting relationships with agents or distributors?
A: A brand's agents and distributors are its sales force and partners in growth. It is important to make sure your sales team is as educated about your brand/story/goals/future as possible. They are your brand ambassadors and represent you to your customers, so it is imperative that you have positive relationships.

Attendance at range reviews is imperative to make sure your sales force is educated about your collection: themes and inspirations, fits and prices, delivery dates, and so on. Every season I try to spend a day or two with each agent and their major customers, and accompany them on store visits. This shows the agent that we support them and the retailer, too, and tells them how important they are to our brand. I also like to do product nights with key retailers and get the agent to come along to those, too. They really appreciate the investment in their business.

Q: What supporting materials should a brand supply to the agent or distributor?
A: It is really important to make sure your sales force is equipped with the right assets. Line sheets, price lists and order forms are essential tools for your agents/distributors to do their job. You will need to make sure they are in the correct currency for the territory.

Fashion is a visual industry, and buyers respond to beautiful imagery that communicates your brand story and expresses its aesthetic. It helps your sales team to understand the perception of your brand and, therefore, where to position the brand in the marketplace. Campaign booklets and lookbooks can be expensive,

because you really want the best quality you can afford, but are still a worthwhile investment. Your sales team can leave the campaign books with potential retailers when canvassing them. If the brand has an online store, the campaign imagery can be used online, but also the books can be sent with online orders. Then the customer can understand the brand more and also see other items they may not have noticed online.

Q: Do you have any tips for avoiding the pitfalls of working in unknown territories?
A: Always have a contract with your sales agents and distributors that has been drafted by legal specialists in fashion law. In the EU, there are directives that will protect the agent or distributor should the arrangement finish. There have been cases of brands having to indemnify agents for up to five years.

Also, be wary of distributors promising to cover too wide a territory. Really, a brand should form a separate arrangement in each territory it wants to enter. Distributors need to know the local market and be present on the ground. Brands can take steps to raise initial awareness in other markets by using tools such as social media or placements on local celebrities.

Q: Do you have any thoughts on the future of the wholesale fashion model?
A: This is an interesting one. We are starting to see movements in when collections are being sold and delivered, because of global climate change. It will be the brands that can capitalize on this and recognize customers who want a buy now, wear now approach to sales, while maintaining the traditional seasonal changeover periods, that will really benefit. It will be the brands that can offer something unique that maintain a strong wholesale business. Independent and major retailers alike are looking for brands that do not compete with an already flooded high-street market.

RETAIL STORE ENVIRONMENT, ATMOSPHERE AND LAYOUT

Just as staff on the sales floor have seen changes caused by online shopping, multi-brand stores and own-brand flagship stores are under pressure to provide an entertaining shopping experience. Bricks-and-mortar stores are servicing well-travelled, highly informed fashion shoppers who are seeking experiential gratification from shopping as a leisure pastime. Retail atmosphere and merchandising have a role in providing an environment for brands in which shoppers will have a pleasurable visit.

Retail atmosphere

More and more stores are investing in the use of quirky architecture, sleek interiors and fixtures and fittings that embody the identity of the brand (own-brand flagships) or the desired retail concept (multi-brand and department stores). In particular for luxury brands, investment in prestigious architects has raised the bar for the luxury shopping experience: Rem Koolhaas, for example, created gallery, shopping and office epicentres for Prada in key world cities. Closely related to the desire to create a high-quality in-store experience is the consideration of retail atmosphere. McGoldrick (2002) cites Philip Kotler on the aspects that make up retail atmosphere, and some notes are added here to suit more current fashion retail.

- *Visual* Colour, brightness, size and shape. Areas are often delineated by product category and a colour, shape or theme concept for that category, provided by the store rather than by individual brands.
- *Aural* Volume, pitch, tempo. As well as providing a background soundtrack, stores may seek to provide appearances by guest or in-house DJs. A brand seeking a more individual identity might provide customizable collections of music for shoppers.
- *Olfactory* Scent, freshness. Often smells of freshly brewed coffee from nearby coffee bars will add to designer brand perfumes; brands without perfumes can use upmarket interior scents. This creates a heady, seductive environment.
- *Tactile* Softness, smoothness, temperature. Modern interiors tend towards smooth, free-flowing units with plenty of space for shoppers to move uninterrupted both visually and physically.

Above Interior of Stone Island flagship store, Rome, Italy. The experimental and sporting nature of the brand is reflected in fixtures and fittings reminiscent of mountaineering equipment, and the use of a clean, large-scale logo adds to the functional feel.

Above right Window display and exterior of Stone Island flagship store, Sylt, Germany.

Below right The space given to brands including J Brand, Victoria Beckham, M.i.h. Jeans, Paige and Frame in Selfridges, London. The contemporary women's department was designed by FAT Architecture in 2009/10.

These factors can be controlled by the brand in the creation of its own retail space, but the concept design of department stores may well provide fewer opportunities for a brand to convey its individual identity through logos and packaging.

Visual merchandising

The consideration of how a mix of brands, or an own brand, may be displayed within store design is known in retail as visual merchandising or VM. Visual merchandising is considered by Alice Chu and M.C. Lam (2007) as a key functional element in store design, which helps shoppers to find their way through the store and make purchase decisions. Department stores or larger multi-brand stores may give over more valuable space or thresholds – typically just by the entrance or at dedicated entrance points such as stairs, lifts and escalators – to brands they are happy to promote. Stores may also have a clear idea of pre-planned, dedicated floor space by category, such as contemporary brands or denim, to which brands will have to conform or risk not being stocked. Fashion merchandise is traditionally displayed by gender, then by colour blocking or by product theme/story and product type, or in branded areas. There have, however, been some newer innovative disruptions, such as & Other Stories' use of items grouped by lifestyle in a location-themed store, or the gender-mixed merchandising used by Selfridges for its pop-up 'Agenda' concept in 2015.

Above The Japanese mass-market retailer Uniqlo is the master of VM by colour blocking. Blocks of merchandise are used to create walls and units of colour and emphasize the brand's USP of affordable basics in multiple colour options. Mannequins are used to reflect the colour walls, and campaign/lookbook images are displayed on digital screens.

Left H&M's & Other Stories style their interiors to reflect the store locations. The London store resembles an industrial-style lab, while that in Antwerp (pictured) has the feeling of an old house.

Retail technology

In recent years a host of retail technology has been employed to bring the advantages of the online world – such as greater access to stock options, assisted delivery, catwalk footage and access to the likes, shares and reviews of online social communities – into the bricks-and-mortar store environment. The Dutch department-store chain de Bijenkorf's app is an excellent example of combining the attractions of in-store shopping with online functionality. Among other services, users have access to a barcode scanner with which they can scan garments in-store and see the full stock inventory. If what they want is not available on the shop floor, they can order it for next-day delivery.

Stores that have got this thinking right, rather than appearing overly invasive or using clunky, problematic technology such as social media-enabled mirrors, include the sports store Pro:Direct. According to Victoria McDermott (2015), they have used retail technology to make stores a social and community space, much more than simply four walls within which to make a transaction. Pro:Direct shoppers, for instance, can view and order products on life-size digital mannequins, but also stay and enjoy screened football matches, live appearances and bespoke shoemaking sessions.

Above Pro:Direct use digital technology to translate their website into an immersive bricks-and-mortar venue. Customers can access large display screens, touch screen monitors and virtual reality to bring products to life.

Above left and right The Brazilian Alexandre Herchcovitch reflected his love of loud prints and bold design in his Studio Arthur Casas-designed flagship store in Tokyo's Daikanyama district.

THE FUTURE OF OFFLINE RETAIL

In the previous chapter we discussed many of the enhanced service options – such as super-fast delivery innovations and smart merchandising – that online selling has taken from a one-to-one selling situation in order to improve on what existed in traditional bricks-and-mortar fashion retailing. The next challenge is to tempt shoppers back to traditional shops by creating an experience, but also by considering embracing omni-channel retail that blends and merges the online and offline experiences across all forms of retail on offer to shoppers.

In addition to the use of retail technology, progressive concept retailers have embraced the idea of stores becoming closer to the experience of visiting a gallery than that of a shop, and have employed a more curated mix of products that are complementary to fashion, such as magazines, books and household lifestyle items. Harder-to-find designer labels and brands sit in a well-thought-out 'experience' for visitors, and sales staff may have to be knowledgeable about a particular theme or even host a nightclub event. These environments can be replicated online by offering downloadable music, galleries of rare books or artworks to go the extra mile to persuade shoppers away from the multi-brand online retail giants.

For brands and retailers with flagship stores, it is ever more important to create a theme that is relevant or sympathetic to the location and the consumer's lifestyle. All retail outlets should consider providing interesting props, atmosphere, appealingly arranged areas of merchandise, and unique events for shoppers. As retail technology moves to blend offline with online and incorporate more intuitive gesture- and sensory-controlled features, with the ability to share thoughts on social media a click away, it is the role of the human touch in personal selling and retailing that will perhaps need to be marketed the hardest to remain relevant.

Above The 66 Gallery by Botas 66 in Prague combines a retail space for the brand's retro-inspired trainers with a gallery. The designer, A1 Architects, used white for the gallery and black for the retail space to contrast the items on display.

Below LN-CC (Late Night Chameleon Cafe) in London hunts down new and hard-to-find labels such as the Danish designer Anne Sofie Madsen and the Chinese-born, London-based Yang Li. These are displayed alongside books, records and a nightclub space for private events. The Gary Card-designed space-age interior is treated as an art installation that can be updated.

REFERENCES

Chu, Alice, and M.C. Lam, in Hines, Tony, and Margaret Bruce, *Fashion Marketing: Contemporary Issues*, 2nd ed., Elsevier 2007

Egan, John, *Marketing Communications*, 2nd ed., Sage 2015

Fill, Chris, *Marketing Communications: Brands, Experiences and Participation*, 6th ed., Pearson 2013

Fritchie, Louise Lystig, and Kim K.P. Johnson, 'Personal Selling Approaches Used in Television Shopping', *Journal of Fashion Marketing and Management: An International Journal*, 7/3 (2003), pp. 249–58

Lea-Greenwood, Gaynor, *Fashion Marketing Communications*, Wiley 2012

Leibowitz, Josh, 'Rediscovering the Art of Selling', *McKinsey Quarterly*, 2 (October 2010), p. 119, www.mckinsey.com/industries/retail/our-insights/rediscovering-the-art-of-selling

McDermott, Victoria, 'Beyond Clicks and Mortar', *Drapers*, 2015. Similar available online at www.drapersonline.com/business-operations/property-special-from-virtual-to-reality/7011434.article

McGoldrick, Peter, *Retail Marketing*, 2nd ed., McGraw Hill 2002

Ruddick, G., (20 October 2014) How Zara Became the World's Biggest Fashion Retailer, www.telegraph.co.uk/finance/newsbysector/retailandconsumer/11172562/How-Inditex-became-the-worlds-biggest-fashion-retailer.html

FURTHER READING

'A Conversation with Mikey Trapstar', *Highsnobiety*, 25 June 2013, www.highsnobiety.com/2013/06/25/mikey-trapstar-interview

Abnett, Kate, 'How Personal Shopping Makes People Spend', *Business of Fashion*, 21 May 2015, www.businessoffashion.com/articles/intelligence/how-personal-shopping-makes-people-spend

Kotler, P., 'Atmospherics as a marketing tool', 1973, www.researchgate.net/publication/239435728_Atmospherics_as_a_Marketing_Tool

DISCUSSION

Reread the panel on Trapstar (p.146). Why do you think they didn't just sell online?

Consider your last experience in a fashion store. What were the positive and negative experiences? Did your experience differ from the observations made by McGoldrick and Lea-Greenwood (p.148)?

What do you think is the future of the fashion store? What features would persuade you to stay, shop and feel loyal to a fashion store?

THE WHITE COMPANY
LONDON

FEBRUARY 2017

Chapter 9
DIRECT MARKETING

Blissful bedroom updates • Your new-season wardrobe edit
• Latest collection from The Little White Company • Plus win a minibreak to Paris

thewhitecompany.com

How is direct marketing useful in fashion promotion? Find out how to:

- Create and maintain a database of customers that can be used as a targeted marketing tool
- Identify customer information that is useful to brands, and focus attention on the best prospects for sales
- Compose effective direct marketing (catalogues, flyers and so on)
- Reach a target audience with personalized and interactive email marketing messages
- Complement other forms of fashion promotion with direct marketing, and help brands get ever closer to audiences via cross-platform messaging

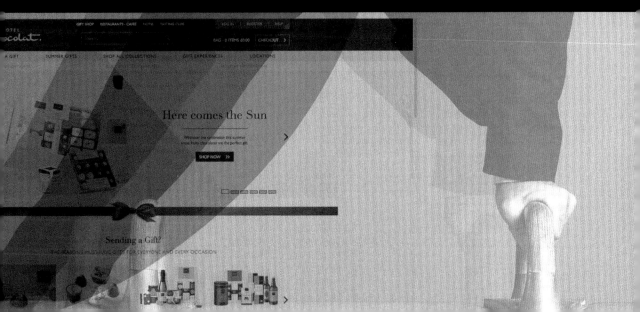

AN OVERVIEW
OF DIRECT MARKETING

Direct marketing (DM) is a form of targeted, personalized and interactive communication that attempts to create and sustain a relationship or ongoing dialogue with specific consumer groups. DM can be used in conjunction with other promotional tools, most typically sales promotions, or advertising messages that are targeted to a consumer group via a database that may be segmented by age, income, interests or behaviour. The aims are:

- To engage customers with the brand, using techniques such as e-newsletters, notification of special offers or events, and range information, and entice them to interact and purchase.
- To collect customer information in the form of personal details, registering of interest, purchasing behaviour and repeat purchasing behaviour, in order to build databases of information to feed future strategies and campaigns and to be able to reach audiences effectively.

Ira Kalb (2015) cites the Direct Marketing Association's (thedma.org) estimate of an industry worth US$2.05 trillion in resulting sales, roughly 8.7 per cent of US Gross Domestic Product. Key to the success of B2C DM is its ability to integrate with other forms of communication, to personalize messages either by using a prospect's name or by targeting their habits and interests, and to establish a dialogue. Direct marketing communication uses a variety of online and offline media, including direct mail such as catalogues and printed invitations, email and telecommunications.

Definitions of DM

DM is most commonly defined with regard to its relationship with other tools. Notification of a sales promotion will often be delivered using a DM technique, but John Egan (2015) defines the difference between the two: once a particular sales promotion has been responded to, it is the role of DM to build and maintain a relationship with the consumer. In order to establish a dialogue, it is essential for brands to communicate in the appropriate tone of voice through being aware of aspects of brand identity, such as personality, characteristics and narrative, discussed in Chapter 2.

Since DM is interactive, it is most similar to the face-to-face nature of personal selling, and replicates that tool's great ability to deliver a personal message. Patricia Mink Rath et al. (2012) note the analytical advantage DM provides over personal selling:

> While personal selling is the full and utmost level of interaction with the consumer, direct marketing is a step removed, allowing marketers to pinpoint key customers and prospects and present them with a variety of communications that are targeted to their needs.

DM is an essential tool in cutting through other promotion clutter, being personalized, directed at consumers' individual preferences and delivered directly to their homes, inboxes or mobile phones.

MIX BY LUCIANBLOMKAMP / WILLEM DAFOE FOR FRAME DENIM / EYTYS X ESTHER MAHLANGU
IF THIS EMAIL IS NOT DISPLAYING CORRECTLY, PLEASE **CLICK HERE**

OKI-ni

LATEST   BRANDS   SHOP   FOCUS   *EDITORIAL*

Mix Series I MS277

SONOROUS by Lucianblomkamp

Melbourne-based electronic musician Lucianblomkamp makes his oki-ni mix debut with SONOROUS, featuring tracks from Massive Attack, Robert Glasper and James Blake.

Play Now >

Left Branded e-newsletters, such as this example by oki-ni, are essential to building relationships with recipients. Access to exclusive content, such as music mixes, news and views on campaigns and collaborations, is key to building engagement with the audience. Clear links to the brand's shopping pages and social media platforms are provided.

MODERN
TAILORING

THE DEFINITION OF GREAT DESIGN IS THAT IT SHOULD
DELIVER A PERFECT COMBINATION OF FORM AND FUNCTION.

AT PAUL SMITH WE DESIGN BEAUTIFUL THINGS TO BE WORN
AND ENJOYED. WE BELIEVE THAT CLOTHES SHOULD NOT ONLY
LOOK GOOD, BUT SHOULD ALSO BE FIT FOR PURPOSE.

THAT IS WHY WE HAVE CREATED A NEW SUIT, TAILORED TO
TRAVEL IN - SOFT AND VERSATILE, IT IS CHARACTERIZED
BY A CONTEMPORARY, NEAT FIT.

HARNESSING THE NATURAL QUALITIES OF 100% WOOL,
THE NEW PAUL SMITH TRAVEL SUIT IS DESIGNED TO MOVE
WITH YOU. THE CLOTH'S STRETCH AND CREASE-RECOVERY
PROPERTIES MEAN THAT WHATEVER YOUR JOURNEY,
YOU'LL ALWAYS LOOK WELL TURNED OUT.

MAX WHITLOCK
BRITISH OLYMPIC, WORLD & EUROPEAN MEDALLIST, MEN'S GYMNAST'CS

Left A direct mail from Paul Smith. Personally addressed, high-quality, well-produced direct marketing messages can attract attention. This fold-out card depicting the Olympic gymnast Max Whitlock contains a swatch of a new pure-wool suiting. This shows attention to detail by the label, and includes the recipient in the design process.

A NEW
CLOTH

100% WOOL CLOTH WITH NATURAL STRETCH AND CREASE RECOVERY.

SHOPS

BOOK A FITTING SESSION WITH OUR TAILOR
IN YOUR LOCAL SHOP.

UK	FRANCE	USA
NO. 9 ALBEMARLE STREET LONDON, W1S 4BL TEL: +44 (0)20 7493 4565	5 RUE DU FAUBOURG ST HONORE 75008 PARIS TEL: +33 (0)142 68 27 10	142 GREENE STREET NEW YORK, NY 10012 TEL: +1 646 613 3000
40-44 FLORAL STREET LONDON, WC2E 9TD TEL: +44 (0)20 7379 7133	22 BOULEVARD RASPAIL 75007 PARIS TEL: +33 (0)153 63 08 74	108 5TH AVENUE NEW YORK, NY 10011 TEL: +1 212 627 6770
WESTBOURNE HOUSE 122 KENSINGTON PARK ROAD LONDON, W11 2EP TEL: +44 (0)20 7727 3553	ITALY VIA MANZONI 30 20121 MILAN TEL: +39 02 763 19121	8221 MELROSE AVENUE LOS ANGELES, CA 90046 TEL: +1 323 951 4800
CANARY WHARF 360-365 CABOT PLACE EAST LONDON, E14 4QT TEL: +44 (0)20 7519 6818	HOLLAND P C HOOFTSTRAAT 136 1071 CE AMSTERDAM TEL: +31 (0)20 670 06 41	50 GEARY STREET SAN FRANCISCO, CA 94108 TEL: +1 415 391 3200
38 MARYLEBONE HIGH STREET, LONDON W1U 4QF TEL: +44 (0)20 7935 5284	BELGIUM KELDERSTRAAT 2 & 3 ANTWERP 2000 TEL: +32 (0)3 231 51 13	THE SHOPS AT CRYSTALS 3720 SOUTH LAS VEGAS BLVD LAS VEGAS, NV 89158 TEL: +1 702 796 3640
WILLOUGHBY HOUSE 20-22 LOW PAVEMENT NOTTINGHAM, NG1 7DL TEL: +44 (0)115 968 1990	GERMANY HOHE BLEICHEN 15 20354 HAMBURG TEL: +49 (0)40 3501 5212	BROOKFIELD PLACE 230 VESEY STREET NEW YORK, NY 10281 TEL: +1 610 965 1000
VICTORIA QUARTER 17-19 KING EDWARD STREET LEEDS, LS1 6AX TEL: +44 (0)113 245 9128		AUSTRALIA 126 COLLINS STREET MELBOURNE, VIC 3000 TEL: +61 (0)3 5639 6110
LONDON HEATHROW AIRPORT TERMINAL 3 TEL: +44 (0)20 8897 8447 TERMINAL 5 TEL: +44 (0)20 8283 7008		

PAULSMITH.CO.UK

It is without doubt the technological advances in database compilation and management of consumer details, and the use of analytical tools to process data, electronic point-of-sale data in retail and analytical tools such as Google Universal, that have enabled DM to become an effective tool when used in conjunction with digital media such as email. These advances have also made DM directly measurable.

Patrick De Pelsmacker (2007) identifies direct marketing as 'contacting customers and prospects in a direct way with the intention of generating an immediate and measurable response or reaction', and it is this cost-effective measurability that has proved attractive to brand stakeholders keen to see a quick return on their investment.

ADVANTAGES AND DISADVANTAGES OF DIRECT MARKETING

Revisiting Chris Fill's (2013) four Cs framework of communications, this time examining the ratings for DM, provides an underpinning for its advantages and disadvantages as a tool. See the table below.

Advantages of direct marketing

- DM can, especially when sent digitally, replicate the customized nature of personal selling.

THE FOUR Cs OF COMMUNICATION TOOLS WITH REFERENCE TO DIRECT MARKETING

Communications	Direct marketing
Ability to deliver a personal message	High
Ability to reach a large audience	Medium
Level of interaction	High
Credibility	
Given by the target audience	Medium
Cost	
Absolute costs	Medium
Cost per contact	High
Wastage	Low
Size of investment	Medium
Control	
Ability to target particular audiences	High
Management's ability to adjust the deployment of the tool as circumstances change	High

- Digital techniques such as email or text messaging are trackable; brands can measure whether or not the message has been read, whether the images or links have been clicked on and if the email contact has led to a sale.
- This measurability allows much more precise budgeting for future campaigns.
- DM integrates easily with other communication tools: it has a high level of management control and can be used as part of the communications mix or to drive sales using techniques such as telemarketing.

Disadvantages of direct marketing

- Even the most effectively targeted DM messages may be considered junk mail or spam and binned or left in junk folders, even those from brands with which the recipient has registered interest.
- Promotional material for printed direct marketing, and targeting specific customers, can be costly.
- Cold-calling in the form of telesales can be deemed annoying and even offensive, and has received negative media publicity as a result of relentless calling tactics, especially to vulnerable people.
- Updating and managing B2C DM databases can be time-consuming and costly.

CUSTOMERS AND DATABASES

As we have established, the primary aim of B2C DM is to reach potential or existing customers with engaging, personalized communications that act as an enticement to shop. The secondary aim is all about consumers: acquiring new consumers and retaining existing ones. However, since all DM activities stem from a database of details, it is impossible to achieve one aim without the other. The next section discusses how consumers are viewed within DM before examining the different methods of DM communications.

Brands and retailers set about compiling lists of consumers in one of three ways.

- *House lists* Start-up fashion brands may decide to begin an exclusive, controlled database by placing an enticing item on the landing page of their website that invites potentially interested audiences to register their interest and sign up with the brand. Alternatively, social media platforms could be used to drive interest through to a sign-up point.

- *Compiled lists* Initial lists of consumer information can be purchased from specialist agencies. According to Paul R. Smith and Ze Zook (2011), these can be basic lists of contact details such as names, email addresses, locations and phone numbers with some form of segmentation, such as age or income. Core information of this kind is taken from public records or directories.
- *Response or mail responsive lists* Lists can also be purchased that are more sophisticated and include a more detailed profile or evidence of behaviour that suggests a more definite interest in the brand.

The value of the list in terms of cost per thousand (CPT) is determined by the value of the information to the brand. The brand then adds additional layers of information, such as reaction to a campaign, response to invitations or take-up of discount vouchers, making the list more suited to its own needs. This way of viewing consumers is linked to the importance of compiling an accurate and detailed customer profile (see p. 10). Once the method to be used (geo-demographic, psychographic, emotive segmentation, etc.) and the terms and description are established, these lists can become the building block of database management and be used to attract similar individuals.

Egan (2015) proposes a 'prospect hierarchy' of consumers. This demonstrates how consumers are viewed in terms of their different strengths as prospects for the brand.

- *Suspects* These are one stage above the general public and are likely to match the brand's existing customer profile; they are, therefore, of potential interest to the brand.
- *Profiled prospects* Have demonstrated purchasing with similar brands and therefore have a stronger likelihood of buying from the brand.
- *Referrals* Have been referred to the brand via an existing customer and are strong prospects.
- *Enquirers* Have contacted the brand directly or expressed interest through a website, email or phone call.
- *Lapsed customers* Have purchased from the brand and need to be attracted back to do so again.

In theory, these groups of consumers can be targeted at first with different types of message to entice them with products relevant to them, then to involve them by invitations to events or other brand activities, or to win them back with exclusive offers or loyalty schemes. This acquisition and tracking of customer behaviour is part of the wider study of customer relationship management (CRM).

JOHN EGAN'S PROSPECT HIERARCHY

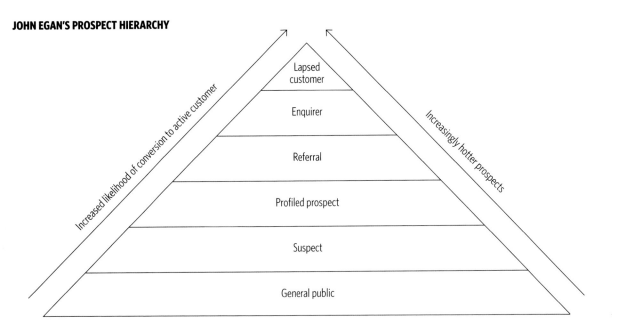

Increased likelihood of conversion to active customer

Increasingly hotter prospects

Lapsed customer

Enquirer

Referral

Profiled prospect

Suspect

General public

DIRECT MAIL AND OFFLINE DM

Direct mail consists of printed promotional materials that are addressed and sent by post to current and potential consumers. Direct mail takes the form of flyers, letters, invitations and catalogues. As Fill (2013) points out, these communications should appear personalized, but in fact they are mass-produced items from a commercial print run. Techniques such as using the recipient's name and incorporating handwritten elements and signatures from the sender reduce the risk of being considered junk mail. According to the UK's Direct Marketing Association (dma.org.uk, 2014), there is still a case for a more 'real' and trustworthy form of printed communication. It cites direct mail as having a 30 per cent higher response rate than

email, with an average of 4 per cent. More importantly, it also works as an effective driver of traffic to websites: 44 per cent of recipients are expected to visit a brand's website after receiving direct mail from it.

Catalogues

Catalogues are the oldest form of DM. According to Egan (2015), they became a popular form of direct sales to the large number of people living outside towns, for whom travel to stores was difficult. In 1888 the Sears catalogue was the first to sell watches and jewellery; clothing was added in 1894. The first fashion-based catalogue in the UK was Freemans, which began in 1905.

Left The White Company Spring 2017 catalogue.

THE WHITE COMPANY
LONDON

FEBRUARY 2017

FALL IN LOVE WITH

Spring

Blissful bedroom updates • Your new-season wardrobe edit
• Latest collection from The Little White Company • Plus win a minibreak to Paris

thewhitecompany.com

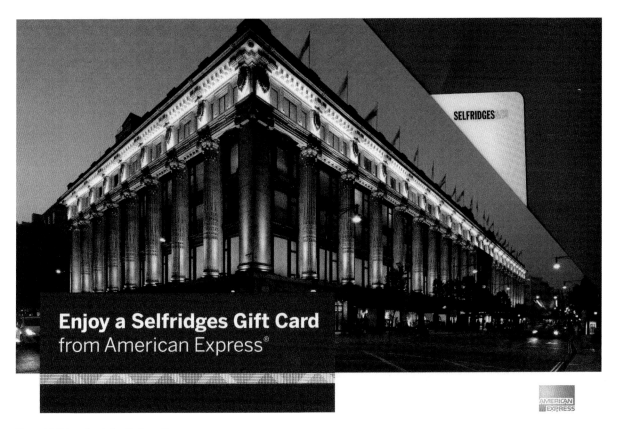

Above A Selfridges gift card offered by the credit company American Express, on spending £150 in Selfridges. This is an example of co-branded direct mail, where the targeted holder or owner of one brand can reasonably be expected to be interested in the other.

Fashion catalogues have had mixed fortunes over recent years. They are expensive to shoot, print and produce, and there are additional costs for packaging and mailing. Previous innovations, such as flexible payment terms or overnight delivery, have been replaced largely by easily available credit and the rise of online shopping. There are exceptions, however, and brands such as The White Company and Boden have identified consumers who do respond to catalogue mail-outs. The White Company was launched in 1994 as a 12-page brochure and has expanded into a multi-channel operation via the catalogue, its online operation, including a US site, and 56 stores. Boden dispatches 6 million catalogues globally every year, and although in 2015 98 per cent of sales came through the website, the brand recognized that 50 per cent of traffic was driven to the site by shoppers receiving the catalogue.

Inserts and flyers

Fashion labels typically use inserts in fashion magazines, including leaflets, flyers and small catalogues. Because it involves a form of mass media at a reasonably low price,

this form of communication is technically an advertising technique rather than DM, and is discussed in Chapter 4 (see p. 70). Leaflets, flyers or brochures that arrive personally addressed through the post, on the other hand, are DM. They can contain purely advertising messages or inform a selected target segment about special offers or financial incentives.

Letters and invitations

Letters and invitations from fashion brands are effective DM tools used by both brands and department stores. They tend to address the consumer in a much more personalized way, inviting them to events such as private views or early sales events or informing them of new collections or even discounts. The London department store Liberty often uses this form of direct marketing: it strikes a chord between the charismatic buying team and targeted customers.

ONLINE DM

The use of internet-based email accounts and an increase in the technology to measure responses have increased the popularity of email messages and e-newsletters used as low-cost DM tools by which to inform consumers about new ranges, products and news. Most websites allow the visitor to sign up to receive messages via email very early in their journey on the site.

Email messages/opt-in email

The Direct Marketing Association (2014) makes the point that email messages have a much more positive response if the recipient knows the sender. On average in 2013, only 3 per cent of email communications resulted in a click-through to a webpage, a response rate of 0.12 per cent. In a message from a familiar brand, the open rate was 38.6 per cent and the response rate 7 per cent, a marked rise. Smith and Zook (2011) give a useful checklist for the content of email messages to minimize the chance that they will languish in a junk mail folder. This has been extracted and adapted here:

- Grab attention in the subject line and in the first sentence. This may be all the recipient will see.
- Be brief and relevant to the target segment (use links from both images and text to the website for more information).
- Be as personal as possible. Direct mail is personally addressed to the recipient. If you can, replicate this for email messages.
- Provide links to social media platforms to give further information on the subject.
- Provide an opt-out or unsubscribe option (required by law in the UK, US, Canada, and across Europe).
- Provide the brand's full address, email address and contact details, or links to them.

As Smith and Zook (2011) also point out, emails to unsolicited accounts in B2C markets is illegal and termed 'spamming', hence the term opt-in email, which involves mailing only those who have expressed an interest (either in-store at point of purchase or by visiting the company website) and agreed to receive communications from the brand. By law, a link to unsubscribe from such communications must be provided in each email.

STRAIGHT UP & #FLARE

TRENDS FOR NOW

Your new wider denim silhouette complete with flattering Diesel cuts and details from the streets of Japan and 70s NYC. You're welcome.

GET MEN'S TRENDS

GET WOMEN'S TRENDS

WIDE CUTS
GOODBYE SKINNY

Shake it up. Your new look is all about the wider cut, straight leg denim Khiro inspired by Japan street style. Authentic vintage details with an easy to wear edge means you can be future forward, while leaning back.

DENIM FOR HIM

Above A Diesel e-newsletter featuring a clear header, attention-grabbing images and small blocks of text. Hyperlinks to the 'New in' section of the website are disguised under boxed-off headings.

Below Diesel provides clear links to social media, an unsubscribe option, links to further contact details and reminds recipients to add its email address to their contacts.

FLARE FOR DAYS
BRIGHTEN UP

Get that contemporary 70s look with the Sandy B denim. Fitted at the waist and thigh with a flare at the knee, this bootcut looks amaze. Pair with under-denim for that new 'Summer of love' vibe.

DENIM FOR HER

DIESEL

To ensure delivery of Diesel e-mail to your inbox, please add digital@diesel.com to your address book.

If you want to update your preferences or no longer wish to receive these messages, click Unsubscribe.

© 2016 DIESEL   STORE LOCATOR   PRIVACY   LEGAL TERMS   CONTACT US

TELEMARKETING, TELESALES AND TEXT MESSAGING

Telemarketing and telesales are not often used by fashion companies. Developments in text messaging, however, are proving relevant to how DM could be used in the future.

Telemarketing

Telemarketing uses the telephone to reach consumers directly. It is divided into outbound, where telemarketers call consumers about new product launches and in-store events, and inbound, where a number is provided for the consumer to call. Inbound telemarketing is most commonly used in the fashion industry to provide customer service and help with problems with returns or website transactions, or possibly to take orders.

SMS and MMS marketing

With the huge change in and evolution of smartphones, the mobile has enabled one of the most effective forms of telemarketing, the targeting of consumers through the use of text messages. Brands keen to reach young audiences, such as Claire's and Vans, found that SMS (short-message service) text messages both reached their audiences and added to their databases of mobile contacts. Instant messaging services such as iMessage, introduced in 2011, allow the sending of MMS (multimedia messaging service) messages such as photos, videos and group messages over the internet, potentially enabling text-based marketing messages to spread to wider audiences than just the initial recipient. Initiatives such as Nordstrom's TextStyle have also used this less formal medium to connect shoppers with staff by putting customers in touch with sales associates or stylists via text to get tips and ideas.

Telesales

Telesales, on the other hand, involves marketers or automated robocalls phoning consumers and trying to push products and services. Telesales is the form of DM that has attracted the most negative publicity, mainly because of its invasive tactics and its association with nuisance calling. The US's Do Not Call Registry and the UK's Telephone Preference Service (TPS) enable anyone who does not want to receive calls to register their details. Unfortunately, this does not seem to be enough to deter determined organizations, which in the UK have included charities. It is hard to think of a positive example or a way in which telesales could be used by a fashion brand to recreate the positive buzz a ringing phone once generated.

HYBRID DIRECT MARKETING

As we have seen, DM is often used as a complementary tool to deliver sales promotion or advertising messages, and in Chapter 4 we looked at problems with lack of interactivity in advertising (see p. 61). We now turn to some of the ways direct marketing is used to enable a route through to an end consumer or a group of interested consumers, and how the lines are being blurred between social and DM channels.

Direct-response ads – print, TV or online

Direct-response ads typically contain a call to action, a section for the consumer to fill in or a number for them to call, to claim an offer or initiate an enquiry. With the evolution of digital and social media, direct-response ads are also used to attempt to blur the lines between traditional print and TV advertising by providing a connection to sales outlets or links to social media.

According to De Pelsmacker (2007), direct-response ads are not targeted at one single consumer, but aim to grab consumers' attention and then engage the consumer by asking them to return a coupon, call a number, visit a website or link to their Facebook and other digital and social media profiles. This means that the advertisement is placed in the mass media but allows individual engagement from current consumers and new prospects.

Direct marketing versus social media

As far back as 2008, marketers were raising concerns about the ongoing effectiveness of email as a form of communication when many target markets were spending much of their time on social media. Matthew Wall (2008) drew an important distinction between the two tools:

Continued on p. 172.

After completing a BSc in International Fashion Marketing at Manchester Metropolitan University, Michelle Crowe took on a role as Marketing Assistant at the lingerie company Figleaves in 2010. The position involved coordinating five catalogues, writing blog entries, posting on Twitter, and PR and events management, as well as proofreading, performance analysis and ensuring the social media strategy was implemented. She became a digital marketing executive in 2011 before joining the footwear and accessories brand Kurt Geiger in 2013 and becoming more specialized in email marketing. There she briefed and approved more than ten campaigns a week, analysing customer purchases and behaviour to develop further accurate strategies and to ensure that key performance indicators (KPIs) were met. She rose to become Senior Email Marketing Coordinator in 2015, managing the planning and delivery of email marketing communications across all Kurt Geiger-licensed websites. In 2016 she joined the award-winning chocolatier Hotel Chocolat as Email Marketing Executive.

Q: What do you find are the differences between marketing chocolate and fashion?

A: I've worked in lingerie, shoes and chocolate now – I'm pretty lucky! The difference is the taste aspect. With shoes and fashion you can see them online – you do need to try them on, but you can imagine what it's going to be like – but with chocolate you don't know what you are getting until you actually try it. The copy we use is a bit more emotive around the sense of taste. At Hotel Chocolat we all work as one team. We all sit altogether, offline channels and online channels, in an aim to get everything more streamlined. We have different campaigns throughout the year. Similarly to fashion, where you have Autumn/Winter and Spring/Summer, we have seasonal occasions such as Easter or Christmas. For Easter we start at least a year in advance. We take the lessons learned from the previous year, discuss the initial feel of the campaign and form the brief. Then we all go off

and work out how we will execute that on each of our channels.

Q: What sort of subjects do you email customers about?

A: I send out newsletters, teasers, etc. – probably a bit more here [at Hotel Chocolat] than I have in the past. It's more behavioural stuff, because the thing about online e-commerce is that you can measure and track customers' behaviour – if they have gone on to the website, if they've gone on to purchase, or whatever. To make the emails more directly relevant, we include first names and information about their nearest store. We also send out more generic trade messages, such as if we're on sale or if we've launched a new campaign, for example for Father's Day. Fashion isn't a necessity and neither is chocolate, but it involves aspiration and luxury with an additional gifting element. Shoes [at Kurt Geiger] were mainly self-purchased, whereas at Hotel Chocolat a big part of the branding is that it's a nice gift to give and it makes you feel good to give it; it's a different edge.

Q: Would you say personalization in emails continues to work?

A: The thing about email marketing is relevance, so you want to make sure you improve the engagement to maximize the return. Every piece of marketing you do is costing money, so you want to ensure you are getting the best return. You can put someone's name in the subject line or recognize that they haven't shopped recently or that they have just shopped – that stuff works as personalization. Email plays a big part in CRM and eCRM. You capture so much data, and in email marketing that's really your first port of call. You are sending them a message, as opposed to search and affiliate, which is all about the acquisition of new customers. You really want to get them into your pot of email subscribers, and then you can try and reach them. You want to be able to turn anyone on your list into customers.

Right The Hotel Chocolat website's landing page highlights celebrations and the pleasure of giving to build positive brand associations.

You can tell who your most important customers are, who spends the most by tapping into an RFM (recency, frequency and monetary) model: how recently they purchased, how often they purchase and how much money they spent. You can tie these three together and identify your best customers.

It has a lot to do with retention, but a proportion of your database will have signed up just because they want to be kept alert. Unfortunately, the big challenge at the moment for a lot of retailers is tying on- and offline behaviour together in one customer view.

We might have a customer who has signed up to our email but has never purchased online, but who comes into our stores and cafes frequently, so it's a big challenge.

Q: How important is the balance of text and image?
A: For any luxury brand, the use of images is really important to build the brand. Along with carefully constructed copy, images help to portray a feeling or emotion. However, in terms of digital marketing, the use of live text plays a huge role in terms of best-practice execution

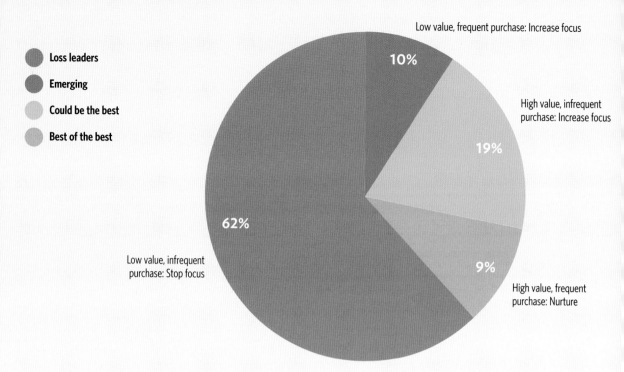

Low value, frequent purchase: Increase focus

10%

High value, infrequent purchase: Increase focus

19%

62%

Low value, infrequent purchase: Stop focus

9%

High value, frequent purchase: Nurture

- Loss leaders
- Emerging
- Could be the best
- Best of the best

Above RFM modelling allows companies to profile the most loyal and high-value customers, who can then be targeted with messages that strengthen the relationship. Similarly, resources to low-value purchasers can be reduced.

of an email or website. Live text is copy that can load in a customer's inbox without internet access. It's important to use live text when possible, especially in today's mobile world. Live text helps a brand to optimize its communication and engage with a consumer when internet access may be limited. In terms of images versus copy, it is a fine balance. A lot of emails (70–80 per cent) are opened on mobile devices, and using a lot of images can slow down the load time of an email. If it is too slow, people will simply be on to the next one. It's about balancing this digital technique: what's best practice and what's best for your brand.

Q: How often do you advise sending out mails for optimum response?
A: Fashion is so fast and trends pop up so quickly that you can get away with sending a lot of content out. Fashion brands do send more frequently, so their engagement is probably a bit less, as people don't open every single mail. I went to a seminar in 2015 in the US and they advocated sending five times a week. They believed the optimum was four days a week, so if you want to hit the optimum response send four, but you could see the same return sending three or five so you might as well send five!

Q: Is it the case that the more you open the more you are sent?
A: It is the case that email service providers (ESPs) will mark you as a safer sender if your emails are getting better engagement rates. They can see that the audience is interested, and it suggests that you are genuine and not just generating spam. ESPs such as Yahoo, Hotmail, Gmail and AOL will recognize the sender's IP address, and if the last mail sent had a low opening rate, they can send the next through quite slowly. Sending to people who are engaged in your brand improves your deliverability and improves your sender score. All the ESPs will then favour you, thinking these are relevant email messages. As a rule of thumb, the more you send out the more revenue/traffic you will generate, simply because you are sending more, but it doesn't mean the value of what you are sending is increased.

Q: How important is brand tone of voice in email marketing?
A: You've got to have one clear tone of voice that sits in line with your brand values, but how that is used across all the brand media will change. Social [media] will be less formal, whereas in print you can be a lot more formal. With email, too, you have only got your subject line, you only have 33 characters. You do have

Right A Kurt Geiger welcome email.

a little more in the preheader to really capture the recipient's attention, but you might have to tweak the tone of voice to improve engagement.

Q: Do you think text- and image-based apps such as WhatsApp will replace email communications?

A: Initially I think it sounds more intrusive, but really it is no different from how email marketing was perceived 15 years ago, and then SMS marketing. There is this statistic that 99 per cent of text messages are opened, which is possibly driving interest. The more you bombard people with SMS marketing or WhatsApp messages, the more engagement will decline to the levels seen in email marketing. I can understand the desire to work in a similar way to social, which is all about sharing – the more people like something, the more likely it is to appear in other people's feeds; the more it is shared, the more exposure your brand will get. I'm not sure; maybe it will work regionally. I personally hate sponsored tweets and ads on social or Instagram. I am all for using it cleverly – Missguided, for instance, will post a really clever quote on a Friday and I'll like it. They've not paid for it to be in my feed; it's in my feed because loads of people have liked it – it's a genuine viral piece. I'm not OK with paid-for posts on social media.

Young people are getting savvy to celebrity endorsements, paid-for tweets and the use of the sponsored hashtag on Instagram. People are way more aware of what's real. You need to work very hard. It's not good enough any more to say these are the top five gifts to get – you have to say exactly why it is you will want them.

for a brand, social media is about pushing messages into communities of followers, whereas email involves communicating with a specific customer. There is an element of control over the response from an email that is missing in social media. Contributors to Wall's article agreed that material designed to be shared must work in conjunction with whatever the brand is communicating via email, but that one could not yet replace the other.

Since then some pioneering campaigns have used social media in a way that replicates DM. The Israeli agency smoyz used Facebook when working for Kleenex in 2011: by using social search keywords, it located people in need of tissues to ease colds or flu and rewarded them with care packs. Marks and Spencer did a similar activity to reward Twitter followers in need of cheer in the run-up to its Christmas 2014 campaign. In other words, individuals can be reached using social media, and rewarded rather than marketed to or sold to. In most cases, recipients of the rewards posted comments and pictures and shared them with friends. It is this element of sharing that the conventional email environment lacks.

Cross-platform mobile messaging

It is with the rise of blended messaging and social platforms such as WhatsApp that the lines between social media and DM have become most blurred. In 2002 the pioneer email provider dotmailer developed a way that email content could be bookmarked, annotated with the user's own comments and pulled into social networks that were willing to support the software, thus placing email content in the desired social environment.

WhatsApp, released in 2009, was developed as a smartphone app that allowed users to send text messages or images, videos and documents accompanied by a real-time messaging component to phone contacts including those who had different makes of phone. By using internet data, WhatsApp had the benefit of avoiding text-messaging costs on standard tariffs. The app became the most commonly used messaging application in the world, and was bought by Facebook in 2014. Although the developers remain resistant to the idea of advertising on WhatsApp, according to an article by Vijaya Rathore and Varuni Khosla (2014), luxury and premium brands such as Cartier, Armani and Diesel are exploring the use of social media DM through WhatsApp in India. The app is extremely popular there, and luxury brand store managers are using it to share pictures, videos and other branded promotional content and to manage customer service with their exclusive clients, in some cases citing a conversion rate to sales of 80 per cent. Much in the way that early mail order grew, clients in more remote areas of India are able to browse ranges and enjoy personal touches such as booking items to try on at home or to collect at a convenient store.

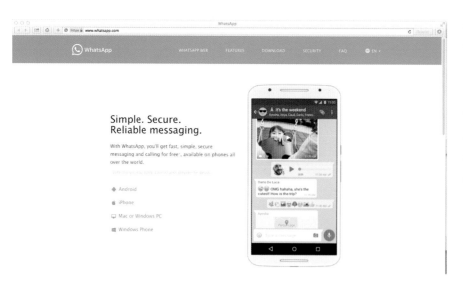

Above A Next sales promotion available in-store at point of purchase. There is a call-to-action section to complete to receive £10 off an online purchase. This fits De Pelsmacker's description of direct response: not targeted at individual consumers, but used in this case to match individual email addresses with a promotional code.

Left WhatsApp was developed by former Yahoo employees Jan Koum and Brian Acton, who became billionaires after Facebook acquired the app for US$19 billion in 2014.

THE FUTURE OF DIRECT MARKETING

In the considered use of DM, two schools of thought exist. One is to consider each receiver environment. Paul Smith is an excellent example of this (see p. 161). At home, when opening the post, it is more pleasurable to receive good-quality invitations, range updates or advice of store openings. People check emails in more professional settings, so Paul Smith keeps shorter notifications of sales or catwalk updates to email content. Behind-the-scenes inspiration, exhibitions of interest and thoughts on objects or garments are reserved for the more entertainment-driven nature of social media. This approach recognizes that the consumer will be located in different circumstances in each case. What they receive should be integrated with other tools and cohesive in terms of brand, but can be different to suit each circumstance.

The other school of thought has brands experimenting with new blended messaging apps, such as WhatsApp or Kik, a similar app that recognizes that Centennial even more than Millennial shoppers are permanently attached to their smartphones. In this way, DM can be closer to the blended bricks-and-mortar shopping experience described in Chapter 8. Retailers can use GPS data alongside the data they have already compiled to text shoppers with personalized, relevant location-based news or offers while they are in a liking and sharing environment.

REFERENCES

Amor, David, 'Why Direct Mail in the 21st Century?', Direct Marketing Association, 6 October 2014, www.dma.org.uk/article/why-direct-mail-in-the-21st-century-1

De Pelsmacker, Patrick, Maggie Geuens and Joeri Van den Bergh, *Marketing Communications: A European Perspective*, 4th ed., Pearson 2007

Egan, John, *Marketing Communications*, 2nd ed., Sage 2015

Fill, Chris, *Marketing Communications: Brands, Experiences and Participation*, 6th ed., Pearson 2013

Kalb, Ira, 'What Businesses Need to Know About Direct Marketing', *Huffington Post*, 30 March 2015, www.huffingtonpost.com/ira-kalb/what-businesses-need-to-k_b_6962236.html

Mink Rath, Patricia, Richard Petrizzi and Penny Gill, *Marketing Fashion: A Global Perspective*, Fairchild Books 2012

Rathmore, V., and Khosla, V., 'Luxury Brands like Cartier, Armani, Diesel and others use WhatsApp to promote products in India', 9 October 2014. economictimes.indiatimes.com/industry/services/retail/luxury-brands-like-cartier-armani-diesel-and-others-use-whatsapp-to-promote-products-in-india/articleshow/44728111.cms

Smith, Paul R., and Ze Zook, *Marketing Communications: Integrating Offline and Online with Social Media*, 5th ed., Kogan Page 2011

Wall, Matthew, 'The Right Bait', *New Media Age*, 14 February 2008, p. 31

FURTHER READING

Bird, Drayton, *Commonsense Direct & Digital Marketing*, 5th ed., Kogan Page 2007

Rogers, Charlotte, 'The *Drapers* Interview: Johnnie Boden of Boden', *Drapers*, 7 October 2015, www.drapersonline.com/people/the-drapers-interview-johnnie-bodens-multichannel-vision/5079711.article

DISCUSSION

Think of a fashion brand. Define the profiles of the consumers that you think would make up their suspects, enquirers and other groups in Egan's prospect heirarchy.

You may have been surprised that catalogues are still relevant in the fashion industry. Can you identify market segments that may be moved to purchase from the content of a catalogue? What content would appeal to them?

Look at marketing emails that you read (as opposed to those you deleted without reading). What made those more appealing?

Chapter 10
CATWALK FASHION SHOWS AND TRADE FAIRS

How can brands use fashion shows and trade fairs to gain maximum exposure to buyers? Find out how to:

- Know when and where the major ready-to-wear fashion events and trade shows happen
- Analyse the benefits of trade shows and events in the promotional mix of a fashion company, and their role in marketing communications
- Understand what is involved in putting on a show, whether at an international fashion week as a designer label or at a trade fair as a premium, mid- or mass-market brand
- Include consumers in shows using livestreaming, by inviting them to previously trade-only events, or by making products available directly from the catwalk

INTERNATIONAL FASHION WEEKS AND TRADE FAIRS: AN OVERVIEW

For fashion brands and designer labels that are seeking exposure to store buyers and the fashion press, to show at one of the international fashion weeks, or to take part in a trade fair, is an effective if costly way to showcase a range to a wide audience of interested parties. These events are essentially a method of B2B (business-to-business) communication (although this is changing, as discussed later in the chapter), and are by invitation only to buyers, fashion editors, journalists and influencers.

The overall aim of exhibiting at a show is to encourage the right store buyers to stock the label, and so it is closely linked with what the brand or label is hoping to achieve by way of personal selling (see Chapter 8, p. 144). As with personal selling, the advantage of showing at trade fairs and fashion weeks is that the return on investment (ROI) is directly measureable against orders achieved. A major further aim is to attract positive press coverage. This can be in the trade press, such as *Drapers* (UK), *Sportswear International* (Europe) and *Fashion Market* (US), for potential stockists to read, or to the end consumer, via magazine or influencer opinion.

Show timings

International fashion weeks and trade fairs take place six months before the goods are due to appear in the stores. Spring/Summer fashions are shown at the August and September shows, and Autumn/Winter ranges are shown in February and March. The finished garments, accessories or footwear are delivered to stores in January/February and August/September respectively. This gives designers and brands the time to accumulate orders after showing, manufacture the styles, sort them and dispatch the goods to the stores that have placed an order.

Pre-collections

In the case of catwalk shows, in addition to the main selling seasons of Autumn/Winter (shown in January/February/March) and Spring/Summer (shown in August and September), designers can also show pre-collection ranges. The largest of these is pre-spring, which is shown in June and July and referred to as Cruise or Resort collections. This concept was developed by US labels such as Donna Karan and Calvin Klein, which sought to offer fresh ranges of lighter-weight clothing to their wealthy clients, who were travelling in the winter to warmer, European climates. This idea has gained huge popularity with European ranges, since it offers buyers the chance to add an injection of more timeless product (pre-spring hits the stores in November) that can remain on sale at full price until the new collections arrive in early spring.

There is now a huge number of global events for buyers to attend. The trend-forecaster WGSN (2015) recommended over 34 shows for the 2016 season, including the international fashion weeks and popular trade fairs such as Tranoï in Paris, WWD Magic and Project in Las Vegas, Pitti Uomo in Florence, Panorama in Berlin, Fenin and Salão Moda Brasil in São Paulo, Scoop in London and CHIC in Shanghai. This figure excludes specialist shows in streetwear, bridal, lingerie, footwear and denim. Many events clash, so buyers plan their calendar and budgets carefully in order to see the best possible combination of interesting and lucrative labels.

Left Alessandro Michele's second collection for Gucci. The recent departure of Gucci from sophisticated and sexy elegance to 'Luxe Geek Chic', as covered in October 2015 by Vogue.co.uk, stole much of the coverage of the Spring/Summer 2016 shows.

CITIES OF FASHION

The shows that take place in Paris, Milan, New York and London are the best known and most established of the international fashion weeks, because of their historical associations with cities of fashion. They are referred to as the big four, and still hold attractions for designers to show because of their heritage, their reputation as a centre of excellence or the origin and associations of the designer.

Today increased spending power, improved economies and the desire to acquire a reputation as a creative centre has caused an explosion of new fashion cities: São Paulo, Tokyo, Mexico City, Seoul, New Delhi, Shanghai, Tel Aviv, Moscow, Lisbon and Porto, among others, now have fashion weeks worthy of international attention and publicity.

Increasingly, there is a trend to select cities because labels have invested in a flagship store there, wish to attract higher-spending consumers, or seek opportunities to build larger customer bases. In particular, pre-collections can be staged anywhere in the world and, therefore, become events that take local press and consumer bases into consideration.

Right Council of Fashion Designers of America (CFDA) award-winning duo Mary-Kate and Ashley Olsen of The Row. The label is thoroughly American in origin, but the Olsens chose to show their Spring/Summer 2016 range in Paris, citing a larger customer base.

SHOWING AT THE INTERNATIONAL FASHION WEEK CATWALK SHOWS

One of the most important limitations designer labels must bear in mind when organizing a show at the international fashion weeks is the staggering cost. In 2014 Fashionista.com gave a breakdown of the costs involved in showing at New York Fashion Week. This is not intended to be academically substantiated, but a guide to how prohibitively expensive the exercise can be (figures exclude the sample costs of the garments themselves).

Venue Between US$15,000 and $60,000, with the most expensive being the Lincoln Center, the largest available space (this venue has since moved). Smaller venues are at the lower end of the price scale. Designers can choose to be part of the scheduled event but show at an off-site venue (known as off-schedule) that may be cheaper.

Stylists Many designers do the styling themselves or use an in-house muse or contact, but an independent top-tier stylist can cost as much as $8,000 per day.

Models The price per model can vary significantly. Fashionista.com cites a post on BuzzFeed claiming that smaller labels can pay around $150 per model, rising to $200–500 for larger brands. International mass brands seeking established names may pay in the region of $1,000 per model. A successful catwalk show may need 15–20 models.

Hair and make-up The brand may be able to save money on hair and make-up if it is happy to use hair stylists, make-up artists and products supplied by the haircare and cosmetics companies that are sponsoring the show.

PR and production Brands may retain a PR person or company who will source a show producer, in which case these costs can be spread over the yearly PR budget, but one-off PR for a show (invitations, organization, press releases, etc.) can cost $5,000–10,000. The production fee for a show producer/designer is $10,000–20,000.

Celebrity appearance Many celebrities now attend shows of their own accord and are happy to generate publicity for the brands they admire. It is still possible to pay a celebrity to endorse the event, whether by payment in kind (in the

Below The cost of staging an elaborate show such as Chanel's for Spring/Summer 2016 in the Palais-Royal in Paris, with its Chanel Airlines set including check-in desk and departure boards, is undisclosed. The show featured models as check-in staff and passengers, wearing what were described as 'dream travel clothes'.

form of clothes and expenses) or a fee of $15,000 paid to a lesser-known celebrity and up to $100,000 for an exclusive appearance by an A-lister.

In total, at the lower end (smaller venue, own styling, sponsored hair and make-up, cheaper models, no paid celebrities) the cost is around $33,000. These shows take place at least twice a year, so that will double. Fortunately, many young designer newcomers receive funding through organizations such as the British Fashion Council's NEWGEN (New Generation) scheme, Fashion East or Fashion Fringe in the UK or CFDA/*Vogue* awards in the US to help with such costs.

International fashion week websites, applications and entry criteria

The show schedules and exhibitor details for international fashion weeks are available through websites such as LondonFashionWeek.co.uk and NYFW.com, for London and New York respectively. These sites give the time and location of all designer shows, as well as designers' profiles, contact details and lookbook photos, press rooms where members of the press can request images, details of how to register, the schedule of events and parties, and sponsors' details. The London Fashion Week site is linked to Facebook, Twitter, Pinterest, Instagram and YouTube, to advise attendees of information such as the late running of shows. It also provides an application form for designers who wish to show. As part of the entry criteria, designers are required to have been in business for three years and have a minimum of six stockists, and to provide two references (from a buyer or journalist, for example). Successful entrants are then subject to approval by a panel. Designers who have been trading for less than three years are advised to apply for NEWGEN support. As well as the option to show on the catwalk, there are also static exhibitions (where ranges are displayed on presentation stands) connected to fashion weeks, providing a more reasonably priced option for newcomers. These also offer a greater opportunity to deal directly with visiting buyers, and, as such, are more similar to showing at a trade fair.

Involving the consumer

The concept of previewing designer labels to an exclusive group of invited customers is not a new one. More familiar in the US is the trunk show, an event hosted by designers in a store such as Barneys or Neiman Marcus in order to take pre-sales from valued clients. The trunk show is gaining popularity with young designers, since the cost of staging a catwalk show is prohibitive for most newcomers. In 2011 *The New York Times*' Guy Trebay cited the admission by the CEO of Marc Jacobs that nine-and-a-half minutes of show cost more than US$1 million.

Above Burberry, Spring/Summer 2016. The catwalk show included a 32-piece orchestra and a performance by the singer Alison Moyet.

The movement to open up the catwalk fashion show beyond the exclusive is gaining momentum. Livestreaming, in particular, has enabled consumers or 'remote attendees' to order items directly from the catwalk, thereby linking such shows more closely to the sales environment. Burberry was the first to livestream an event of this kind, with its Autumn/Winter 2011–12 catwalk show. Registered clients were able to interact on social media channels and purchase items directly from the catwalk during the week after the show, and were promised delivery within seven weeks. This was the first time end consumers had been considered alongside the needs of store buyers, and, crucially, they did not have to wait six months before the items were available in-store. For subsequent collections, the brand has livestreamed on Twitter via an app, and it was the first luxury brand to use Twitter Buy, enabling sales to come through a social media channel. Its show for Spring/Summer 2016 achieved another first. The evening before the scheduled slot at London Fashion Week, the brand previewed the collection on new favourite, Snapchat. Viewers were given a unique real-time glimpse as finishing touches were added to the show. In line with the fleeting nature of Snapchat, the footage disappeared 24 hours later.

In 2015 Givenchy showed its Spring/Summer 2016 collections at Pier 26 as part of New York Fashion Week. The Parisian label showed in New York to coincide with the opening of a flagship store on Madison Avenue. For the first time members of the public were invited to a fashion show of this standing, via 920 tickets that were made available in a first-come, first-served draw, with a further 280 reserved for students at local fashion colleges. The show achieved positive press coverage for

Left Givenchy's Spring/Summer 2016 show in New York, September 2015. A sales promotion giveaway integrated with an event, the sales environment and PR news coverage.

Below Front row of Henry Holland's Spring/Summer 2016 show in London. Alexa Chung and Daisy Lowe (pictured with Poppy Delevingne) wear bespoke payment rings that incorporate near-field communication technology into an oversized insect design. Pieces from the collection were fitted with corresponding tags that enabled a Bluetooth connection to Visa's payment network.

its inclusiveness, and for the fact that it took place on 11 September, the anniversary of the 2001 terrorist attacks on New York, a positive move for trade and industry. It was also the designer Riccardo Tisci's tenth anniversary at the helm of the label.

Another pioneering innovation was used by Henry Holland, which – in line with trendwatching.com's 'No Interface' prediction (see p. 25) – used wearable payment technology in partnership with Visa Europe. Invited guests were able to use a bespoke ring fitted with communication technology and preloaded with £500. When contact was received between the ring and tags fitted on available items, payment was immediately made and the goods were bagged up backstage, ready for the purchaser to take away. This astonishing new development allows the possibility that catwalk shows will expand into direct shopping experiences, possibly one day available to the general public.

In a radical shake-up to the fashion industry, and one that may disrupt the long-standing fashion seasons, Burberry announced in February 2016 that a men's and

women's collection of season-less garments, suitable for all climates, would be available directly from the label's catwalk shows in September of that year. The collections, which will be previewed to the media, are designed to integrate previous pre- and main season collections. This is a bold move that ends any form of consumer wait for product at all: they see the catwalk images and an immediate release of campaign material and can purchase straight away, either online or in-store. At the time of writing there is great speculation in the industry about how suppliers will have to alter their timings to meet orders, and how smaller brands that do not have their own retail outlets will service this initiative.

SHOWING AT TRADE FAIRS

For brands and labels with the budget, international fashion weeks offer an exciting, vibrant and increasingly progressive showcase with a wealth of opportunities for sales and publicity. For some premium brands, mass- and mid-market brands, however, to show at a trade fair offers a more economical and direct way of engaging with potential buyers.

The trend-forecaster WGSN (2015) lists a huge number of trade fairs that showcase RTW brands globally in the areas of:

- Accessories, such as Accessorie Circuit in New York.
- Beauty, such as Indie Beauty Expo in New York.
- Men's denim, casualwear and accessories, such as Selvedge Run in Berlin.
- Footwear, such as The MICAM in Milan.
- Intimates and swimwear, such as Miami Swim Week in Miami.
- Jewellery and watches, such as Goldsmiths' Fair in London.
- Licensing opportunities, such as Licensing Expo in Las Vegas.
- Menswear, such as Jacket Required in London and The HUB in Hong Kong.
- Womenswear, such as Premium in Berlin and Rooms in Tokyo.
- Youth and streetwear, such as LA Majors Market in Los Angeles.

RTW trade fairs follow the main Autumn/Winter and Spring/Summer fashion seasons, taking place in January or February and July or August respectively, usually slightly before the catwalk shows. Brands will be hoping to take orders for delivery in six months' time, known as forward orders. Increasingly, however, buyers are looking to reserve budgets for product for immediate delivery to take advantage of later sales and information on colour and trend. In this sector, rather than show a later pre-collection, it is normal for a brand to show two seasons at once: the main season for which it is hoping for forward orders, and available current-season stock items that it can deliver in a few weeks.

For smaller brands showing at static exhibitions connected to international fashion weeks, or at smaller trade shows, one sample range may be adequate to bring prospective buyers and press visitors to the stand. Larger brands, however, may seek to greet visitors from several territories or countries in which they are present. A brand normally provides each member of the sales force responsible for a certain region or country with their own full range of samples, available colour options, wholesale prices and product details to sell to buyers effectively, in their own language if necessary. These sample ranges are known as salesmen's samples and are a large part of the pre-organization and expense that brands have to undertake for trade fairs; these samples cannot be late or missing.

Entry criteria and costs

Over recent years Berlin has become a European hub for fashion trade fairs, playing host to Selvedge Run, Premium, Seek, and Bread & Butter by Zalando. Application forms for potential exhibitors and entry criteria are available via the shows' websites, such as SelvedgeRun.com and PremiumExhibitions.com. These sites also provide links to information about the exhibiting brands, press contacts, press reviews and practical details such as registration and accommodation for visitors. The entry criteria are not as rigorous as for catwalk shows, but many fairs now create an intimate, curated setting and want to make sure the brand fits in with that ethos. Brands are often asked to provide images of their collections and to meet other criteria, such as a specific level of workmanship or transparency of approach.

As with the international fashion week catwalk shows, the cost of exhibiting at a trade fair varies depending on the kudos of the show and the size of the stand. This information is not given out to non-exhibitors, but as a very general indication, budget-holders should allow around £1,000 for smaller, less well-known fairs, up to around £3,000 for an average-sized stand at a more prestigious fair. Larger brands spend much more than this; in the heyday of the Bread & Butter exhibition, Tommy Hilfiger installed a usable ice rink complete with model penguins, G-Star RAW staged elaborate catwalk shows and live performances, and Diesel created an island concept complete with a sandy beach.

Some trade fairs feature catwalk shows, to which brands can contribute items. The shows are arranged by the organizers of the fair, at no extra cost to brands. Many brands hire models by the day to show off the range to best effect on their stands, but usually only one or two models are needed to help with the selling process.

Considerations for showing at a trade fair

It is important that a brand selects the trade fair at which it will be both noticed and able to exhibit among complementary brands. For newcomers, especially, it is important to ensure that visitors to the show will be interested in stocking new or undiscovered brands, otherwise they will be overlooked in favour of established business. Trade fairs also fall in and out of fashion, and positive press concerning one above the other will drive buyer attendance. Graeme Moran in *Drapers* (2015) reported a generally flat Spring/Summer 2016 season, with sluggish attendance across Florence, Berlin and the UK, and raised the question of the future direction for trade shows. In contrast, Raven Projects, part of the Copenhagen International Fashion Fair (CIFF), attracted positive reviews, demonstrating an ongoing trend for tightly curated brands but this time displayed in the manner of a spacious concept store. The show was co-curated by John Skelton, the founder of the London-based concept store LN-CC (see p. 157), and included showing garments on high-quality and interesting fixtures and fittings. The experience merged a B2B sales platform with a B2C sales environment and enabled buyers to envisage product more clearly in their stores. Organizers are now being asked to consider similar concepts, and to come up with ideas for busier shows to help boost buyer attendance.

Involving the consumer

In December 2013 Karl-Heinz Müller, organizer of Bread & Butter, the most popular and largest trade fair on the international circuit, put forward the idea that end consumers should be invited to the fairs to experience how such events work, and attend some of the organized parties and other events. The idea was dropped in the face of huge industry objection. Negative comments focused on the fact that consumers would want immediate goods and would not understand the forward-order timings involved. Brands were also concerned that they would need to go to the additional trouble of providing consumers with something they could take away or buy on the day.

The show's new investor, the German e-tailer Zalando, however, on acquiring the event from insolvency in 2015, pushed forward with this idea to launch a truly democratic 'festival of fashion', open to the public and running alongside the other Berlin trade events. Zalando Fashion House appeared in Berlin in July 2015 in collaboration with the designer platform Not Just a Label (NJAL). The event showcased designers from under the Zalando and NJAL umbrellas, and made panel discussions on music and fashion, live performances, films and talks on new fashion technology open and accessible to the interested public. This event demonstrates that, as with the international fashion weeks, slowly and in some cases somewhat reluctantly, the fashion industry is democratizing and opening up its practices to the general public.

The future and ongoing relevance of fashion and trade shows is under debate within the industry. In theory, buyers could attend far fewer shows and watch livestreamed video footage, or research and approach brands directly through social media. However, for the moment at least, these events continue to act as vital forums in which all interested sectors of the fashion industry can meet and exchange and report ideas. In particular, they enable buyers to keep an eye on labels they are interested in stocking, to test that they are financially viable and able to take on the responsibilities of handling orders and deliveries. For brands, they still represent a chance to get a message across in one hit; such events also help them to consider how many accounts they wish either to achieve or to grow by, and how they will manage visits by new and existing accounts. The case study on the next page illustrates the benefits of both positive press coverage from events and thorough research into the nature of potential stockists.

All brands and designer labels must, however, now think about inviting consumers to or involving them in these events, and how they can manage the new 'see-now-buy-now' culture that has caused consumer demand for immediate product to challenge a RTW selling model that has been in place for more than 40 years.

Below Premium Berlin. Trade fairs are typically laid out with stands along aisles. Brands are usually grouped by product so that prospective buyers can make their way to areas of interest.

Below Diesel Island at Bread & Butter, Berlin, 2012.

Bottom As part of Raven Projects at CIFF in Denmark, 2015, brands were displayed in an installation environment more similar to an upmarket department store or independent concept retailer.

Above Racil lookbook,
Spring/Summer 2016,
tuxedo jacket in Sunrise.

Racil Chalhoub launched her eponymous brand in March 2015, with a 20-piece concept collection that focused on tuxedo dressing for women. When interviewed, in March 2016, she was about to make her third appearance at Paris Fashion Week, with a 65-piece collection presented to buyers in a private hired showroom. Chalhoub's previous life as a buyer for her own store in her native Beirut, combined with her studies in both fashion design and marketing, has afforded her a business awareness both of how to build a brand and of what women want from a piece of investment dressing. Her collections build on the lasting appeal and day-long versatility of an expertly tailored dinner suit for women. Details such as scatterings of Swarovski crystals, innovative takes on traditional cuts and injections of colour firmly update the tradition of *Le Smoking* to meet the needs of twenty-first-century women. Since its launch, Racil has attracted a wide range of attention, including coverage by international editions of *Vogue, Grazia* and *Glamour* magazines and endorsement by influential bloggers such as Leandra Medine and Garance Doré. In February 2016 some 15 stockists globally were in receipt of their Spring/Summer 2016 orders, including accounts in France, Italy, the US, Russia, Saudi Arabia and the UK. Chalhoub divides her time between working at her headquarters in London, sourcing sampling and production in Paris, England and Eastern Europe, and presenting her collections to buyers in Paris.

Q: Paris Fashion Week is not far away now! What stage in the planning process are you at?
A: Once you are eight weeks away from fashion week, you are also six weeks away from delivering all the previous season's orders, so right now we are dealing with both seasons at the same time. I am getting everything finalized with production and producing the new samples for the next fashion week. We are starting to get patterns back and waiting for sampling fabrics to come in, and we have a plan on the wall with every item – and who is making it. When we

receive the fabrics, they are allocated so they are ready on time. It is always very stressful. Ideally I like to have everything ready two weeks before the shows to give me time to shoot and produce the lookbooks. We like to take all the orders within a month from showing. This season we are hoping to make that shorter, perhaps two to three weeks. It can be tricky: you want to close your order books as soon as possible after fashion week, but you want to stay as accessible as possible. The two or three main stockists that I have, for instance, I got a month after fashion week.

Q: Do you show any pre-collection ranges or stick to the twice-yearly fashion schedule?
A: I do not show pre-collection yet, just main season collections. I do not take part in the official Paris Fashion Week fashion shows, but I take part in the schedule. I show during Paris Fashion Week dates, but I take a private suite in a hotel where a lot of brands show, and I invite buyers and press to visit what I term a showroom because it becomes a branded space. I am getting a lot of pressure now to show pre-collections, mainly from the big stores

and department stores. They are allocating more budget to buying pre-collections, mainly to get the merchandise in sooner, as it has a longer shelf life. Pre-spring, for instance, comes in before the winter holiday season and remains at full price until almost June.

Q: What made you choose Paris above the other international or newer fashion cities?
A: Country of origin is not so important any more, but where you show is important for the ethos of the collection. We chose to show in Paris because, although I understand and learned a lot about fashion in London, my love of fashion began in Paris [where Chalhoub was brought up]. I believe that for the type of product I sell Paris was the correct place to launch. We have fairly equal numbers of retailers in each country; I do not know if the larger international retailers will cover all the fashion weeks, but everyone will go to Paris. They manage to keep everything restricted to a golden triangle of events where everything is happening; New York, for instance, is much bigger and harder to navigate.

Q: I notice you got some really good coverage from Vogue.com in March 2015 that placed you as the most interesting thing they saw at Paris Fashion Week. How did they find you?
A: That was amazing. That was my first season and the very first bit of coverage I got. I was overwhelmed. I realized early on that if you are going to launch in Paris, you need to create as many opportunities as you can. Normally as a single designer you invite all the press, but you are one in a million. I did think I could do everything myself – I could email all the press, but then you need to get them to come. Then I found a press office in Paris that liked the brand, and I signed with it before showing. The first day of showing at Paris then became a press day for editors invited by the press office. Some came, some did not; you can invite them, but you can't force them to write about you. It can be incredibly effective; for example, Vogue.it (Italian *Vogue* online) also came to visit and wrote a piece, and that is how my two Italian stockists came about. They saw it online and contacted *Vogue* to see where we were showing. It is important, you want to show your collection and then you need the press coverage, because that will either help the stores that have

Below Racil lookbook, Spring/Summer 2016, crystal-embellished dinner suit.

already bought you to sell it, or bring you to the attention of new stores.

Q: *Do you find the way you show, in a hired suite, makes it easier to meet buyers and talk face-to-face?*
A: I love interacting with people and I love doing my own sales, but there are pros and cons to everything: if I were to be part of a trade fair such as Tranoï, I could get more exposure from more footfall, whereas in a private room you may see two people a day. It depends what you want. I wanted to work towards a more exclusive brand positioning, and I knew the stores I wanted to target; this knowledge defined how I showed the collection. It is a shame that a lot of sales showrooms are not interested in working with small brands. They want to see you when you are larger and more established, so they can be sure they will make a lot of sales. I approached some who were not interested yet. There is a benefit in doing sales yourself. If I do take on this type of sales agent, I also have to consider the percentage of my margin they will want to take.

Q: *How do the shows link in with the other ways you promote yourself as a designer label?*
A: For every season we do a lookbook and a press release, which we send to the press and the buyers before showing. Nowadays we are lucky to have channels such as Facebook and Instagram that are really important for self-promotion. I don't like this so much, but it is a way to share the press you get. More people, even stores, see it and you get on people's radar. I can put photos of my lookbook up and, since it is still my third season, maybe 90 per cent of the press coverage I get. If you are trying to reach out to stores, the first thing they do is look at your Instagram, searching for that affirmation that you are getting talked about in *Vogue, Harper's Bazaar* or the *Telegraph*, etc. They can feel reassured that the brand is respected.

Q: *Do you feel that you personally are part of promoting your own brand?*
A: Absolutely. If I put a plain picture featuring my lifestyle on my personal pages on social media, I notice that it will attract more likes than anything else. Readers like to relate to the person. On another note, my best friend is a cookbook author and food blogger. Before posting say a recipe every day on her blog, she writes an introduction about how her day went or why she is doing a particular recipe, or how her kids made her feel. Most of her positive comments are about the introductions. There is so much out there now that followers are looking for something to relate to.

Q: *What are your thoughts on the future of fashion shows – are you interested in the use of technology or involving the customer at some point in the future?*
A: In a way, I like the old-school ways while trying to build a brand. I think it is amazing that you can watch a fashion show live – you used to have to wait for coverage in a magazine, but now you can see it online an hour after the event. It is also interesting for brands to get an idea of customer pre-orders from shoppable collections. For brands with their own stores, the buyers can get an indication of which

Below The actor Annabelle Dexter-Jones in Racil's launch collection, Autumn/Winter 2015–16.

styles will be the strongest to produce more of. When you are still a young designer, however, initiatives such as involving the public in fashion shows are very stressful, because you need to focus on your store buyers and your press. Afterwards, when you have a company that is big enough, it is part of promotion, as everyone who attended that show will go out and spread the word. It is of interest because of the way social media is used by everyone. This type of promotion can be used to create further buzz about the event and the brand.

REFERENCES

Mau, Dhani, 'How Much it Costs to Show at New York Fashion Week', 5 February 2014, fashionista.com/2014/02/new-york-fashion-week-cost

Moran, Graeme, 'A Project to Rave About', *Drapers*, 22 August 2015, p. 28

WGSN.com

FURTHER READING

Amed, Imran, 'Why Stage Fashion Shows?', *Business of Fashion*, 2 October 2015, www.businessoffashion.com/articles/week-in-review/why-stage-fashion-shows

Breward, Christopher, *Fashion*, Oxford University Press 2003

Buxbaum, Gerda, *Icons of Fashion: The Twentieth Century*, Prestel 2009

Drapers, 'Show Calendar Spring 17', 20 May 2016, www.drapersonline.com/product-and-trade-shows/drapers-show-calendar-spring-17/7007630.article

Harris, Sarah, 'Show Business: Are Fashion Shows Still Relevant?', *Business of Fashion*, 8 January 2014, www.businessoffashion.com/articles/intelligence/show-business

Hounslea, Tara, 'Bread & Butter Berlin to Transform into Consumer "Festival of Fashion"', *Drapers*, 8 July 2015, www.drapersonline.com/news/bread-and-butter-berlin-to-transform-into-consumer-festival-of-fashion/5076817.article

O'Byrne, Robert, *Style City: How London Became a Fashion Capital*, Frances Lincoln 2009

Sowray, Bibby, 'Burberry to Preview SS16 Show on Snapchat', *The Telegraph*, 18 September 2015

Todd, Luke, 'Shows of Intelligence', *Drapers*, 26 October 2015

Trebay, Guy, 'At Marc Jacobs, The Show Before the Show', 16 February 2011, www.nytimes.com/2011/02/17/fashion/17Curtain.html

Zargani, Luisa, 'Lagerfeld, Armani Remember Krizia's Mariuccia Mandelli', WWD.com, 7 December 2015, www.wwd.com/fashion-news/fashion-features/krizia-mariuccia-mandelli-dies-obituary-10291751

DISCUSSION

Consider ways in which fashion consumers could be involved with catwalk fashion shows, beyond those outlined in this chapter.

If you owned a start-up fashion business, which shows would you present your collection at, and why? Answer for a designer label and a mass-market label.

What are the threats to the conventional trade shows? Are they still relevant? What is current opinion about shows in the trade press and on industry forums? What are buyers doing instead of going to trade fairs, and what are the fairs doing to be more attractive to buyers?

Chapter 11
SALES PROMOTION AND PACKAGING

FIT YOUR ATTITUDE

A CLASSIC DENIM LOOK
BUT WITH AN ICONIC IDENTITY

GET SLENDER LO
MORE C

What incentives can brands use to persuade consumers to try or buy?
Find out how to:

- Apply the tactics of customer promotion used in fashion, from online flash
  sales to loyalty schemes
- Add value to consumer experience and build a credible brand image with
  creative promotions that go beyond simple discounting
- Time promotions for best effect, whether for new or established brands
- Promote trade-based initiatives between brands and retailers
- Boost brand identity, add value and increase sales by utilizing packaging and
  the point-of-sales environment

DEFINITIONS OF SALES PROMOTION

Sales promotion is the considered use of an incentive, such as a discount, a giveaway, a free sample or a competition, to entice people to buy or at least try a product. John Egan (2015) defines sales promotion in this way, adding:

> By its nature, it implies there is a built-in urgency to purchase (or otherwise act), either within a time period or until the offer is sold out. It has the function of accelerating purchases, being designed to increase the volume of sales by directly influencing the choice-making process and influencing the speed of the decision.

The primary use of sales promotion by brands is to accelerate sales within a short period of time. The use of promotions can also measure interest in an item or generate new leads through the data that is captured when customers complete forms, enter competitions or use vouchers.

ADVANTAGES AND DISADVANTAGES OF SALES PROMOTION

In relation to Chris Fill's (2013) framework of effectiveness, sales promotions have the following ratings (see below).

Advantages of sales promotion
- As can be noted from Fill's high control ratings, the start and end of sales promotions can be controlled by the brand or retailer. Promotions can also be relatively easily withdrawn should problems occur.
- Brand-owned databases can be used to target specific consumer groups with notifications of promotions. Technology is allowing more measurable interaction with promotions and giving brands the ability to personalize the message.
- Promotions can help to shift excess stock (this is particularly true in fashion, with styles that have not performed so well or are definitely last season) to help make way for the new season's styles.
- Sales promotions integrate extremely well with other tools; Egan (2015) terms this the ratchet effect, in which promotions are often delivered through use of direct marketing, personal selling, PR and social media, even advertising if the budget allows, in turn building credibility and further PR.

THE FOUR Cs OF COMMUNICATION TOOLS, WITH REFERENCE TO SALES PROMOTION

Communications	Sales promotion
Ability to deliver a personal message	Low
Ability to reach a large audience	Medium
Level of interaction	Medium
Credibility	
Given by the target audience	Medium
Cost	
Absolute costs	Medium
Cost per contact	Medium
Wastage	Medium
Size of investment	Medium
Control	
Ability to target particular audiences	High
Management's ability to adjust the deployment of the tool as circumstances change	High

Disadvantages of sales promotion
- Collaborative promotions, or those that need external agencies to participate, require scrupulous preparation and organization. Costs can also mount.
- Consumers are drawn to promotions such as discounts, but the intention is transparent and therefore consumers award discount promotions little credibility or loyalty.
- A sales promotion can result in a rise in sales that immediately falls away when the promotion ends.

PORTER
invites you
to become a subscriber
for just £17

Plus, receive a **FREE GIFT**
from REN *worth* £32*

NEW

'Wake Wonderful
Night-Time Facial'
leaves skin more
radiant, invigorated
and nourished
by morning.

PORTER – the global fashion magazine you have
dreamed of, powered by NET-A-PORTER.COM

TYPES OF SALES PROMOTION USED IN THE FASHION INDUSTRY

We first discuss the brand-to-consumer tactics of discounting, competitions, giveaways, free samples and loyalty schemes used by the fashion industry. By far the most familiar and even overused form of promotion is discounting. The more powerful buying forces of department stores and online retailers are able to mark down fashion goods earlier and earlier in the season, making it much harder for small independent stores to compete. The already low prices on some fast-fashion goods combined with the overuse of discounting has led to a culture in which shoppers expect a bargain and will actively search for discounts or wait for the sales rather than buy goods at full price.

Discounts and online discounters

Marking down the price of a garment at retail may be good news for the consumer, but for the retailer it means taking a hit on the retail markup (of 2.7–3 times the landed price) that has been applied (in the case of own-label goods) or the wholesale price (in the case of bought-in brands). That can affect profit margins. In fact, many international fast-fashion retailers, such as Zara, H&M and Uniqlo, keep a tight grip on discounting. Zara, in particular, typically marks down by only about 15 per cent, whereas mid-market and premium US department stores regularly discount by 50–70 per cent, according to Steve Denning (2015), who examined Zara as a business model for US retailers to consider. Zara items that are discounted are

kept small in number, never dominate the stores and are clearly those that are to be replaced by newer, more exciting styles. Zara aims to discount less because of the necessity to shift excess stock; instead, it favours using consumer feedback from the shop floor and practising postponement, keeping cloth ready to make at short notice based on demand. This reduces the likelihood of overproducing risky fashion styles.

It is, however, the online environment that has seen the biggest growth in the use of discounting as an incentive. Membership of sites such as Vente-Privee.com in France, Gilt.com in the US or the UK's SecretSales.com allows access to daily flash sales of 50–70 per cent off items including luxury fashion, footwear and accessories, so that consumers no longer have to wait for store-based discounts. Unlike designer store outlet villages, which sell the previous season's stock at discounted prices, flash sales provide a quicker route to sale for desirable, excess stock items for limited periods of time. Luxury labels are wary of in-store discounting because it can lead to a downmarket look, but sites such as the Japanese Glamour-Sales.com, Reebonz.com from Singapore and India's Fashionandyou.com have proved a successful

Below Zara typically keeps discount promotions to small quantities of end-of-season lines, and releases understated supporting campaign material. It has, however, participated in US initiatives such as Black Friday.

SALE

SPRING SUMMER

method of rolling out flash sales of luxury goods across the world.

A similar phenomenon originated as an online/offline activity from the Chinese practice of group shopping or *tuangou*. Interested parties would discuss an item in online forums, then arrange to meet as a group to 'mob' surprised retailers with the aim of obtaining a discount for sales of a large quantity of one product. This is now largely an online practice operated by group buying websites such as Lashou.com and 55tuan.com that allow merchants to offer their own daily deals directly to shoppers based on a minimum number of people taking up the offer. In the UK and the US, Groupon works in the same way.

In-store and online, the take-up of the US sales incentive Black Friday, a weekend of discounts designed to kick off the Christmas shopping season, is spreading across Europe, South America, Canada and India. According to *Drapers* (2015), in the UK, sales figures for Black Friday in 2015 were expected to be in excess of £1 billion, with retailers looking strategically to discount heavy winter items. Despite concerns that the public will become used to waiting for a short spell of drastic discounting before purchasing, many retailers now accept the practice and seek to make more targeted offers rather than blanket discounts. Previous scenes of in-store chaos have led to better planning to cope with the increased strain placed on e-commerce systems, deliveries and returns.

Clearly, consumers have become accustomed to discounting and have even developed their own systems

Above The French flash sales site Vente-Privée operates in eight European countries. Members register for free and can receive alerts of sales of products they are interested in, or see what the platform has to offer each day.

for negotiating better deals, disrupting the retailer's traditional control over the matter. Trendwatching.com's 'Sympathetic Pricing' trend (see p. 20) provides suggestions for targeting consumers with more personalized discounts, or with discounts aimed at solving genuine concerns or money problems in their lives. To target consumers with a discount voucher for accessories to accompany an expensive occasion dress would, for example, be a less obvious, more feel-good form of discounting that would have less impact on the store and be more similar to the Zara model of understated discounting.

Above Luxury retailer Lane Crawford in Pacific Place shopping destination in Hong Kong.

Filippo Gori has a background in pure finance. His desire to bring a rational, common-sense balance of effective merchandising to a creative field drew him to the fashion industry. He began his career at Emilio Pucci as a retail controller and in 2005 moved to Gucci, where, after starting in financial planning and accounting, he rose to the position of Chief Financial Officer for Greater China in 2011. At Gucci he found himself responsible for pretty much all the general management duties: deciding strategy, business development, merchandising and human resources. He then moved to the Italian denim brand Replay, where, after a short time as Hong Kong-based Country Manager and Wholesale Business Development Manager for South-east Asia, he was quickly promoted to Chief Executive Officer for Asia. He is currently director of a new sales outlet project in Hong Kong, and is setting up a fashion start-up business. Here, he uses his experience to reflect on the Far Eastern perspective on sales promotions.

Q: In the UK at the moment we have crazy discounting – labels are only selling at full price for about six weeks. What is the discounting situation in Hong Kong and China?
A: A little better than Europe in terms of timing and level of discounting, but it is getting worse. In Hong Kong especially, since the Occupy Central [peaceful civil disobedience] protests of 2014, business has decreased significantly. An outcome of the protest was that the Chinese government banned travel agencies from selling group tourist packages to Hong Kong. That is why there has been a substantial shift among Chinese tourists towards travel to destinations such as Japan and Korea. Last season, for the first time, the well-known Hong Kong multi-brand, luxury retailer Lane Crawford offered 70 per cent discounts. In China, sales simply decreased because of the price differential between China and Europe or Japan. Although negligible in terms of the currency's growth in value over the last seven or eight years, the

Right Alibaba CEO Daniel Zhang stands in front of total sales figures of ¥91.2 billion (US$14.32 billion) transacted during the Singles' Day Shopping Festival in November 2015.

unexpected devaluation of the yuan in 2015 by the Chinese government did not ease the situation. Also, generally Chinese customers love discounts and love to ask for them.

The Japanese, too, are bargain-hunters; they plan their holidays depending on currency fluctuations to maximize their discounts. Some customers (especially in HK) have become VIP members of stores in Paris, London and Milan and get products shipped directly with sales tax deducted. In Australia customers would buy online from us in China with fake PO boxes, all to save on prices. We seem to have reached a point where brands factor higher-than-average discounting into the full retail price.

Q: Do you think premium brands are more protected from the need to discount?
A: They used to be, but in 2014 for the first time Hermès offered discounts on ready-to-wear (RTW) in China, and Gucci – using the reason of a change in designer – discounted everything in the Spring/Summer 2015 range by 50 per cent. Usually the approach is differentiated by category: RTW and shoes are discounted more than accessories and bags. There is no discounting on successful styles that are carried over from a previous season.

In the premium denim industry, it is common to add additional discounts such as buy more than five pieces and get an extra 10 per cent off, or buy a pair of denims and get 10–20 per cent off shirts or jackets. Generally speaking, in countries where a brand has both wholesale and retail customers, it cannot go too crazy with discounts because it needs to try and protect the wholesalers' margins.

Q: Have you noticed any impact from flash sales sites? Do you feel these are a good way to offer luxury goods at short-term discounts without damaging the brand image?
A: In Hong Kong there is pretty much no local e-commerce (except from the US and Europe). In China, however, there are three main players, and one of them, Vip.com, is owned by Sequoia Capital and is definitely effective at flash sales. The Alibaba Group also does promotions on particular days, similar to Black Friday in the US. Its Singles' Day (a Chinese response to Valentine's Day) in 2014 generated over US$9 billion in sales from both Chinese and overseas shoppers, who bought heavily discounted goods. I personally consider flash sales better than retail outlets, especially in Asia, where the tendency to purchase online is more prevalent than in Europe.

Talking generally, there is way too much discounting, and also brands are expecting to make too much margin in the first place. I almost feel there is a need to restructure pricing. It is hard for the customer to buy at full price and spend £2,000–3,000 on a bag or jacket when they know a month later it will be sold for half the price.

Q: Have you seen any other evidence of discounts becoming more personalized – or technology being used to target shoppers more efficiently with discounts?

A: All brands are beginning to implement standard VIP programmes. Some brands are taking loyalty programmes and customer relationship management (CRM) to the next level. VF International, for instance, whose labels include Vans, Timberland and North Face, is pretty active in Asia. It uses loyalty programmes to collect data on customers and propose tailored online cross-selling. This has more of a focus on existing customers and uses their purchasing history to make informed suggestions of additional items from the same or complementary brands. The data can also be used to predict *when* they might need items, as well as *what* they might need. I consider this the future instead of the standard undifferentiated emails.

Q: Loyalty cards are becoming more popular in the UK. Have any of the companies you have worked for had a loyalty scheme?

A: All of them. Loyalty schemes should provide important data, which then needs to be analysed. Some, however, have been misused. There was an example of parallel Chinese traders (traders who are buying tax-free goods in one country and selling them on in the Chinese mainland at a profit) becoming VIP customers in European stores and obtaining extra discounts on top of the VAT deduction.

Q: Would you say loyalty cards have become about more than collecting points alone? The latest schemes involve previews of the ranges, entry to exclusive events and tier systems of rewards depending, of course, on how much people shop.

A: I think it has not evolved yet to the level it should. I consider loyalty programmes together with advanced CRM (for example clustering of segments of customers, tailored cross-selling) as the tools by which it will be possible to transfer more offline business into online. In the future retailers may need fewer bricks-and-mortar stores, which may allow them to make

those that remain into more interesting places where customers can experience the brand more deeply.

Q: Any other thoughts on the future of sales promotions as a way of attracting and keeping shoppers?

A: I'm thinking here about models that exclude discounts. For sure, in the luxury high end, instead of offering discounts it would be much more interesting and valuable to offer experiences. A luxury retailer of leather goods, for example, could bring in some customers to show them how handmade bags are really produced, or how the shoe factory works. Instead of being used just to fuel discount business, a portion of old or slow-moving stock could be gifted to VIP customers. If they are asked to collect their gifts in a store, it becomes an occasion to introduce new items to customers or to 'reactivate them' if their frequency of purchase has declined. This turns a potential discount into a new sales opportunity.

Competitions

Competitions are more usually employed in the fashion industry to promote young design talent, and are underwritten or sponsored by organizations that benefit from the resulting publicity, which connects them with the mentoring and support of new designers. The coveted LVMH Prize is an annual competition that allows entrants to compete in either the Young Fashion Designer category, to win a prize of €300,000 and 12 months' mentoring from LVMH, or in the Graduates category, in which three graduates can win €10,000 and the chance to work for an LVMH brand for a year. In 2016 the judges included such prestigious designers as Phoebe Philo, Riccardo Tisci, Marc Jacobs and Karl Lagerfeld in their role as ambassadors for LVMH-owned labels.

Many fashion magazines host competitions, such as the CDFA (Council of Fashion Designers of America)/ *Vogue* fashion fund initiative. One winner and two runners-up compete for a prize of US$400,000 and $150,000 respectively, and mentorship from the associated industry experts. In 2015 the competition was held in partnership with Uniqlo and underwritten by a further 20 companies, including Theory, J.Crew and Nordstrom, which were represented on the expert judging panel. Very occasionally, such competitions may be open to the public, offering the chance to design product for a particular brand. John Fluevog (see p. 135) is an example of a fashion shoe brand involving the public in an inclusive experience.

In 2015 the H&M Foundation launched the Global Change Award, a competition open to anyone with an early stage innovation that aims to reduce waste and needless consumption within the fashion-industry supply chain. The first round attracted over 2,700 entrants from 112 countries. A panel of experts selected the top five, whose share of a million-Euro prize fund was decided by public vote. Winning ideas included a Polyester Digester, which uses microbes to recycle polyester waste, a plan to create a new textile from citrus waste by-products, and 'growing' textiles under water using algae as a source material. To ensure further impact, 2016 winners will have access to a one-year Innovation Accelerator organized by the H&M Foundation in conjunction with Accenture and the KTH Royal Institute of Technology in Stockholm.

Many competitions now involve techniques such as the formation of a community, or request participants to obtain their own votes from their followers on social networks. The person with the most votes is chosen as the winner, but the wider participation also spreads the credibility and name of the hosting brand further than among the contestants alone.

Giveaways

Giveaways can also be used for the mutual benefit of the brand or retailer and the consumer. These can take the form of small promotional objects, such as branded bags,

Above Artwork from the H&M Global Change Award, which aims to reduce waste in the fashion supply chain.

Right Grace Wales Bonner, winner of the LVMH Young Designer prize in 2016.

stickers, badges, items of stationery or even lookbooks, given away at point of sale with a purchase. Retailers may also decide to reward loyal and high-spending customers with a gift to encourage repeat purchases. Giveaways may also require an interested party to sign up or register their details to receive the gift directly from the hosting brand; this can lead to positive posts on the brand's site or social media, and sharing of the opportunity, as well as great blog, social or newsletter content for the brand.

Free samples

Free samples are more frequently used by the beauty industry both at point of sale and as a form of advertising in fashion magazines. Their primary use is to encourage the trial of a new product or a product that is complementary to the purchase made. Occasionally, a fashion brand may offer a 'try before you buy' incentive or give a free sample in return for consumer feedback, but this is a more costly exercise, since items such as clothing and footwear are, for obvious reasons, not available in mini sample sizes.

Loyalty schemes

Loyalty programmes have been popular since the 1980s. Egan (2015) cites UK figures from 2012, which show that 86 per cent of adults owned at least one loyalty card, and 29 per cent owned more than five. As the name suggests, loyalty schemes are used to retain customers by rewarding them with points for various actions such as purchasing, signing up for newsletters, promoting the name of the store further or recommending friends to join. As a device, they recognize the importance of keeping existing customers rather than attracting new ones. As well as innovating to reward purchasing, retailers are providing a feel-good alternative to discounting, and acting to spread the name of the brand. The flash sales site Gilt.com and the US department store Nordstrom offer tiered systems of rewards. Members are rewarded for visiting as well as for purchasing, and gain more points for referring friends or – in the case of Gilt.com – visiting the site five weekdays in a row. The benefit of accruing points is access to the higher tiers of rewards, which include exclusive previews of sales, VIP customer service and priority on waiting lists of popular items. Some loyalty schemes are now available as downloadable apps, such as Rewards by Harvey Nichols, which allows users access to tiered rewards including gift-wrapping, a make-up artist, garment alterations and an at-home stylist. Harvey Nichols uses the data collected via the app to refresh content and offer surprise personalized rewards depending on the amount spent.

The US site Prima Donna also rewards customers who pin store items of interest on Pinterest's highly visual storyboards. The UK shoe retailer Van-Dal goes a step further by rewarding customers for reviewing their products.

VALUE-INCREASING AND VALUE-ADDING PROMOTIONS

In the examination of the types of incentive, Fill (2013) refers to the important demarcation made by Ken Peattie and Sue Peattie (1993) between promotions that can be applied as a tool to increase value and those that add value.

Value-increasing promotions

Promotions that increase value are those that reduce the price, such as discounts, money-off coupons and two-for-one offers. Changes can also be made to the quality of make or manufacture to result in a better price point for the consumer. Both are generally used as a short-term incentive to buy.

Value-adding promotions

Promotions where value is added leave the price and quality unchanged but add an extra incentive, such as a loyalty card, a free gift, or entry to a competition or prize draw. According to Fill, this can also apply to features such as limited editions, collectable packaging and in-packaging gifts. It is these feel-good, more personalized incentives that add value over the longer term. A theme also emerges from the discussion of competitions and tiered loyalty schemes in which such promotions enable the customer to interact more and further promote the host brand among extended networks of potentially interested people.

WHEN TO USE SALES PROMOTIONS AS A TOOL

One final factor to consider when contemplating using customer sales promotions as a tool is that theorists say they may not be as effective for unknown start-up brands wishing to raise awareness, for brands entering new markets, for purchases of high value or for the consumer purchasing luxury goods. Fill (2013) suggests a grid to summarize the use of sales promotions against the longevity of the brand in the market, with regard to the consumer's level of involvement in the purchase; this has been extracted and adapted below with reference to the fashion industry.

FILL'S SALES PROMOTION OBJECTIVES GRID

	High involvement (luxury goods, high-investment purchases)	Low involvement (mid- or mass-market goods, fast fashion or basic purchases)
New product/brand or new market sector for either	Suggest to withhold use of sales promotion.	Use value-added sales promotion to promote trial. • Giveaways, free samples
Established product/brand or established market sector	Use value-added sales promotions to tempt new customers. • Better/more innovative loyalty card rewards than a competitor • Chance to take part in a credible design-based competition or prize draw to win a place at an event Use value-added tactics and value-increased discounts to reward existing customers. • Tiered reward schemes • Personalized discounts	Use value-added and value-increased promotions to encourage trial in new customers and further promotion among potential new customers. • Giveaways, free samples, entry to democratic competitions with high sharing potential • Short-term two-for-one offers, or flash discounts Use value-added and value-increased promotions to reward existing customers. • Loyalty card rewards such as points for purchases and/or gifts and giveaways • Short-term discounts • Sympathetic discounts

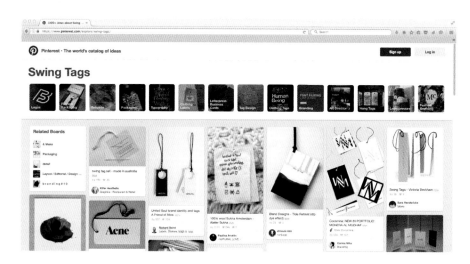

Left Pinterest swing tag and packaging boards, where compilers Pin and discuss interesting packaging.

Below left The ethical Dutch brand Kuyichi has developed a clear policy of how it should appear in its own stores and in stockists. In its own flagship stores, the logo, strapline and product packaging are evident and reflect the brand's ethical stance. The fit-out features natural stone, exposed brick and sustainable wood.

Below right A Kuyichi shop-in-shop layout, as used in multi-brand stores. Here the use of showcards depicting the latest shoot and labelling information is more evident. The brand philosophy/mission statement is also prominent.

PACKAGING AND
RETAIL POINT OF SALE

Swing tags and other packaging can be value-added promotional items that convey brand identity to the consumer, and they are popularly used by fashion companies to add value and convey brand identity. Considered packaging can be collectable, engaging and useful. It also enjoys an extended life on social forums, especially on Pinterest, where items of interest are Pinned for further comment.

Generally, fashion is displayed in-store in two scenarios: in an own-label retailer or brand flagship store, where the shopper is aware that they are in a single-brand environment; or in a multi-brand situation, where a retailer or department store stocks a number of selected brands that it has bought in. Packaging and retail point of sale are important in both situations, since they convey the identity of the brand in-store. In fact, packaging should trigger all the emotional connections intended by the brand, as discussed in Chapter 2. It is in the second scenario

that packaging is doubly important to help the shopper differentiate between the brands stocked.

Packaging

Both Egan (2015) and Paul R. Smith and Ze Zook (2011) mention the role of packaging, including swing tags, boxes, bottles and product holders, as a 'silent salesperson'. In an increasingly self-service retail environment, packaging should be seen as a final, if not the only, opportunity to convey information such as price, fit and product details. Egan provides the following checklist for good packaging, which has been amended here to suit the fashion perspective.

- It should gain attention.
- It should be distinctive.
- It should instruct and inform by giving, for instance, fit information, fabric features, sizing details and country of origin (if this is marketable).

- It should help to persuade the purchaser to buy through indicating special offers or through its usefulness or collectability.
- It should reflect the identity of the brand.
- It should motivate brand choices.

Environmental factors also govern the choice and future development of packaging materials. According to a World Packaging Organisation report of 2008, the North American markets (Canada, Mexico and the US) are the world's largest consumers of packaging, worth US$132 billion and accounting for 32 per cent of the world's production of all packaging types. Western Europe and Asia each account for 26 per cent of packaging consumption. In the member states of the European Union alone, according to figures measured in 2012 by Eurostat statistics, each inhabitant accounted for 156.8 kg of packaging waste, with paper and board packaging accounting for the largest amount by material. Concern about this prompted the EU Packaging Waste Directive (1994), which encourages producers to take measures to end the production of packaging waste by:

- Reusing packaging.
- Recycling packaging.
- Reducing the likelihood of end disposal of packaging waste.
- Lightening the weight of packaging.

Brands could consider using compostable materials, materials that close the loop on supply (i.e. by-products or recycled items of the brand's garments, footwear or accessories) or materials that use ground-up waste products, such as those used for 3D printing.

Swing tags

Swing or hang tags are detachable branded tags attached to the item and taken home by the purchaser. The illustrations here show how swing tags have been designed as a device to offer further information, to be distinctive through the use of materials, and perhaps to be kept as collectables or for future use by the purchaser.

❶❷❸ Clear features and benefits of swing tags can take the form of visible features such as buttons to repair or replace (Acne), the extra information given in Diesel's mini lookbook swing tag, and seals of approval and authenticity (Franklin and Marshall).

❹❺❻ Unusual and touchable materials: orange chiffon Boss swing tag with a fragment of crystal for energy and well-being, enclosed in a fabric sachet; a lenticular 3D-style print used on a Paul Smith swing tag; and a neon plastic wallet containing a David Bailey mini print for a range of limited-edition T-shirts, a collaboration between Bailey and The Bleach Room.

❼❽❾ Swing tags with another purpose or possible use instead of disposal: a Fake London rosette with a safety pin to attach to other garments; Lost Propertee's printed fabric sticker with a peel-off back to resemble a backstage pass; Roxy's mini ice-scraper to accompany snow wear.

Boxes and holders

In a similar vein, larger items of packaging should also inspire love of the brand, while being consciously designed to consider issues of disposal. Fuseproject in association with Puma came up with a solution to the problem of waste shoeboxes by developing reusable fabric bags that were supported for display and sale purposes by a single piece of die-cut cardboard, drastically reducing the amount of cardboard that would usually be thrown away.

The eco-conscious activewear brand howies gained PR coverage for its use of 14 recycled wardrobes, decorated by artists, as in-store display units (see p. 5). Recycled flower-bulb packages also made cost-effective and on-message statements as T-shirt packaging for the brand.

Luxury brands have not escaped the pressure to think sustainable as well as luxurious in terms of packaging. Gucci, for example, was the first to introduce FSC (Forestry Standards Commission)-certified materials that are fully recyclable. The brand also reduced the amount of paper it used and changed the composition of its ribbon and its garment bags from polyester to cotton to achieve a fully recyclable packaging range.

Retail point of sale

Retail point of sale (POS) such as posters, showcards and product display units (such as howies' wardrobes) is used in a similar way to packaging, but serves the additional purpose of reflecting in-store the campaign material that shoppers may have seen in other settings. In this way, the consumer is given a reminder of the brand in-store to trigger recall of previous associations, which can give a strong impulse to buy. It is vital, therefore, that campaign material is integrated with retail POS. Pepe Jeans London (see p. 51) is a good example of how branded designers take a holistic approach to the development of product, retail and campaign material.

The ideal retail-based scenario is termed 'bathing in the brand' by Gaynor Lea-Greenwood (2012). This is where a shopper has seen some advertising or PR about a label they intend to purchase, is reminded of this on the way to the store, possibly by some location-based outdoor advertising, is attracted into the store by an inviting window display and is then led to a branded area demarcated by branded graphics that reflect the campaign they have seen.

This page Fuseproject's sustainable solution for Puma shoeboxes resulted in a 65 per cent reduction in the use of cardboard, a saving of 8,500 tons of paper and 1 million litres of water.

In summary, retailers, industry commentators and consumer trend-forecasters agree that we will not backtrack from our new culture, in which we expect to seek discounts, but that those discounts can be more considered, more targeted and take up less of the valuable floor space in a store. Brands must also think of ways of maintaining a positive brand image through providing experiences such as meet-and-greet, behind-the-scenes knowledge or gifts as a prompt to buy, thus adding value for both consumer and brand. It is this area of experience that leads into the consideration of all the manifestations of the brand in-store, such as packaging and retail point of sale.

REFERENCES

Denning, Steve (2015) 'How Agile and Zara Are Transforming the US Fashion Industry', *Forbes*, 13 March 2015, www.forbes.com/sites/stevedenning/2015/03/13/how-agile-and-zara-are-transforming-the-us-fashion-industry

Egan, John, *Marketing Communications*, 2nd ed., Sage 2015

Fill, Chris, *Marketing Communications: Brands, Experiences and Participation*, 6th ed., Pearson 2013

Lea-Greenwood, Gaynor, *Fashion Marketing Communications*, Wiley 2012

Smith, Paul R., and Ze Zook, *Marketing Communications: Integrating Offline and Online with Social Media*, 5th ed., Kogan Page 2011

Sutherland, Emily, 'Get Set for Black Friday', *Drapers*, 29 July 2016, www.drapersonline.com/news/how-to-stay-ahead-of-the-pack-this-black-friday/7009176.article

World Packaging Organisation, *Market Statistics and Future Trends in Global Packaging*, 2008

Below Carter Wong Design in association with howies, recycled product packaging, 2007.

Bottom Gucci FSC-certified and fully recyclable packaging, introduced in 2010.

FURTHER READING

Jourdan, Adam, 'Alibaba Reports Record $9 Billion Singles' Day Sales', Reuters, 11 November 2014, www.reuters.com/article/2014/11/12/us-china-singles-day-idUSKCN0IV0BD20141112

Madden, Normandy, 'China Did Group Buying Discounts Before Groupon', *Advertising Age*, 15 December 2010, www.adage.com/china/article/china-news/china-did-group-buying-discounts-before-groupon/147676

Peattie, K. and Peattie, S., in Michael Baker, *The Marketing Book*, 5th ed., Routledge 2012

Rogers, Charlotte, 'The Rise of Loyalty Schemes', *Drapers*, 14 March 2016, www.drapersonline.com/retail/the-rise-of-loyalty-schemes/7005465.article

Sutherland, Emily, 'Flash Sales Sites', *Drapers*, 25 July 2016, www.drapersonline.com/news/analysis-flash-sales-sites-enjoy-summer-boost-from-surplus-stock/7009572.article

DISCUSSION

Incentives such as discounts are thought by many to be a main driver of the success of online fashion retail. Do you think this will change as e-commerce gains a larger market share? What incentives will take its place?

Take a look at the loyalty cards you own. How could they be modified to make you spend more? Consider value adding rather than value increasing.

What new packaging initiatives have you noticed recently? Do they meet any of Egan's critera (p.200), or address consumers' environmental concerns?

Chapter 12

PLANNING, COSTING AND MEASURING EFFECTIVENESS

How does a brand plan a promotional campaign and evaluate its success? Find out how to:

- Assess which integrated communication tools will be most productive for a brand
- Work out a budget and gauge affordability
- Make a marketing communications plan for a new campaign and also use it as an analytical tool to examine the elements of existing campaigns
- Analyse the effectiveness of a promotional campaign, to test if there has been a rise in sales and the creation of a positive brand image as a result

A REVIEW OF MARKETING COMMUNICATIONS PLANNING

You should now be armed with a strong grasp of how to build a detailed customer profile, how to create a powerful and evocative brand identity, how to form campaign objectives and use them to suggest communication types, and have had an overview of successful examples of the use of each tool in the communications or promotional mix. It would now be the role of a marketing communications planner to finalize which of the tools would be employed to create the campaign. A review of the following should take place.

- The consumer. Keeping constructed knowledge of the consumer throughout the design of a campaign ensures that the desire for creativity does not override awareness of who will be the ultimate buyer of the brand.
- The brand identity. This should be at the core of all the brand's communications.
- Brand positioning. All communications should consider what other brands the viewer may already know and have formed opinions on.

Left Nike's 'Better For It' campaign, 2015. Nike's objective was to widen its appeal in the women's market. A witty film demonstrated knowledge of the consumer in the form of the internal conversations women use to put themselves off sporting activity. The campaign encouraged women to motivate themselves by sharing accomplishments via apps and social media using #BetterForIt.

Opposite Mango's Violeta range, designed for sizes 40 to 54 (available in UK sizes 14–22 and US sizes 10–18). The retailer responded to consumer demand for inclusive, young, feminine and modern styles in larger sizes.

- The objectives. These should formalize the areas in which the brand or retailer is hoping to gain attention, build interest, provoke desire and achieve sales.
- Strategic choices of tools suggested by using the AIDA or DAGMAR models in Chapter 3 (p. 55).

Following a review of the objectives and the consideration of the AIDA and DAGMAR models, another method of strategically planning the choice of communication tool is to use Fill's 'key characteristics of marketing communications' framework (2013) and then assess the advantages and disadvantages of each tool in turn. In this book, each chapter on a particular communication tool rates that tool according to Fill's system in terms of personalization, interaction, credibility, cost and element of control for the brand. If a brand can recognize that a tool has a low rating in one area, it can be tackled directly, or combined with another tool with a higher rating in the same area. A review of the Chapter 3 Synergy, Technology, Disruption, Consistency, Continuity integration framework is also suggested (see p. 54).

Traditional TV advertising has a low rating for credibility from the target audience and for interaction with the audience. If we return to the House of Fraser example pictured in Chapter 2 (p. 41), however, the retailer used an award-winning 23-year-old choreographer whose distinctive style, known as polyswagging, viewers may have recognized from the video for Beyonce's song '7/11'. This afforded it credibility by association. One week after its release, placing the ad on YouTube had garnered 121,038 views, 573 likes and 77 mixed – but nonetheless treasured – viewer comments by way of interaction. House of Fraser, therefore, tackled both the major disadvantages of TV advertising in this campaign.

THE EFFECT OF BUDGET ON THE CHOICE OF COMMUNICATION TOOLS

The type of campaign material a brand or retailer can launch is also highly dependent on the budget. Theorists suggest several methods to help assign budgets to communications plans.

Objective and task (after Smith and Ze Zook, Egan, Micael Dahlén et al.)

This method advises expanding the objectives into what needs doing to achieve them, and calculating how much that will cost. A communications budget is therefore drawn up to an ideal scenario, one that may be subject to management approval. To return to the example in Chapter 3 of Louisa Clayden's small-business start-up objectives for Head, Heart and Base (see p. 56), the table below shows the objectives and task method in action.

HEAD, HEART AND BASE OBJECTIVES AND TASKS WITH COSTINGS

Objectives summarized	Task	Cost estimate and basis
Objective 1: Begin a blog on the Head, Heart and Base website.	Assign a morning to set up and half an hour daily to post.	Free, but labour-intensive.
Objective 2: Send gift samples to 20 external bloggers.	Research relevant blogs and addresses. Package up.	£132.80 20 x cost-price samples @ £3.24 Postage and packing @ 20 x £3.40 (first class)
Objective 3: Organize workshop events.	Research and pay for venue hire. Base on 35 attendees over four days of seven sessions. Arrange oil sampling to work with. Catering and props. Arrange photos on the day.	£696.11 Based on: Venue £50.00 per day x 4 = £200 Glass jars x 48 = £51.96 (allow 13 extra) Carrier oil, based on 300 ml per person £1.69 x 35 = £59.15 Essential oils, based on 20 ml per person (average price £2.50/10 ml) = £5 x 35 = £175 Customizable labels x 35 = £35 Catering and sundries @ £5.00 per person per session = £175
Objective 4: Achieve editorial coverage in a magazine.	Research potential online and offline titles. Prepare press release and images.	Free (arrange to take own product photos).
Objective 5: Ensure the website is able to capture data in order to build a database.	Ensure website designer enables this function. Compile email addresses from interested parties from blog and website.	Free if included with website price.
Objective 6: Ensure business accounts are set up with Twitter, Instagram and Facebook.	One day to set up, then assign an hour a day for upkeep and creation of posts. Take inspirational photographs each day.	Free, but labour-intensive.
Objective 7: In mid-November release discount codes to all subscribers for Christmas purchases.	All social media followers and those registered through the website to receive discount codes.	Assess impact on normal sales of 20 per month. Sales may increase but margin may be less.

Total: £828.91

Percentage of revenue

Fill (2013), Egan (2015) and Smith and Ze Zook (2011) recommend that a percentage of forecasted sales revenue or turnover (sales figures with nothing else deducted) be assigned to the communications budget. Fill mentions 5 per cent as a suitable amount. As a general indication, figures provided by Dahlén et al. (2010) suggest that Gap, which advertises extensively, spends 4 per cent of its turnover while H&M, which uses advertising and celebrity endorsement, spends 3.5 per cent.

The first-year revenue for Head, Heart and Base was predicted at a very conservative £5,148, based on slowly building online sales only. At 5 per cent of revenue the company had roughly £257.40 to spend on the promotion of its products. This explains the reliance on cheaper or free PR tools such as reaching out to third-party bloggers; a carefully controlled event; activities such as database building for direct marketing and sales promotions; and a focused social media strategy.

Affordability

This method is also referenced by the authors mentioned above, and suggests that a communications budget could come from a share of the total profits (revenue minus operating costs) after an assessment of what would be affordable for the company. Head, Heart and Base predicted cautious revenue, but its outgoing costs of £4,780 in the first year were low, based on a one-person start-up with a lean stock holding, acting on internet orders. According to the affordability method, therefore, if the company decided to invest 70 per cent of its profit (£5,148 – £4,780 = £368) in communications (the amount is arbitrary, but could depend on factors such as what needs to be reinvested in product development or space for expansion, for example), that sum would be £257.60.

Running both the percentage-of-revenue and affordability-calculation methods gave Head, Heart and Base an indication that around 5 per cent of revenue was realistic until revenues increased. Costing to an ideal or objective/task method, however, indicated that the cost of an interactive event, such as a workshop where visitors could blend their own perfumes, would take the company over that amount. In practice, Head, Heart and Base would have to look at keeping costs to the minimum for the venue and tightly controlling the nature of the workshops. The company could, however, decide that the opportunity for face-to-face encounters with the target market would be so valuable that a case for increasing the budget could be made.

For start-ups in general, should revenues increase, the type of communications must also change (to reflect the money needed for personal selling activities and rewards for the loyalty of existing customers), while maintaining a level of awareness in the target market.

REGULATORY FRAMEWORKS

The role of regulatory frameworks is to ensure that advertising and other communications are not misleading, harmful or offensive. Such organizations exist in the US (Federal Trade Commission, FTC), Canada (Advertising Standards Canada, ASC), New Zealand (Advertising Standards Authority, ASA), Australia (Advertising Standards Bureau, ASB) and South Africa (Advertising Standards Authority of South Africa, ASA). In the UK, since the closure of the Office of Fair Trading in 2014, the Advertising Standards Authority (ASA) is now the principal place for audiences to complain, should a marketing message have offended or misled them.

The ASA in the UK works both to monitor proactively and to investigate complaints about advertising, direct marketing and sales promotion messages. The Direct Marketing Association also exists to provide additional codes of practice for direct-marketing activities. If all or part of a campaign that could be causing offence in a particular media or location is found to be in breach of the UK codes of advertising, the brand is asked to withdraw or amend the offending message.

The ASA is funded by a 0.1 per cent levy on the cost of advertising space and 0.2 per cent on the cost of some direct marketing (ASA.org.uk, 2015), which enables it to provide a service that is free to the taxpayer. Broadcast (TV and radio) and non-broadcast (outdoor, print, sales promotions and direct marketing) advertising codes of practice are self-regulated, since they are written by two industry panels of advertisers, but are independently enforced by the ASA. A link is provided in the references on page 217 to the full UK advertising codes of practice, and planners should familiarize themselves with what might cause unexpected offence locally or be considered misleading or irresponsible.

Legal issues surrounding advertising practices on social media sites engender much debate. In 2013, in the UK, Channel 4 broadcast the documentary *Celebs, Brands and Fake Fans* as part of the channel's 'Dispatches' series. The programme highlighted the practice of buying fake 'likes' from 'click farms' in Bangladesh, which generates thousands of likes for branded social media profiles. In addition, a moral dilemma was raised. When a celebrity receives free products and then tweets for the brand in return, is this advertising or a thank-you from a grateful celebrity who enjoyed the product? In general, promoted or boosted posts must feature the devices listed on page 82. For example, a tweet that is obviously advertising a product must feature the #Ad sign so that it is clear to viewers that the post constitutes paid-for advertising. The boundaries between advertising and endorsement remain confused, but both the FTC and the ASA provide further guidelines.

Below In 2015 an Yves Saint Laurent print campaign in *Elle* magazine was banned by the UK ASA, which deemed the model to be unhealthily underweight. The organization felt the image of the model's very thin legs and visible ribcage was 'irresponsible' and should not be promoted. Complaints by viewers were upheld and the image was judged to have breached section 1.3 of the Committee of Advertising Practice code, which states: 'Marketing communications must be prepared with a sense of responsibility to consumers and society.'

DESIGNING A MARKETING COMMUNICATIONS PLAN

Below The marketing communications mix. This lists most of the communication types covered in this book, with a cross-reference to objectives, timelines, measurement of tools, costs and integration.

A table is helpful for planning communications in greater detail.

THE MARKETING COMMUNICATIONS MIX

Communication tool	Description	Objective met	Time schedule	Effectiveness rating as a choice of comms tool (Fill, 2013)	Cost indication	Means of measuring effectiveness	Notes on integration and disruption, use of technology, consistency, synergy and continuity
PR, including editorial publicity, third-party seeding including celebrity gifting, basic level of product placement, events							
Advertising							
Celebrity endorsement							
Trade/international fashion week shows							
Enhanced and integrated product placement							
Sponsorship							
Personal selling							
Sales promotion							
Direct marketing							
Social media							
Budget total (objective and task)							
Budget as percentage of revenue							
Budget as affordable							

Sequence of events

A further advantage of using a Gantt chart (see Chapter 3, p. 56) for communications planning is to give an indication of the sequence in which the various elements of the campaign should occur for maximum impact. It may be necessary for start-up brands to begin PR activities immediately before attending a trade show, for example, or plan to leave a sales promotion until the brand has achieved some recognition.

The flow chart below summarizes the processes discussed so far, and introduces the role of evaluation, discussed in the next section.

A FLOW CHART OF MARKETING COMMUNICATIONS PLANNING

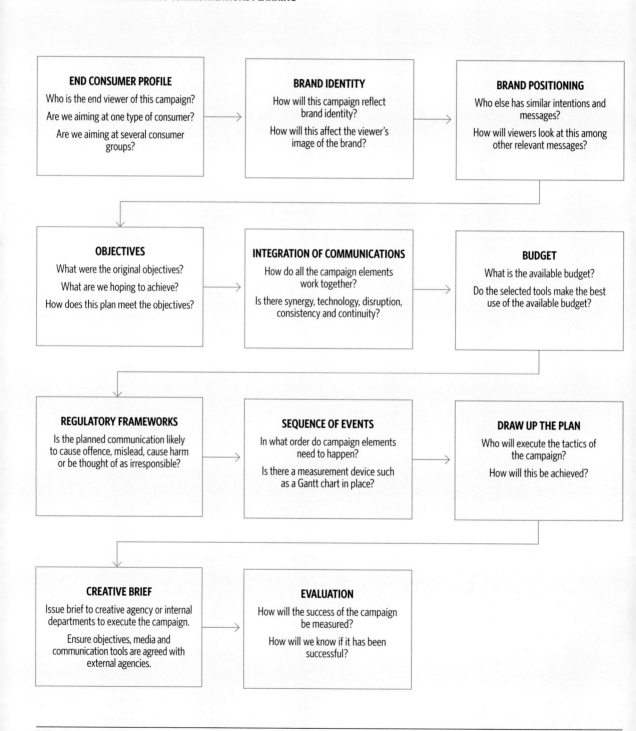

END CONSUMER PROFILE

Who is the end viewer of this campaign?

Are we aiming at one type of consumer?

Are we aiming at several consumer groups?

BRAND IDENTITY

How will this campaign reflect brand identity?

How will this affect the viewer's image of the brand?

BRAND POSITIONING

Who else has similar intentions and messages?

How will viewers look at this among other relevant messages?

OBJECTIVES

What were the original objectives?

What are we hoping to achieve?

How does this plan meet the objectives?

INTEGRATION OF COMMUNICATIONS

How do all the campaign elements work together?

Is there synergy, technology, disruption, consistency and continuity?

BUDGET

What is the available budget?

Do the selected tools make the best use of the available budget?

REGULATORY FRAMEWORKS

Is the planned communication likely to cause offence, mislead, cause harm or be thought of as irresponsible?

SEQUENCE OF EVENTS

In what order do campaign elements need to happen?

Is there a measurement device such as a Gantt chart in place?

DRAW UP THE PLAN

Who will execute the tactics of the campaign?

How will this be achieved?

CREATIVE BRIEF

Issue brief to creative agency or internal departments to execute the campaign.

Ensure objectives, media and communication tools are agreed with external agencies.

EVALUATION

How will the success of the campaign be measured?

How will we know if it has been successful?

EVALUATING MARKETING COMMUNICATIONS

Once a campaign has been implemented, brands and retailers must consider how effective it has been as a brand message. There may, for example, be key differences in the brand's own identity and brand image in the mind of the consumer that need tracking and measuring. Such results provide key feedback that should be used to shape future communication strategies. The process of evaluation involves identifying the metrics available to brands to measure how effective the campaign has been against the objectives set.

The role of control

Setting a system of control at the objective-setting stage, as in the example given in the Gantt chart of Chapter 3 (see p. 56) – using the M of the SMART model to suggest how objectives will be measured – can help to suggest a good deal of evaluation practice. For instance, specifying the number of third-party bloggers to target with gifts can enable a brand to set a realistic target of blog posts, which can be counted after an agreed period of time. Some tools are more readily quantified than others. The success of personal selling, for example, can be measured directly by the number of orders achieved against the objectives set.

It is also possible to research the number of Instagram or Facebook followers a similar brand has, set the objective of achieving a similar number, and simply counting new followers after a period of time. The increase in digital communications, too, has made online responses to direct marketing emails, advertising on social media, traffic from affiliates and search-engine optimization exercises directly measurable and possible to set as a control. Tools such as Facebook Insights and Twitter Analytics can measure the impact of social campaigns by counting reach, likes, shares and who is talking about the campaign. By using tools such as Google Universal Analytics (see p. 140), responses and views can also be tracked through to conversion to sales, to provide direct return-on-investment (ROI) figures as a simple number.

MEASURING THE EFFECTIVENESS OF ADVERTISING

Since advertising is often the most expensive part of a marketing communications plan, it is the effect of traditional TV, billboard and print campaigns that managers will be keenest to quantify, but which remains the hardest to measure directly. Brands should maintain good relationships with stockists to get frequent updates on sales during the course of a campaign and afterwards, to see how long the effect lasts. Some objectives, however – such as the repositioning of the brand image – may change opinion of a brand but will not be reflected directly in sales figures.

Evaluating advertising is the most documented of all the tools, and it is possible by way of pre-testing to assess who will be exposed to the campaign. The breakdown of aspects given by Dahlén et al. (2010), including reach, opportunity to view, share of market and share of voice, is summarized here, with additional thoughts relevant to the fashion industry.

Reach

This is the calculation of how many people are likely to view the advert over a certain period of time. According to Gaynor Lea-Greenwood (2012; and see Chapter 4), circulation figures for magazines can be multiplied by 2.3 to give their readership figures and, therefore, a more accurate idea of the reach of a print campaign. Evaluators should consult media-specific data-collection agencies for each type of media used.

Gross reach

Gross reach is the outside figure for campaigns that use several overlapping media to broadcast the same ad. A campaign may, for instance, feature in two or more fashion magazines in the same month, or be broadcast at the same time on different TV channels. Gross reach calculates each viewing as one, regardless of how many times the viewer may have seen the same thing over a period of time.

Opportunity to view

This figure refers to the probability that a viewer will see a message, and is the gross reach divided by the reach.

Share of market

Share of market (SOM), as its name suggests, refers to the market share a brand holds in a particular category, and can provide the context for figures such as opportunity to see. For example, a brand could hold 25 per cent of the men's tailoring market.

Share of voice

Share of voice (SOV) measures the percentage of time a company is 'heard' in the market category in relation to its competitors. The figure equates to the amount a company spends on advertising against the total adspend of the category. If, for example, the total adspend on tailoring is $600 million (not actual figures) and a tailoring brand makes available $110 million to advertise men's suits, its SOV is 18 per cent ($110 million divided by $600 million, multiplied by 100).

Equilibrium

Equilibrium is said to be reached when SOM and SOV are the same figure. In the example given above, the brand's SOV is lower than its share of the market (SOM), implying that it should invest more in advertising.

Knowledge of communication costs and the number of probable viewers gives an idea of the cost of the use of the communication tool per contact or per 1,000 contacts. This is useful for marketing managers to view alongside ROI figures so that they can assess the tools and adjust if they prove to be too expensive and fail to bring the expected results.

Market research

The only way to analyse or post-test the effect of a campaign more fully and add some quantitative analysis (thoughts, opinions and feelings) to qualitative analysis (data sets and number counts) is to conduct deeper market research. This could be in the form of focus groups, observations, surveys, interviews or on-site field tests to assess viewers' recall, recognition, attitude to or processing of the message. Dahlén et al. (2010), Fill (2013), Egan (2015) and Lea-Greenwood (2012) mention some of the tests advertisers can use, among them:

- Advertisement recognition. This can be tested by showing an ad campaign and measuring direct responses. Alternatively, the logo, packaging and name, if not part of the logo, can be obscured (this is known as masked brand recognition). This helps to test what has been retained in the memory regarding the image of the brand.

	-3	-2	-1	0	1	2	3	
Modern		●	○					Old-fashioned
High quality		●		○				Low quality
Stylish			●	○				Basic
Reliable		●	○					Unreliable
Caring			●		○			Uncaring
Expensive			●○					Inexpensive

Key
- ○ Pre-campaign
- ● Post-campaign

Above Respondent attitudes are placed on an attitude scale against opposing pairs of statements. This takes place before exposure to a campaign message and afterwards.

- Day-after recall. This technique measures the percentage of viewers who recall the brand and key elements of the new message soon after exposure.
- Brand-prompted recall. This checks whether recall of the message matches the image the viewer associates with the brand, and therefore if the viewer has processed the information in the advert as expected.
- Attitude scales. Egan (2015) demonstrates the use of attitude scales for measuring effectiveness (see the table above). Sample respondents plot attitudes to a brand using a sliding scale against a pair of opposing statements, before exposure to the campaign and again afterwards. These can be useful to test how effectively a brand has repositioned itself.

Eye-tracking studies

Eye-tracking technology monitors the movement of a viewer's eye over a computer screen, or in a mobile situation via a camera mounted on glasses. This can capture which element a viewer spent looking at on a TV programme, billboard, magazine or in-store shelf and, therefore, what engaged their interest most. Practitioners who offer this service believe the results to be superior to recall and recognition tests, which convey what the respondent *thought* they saw rather than what they *actually* saw. Eye tracking is now on offer to measure the effect of product placement, direct-marketing mail or email shots, billboards, print and TV campaigns. Brands that pay for this service can see the evidence as though through a potential consumer's eye, revealing the hotspots of viewing attention.

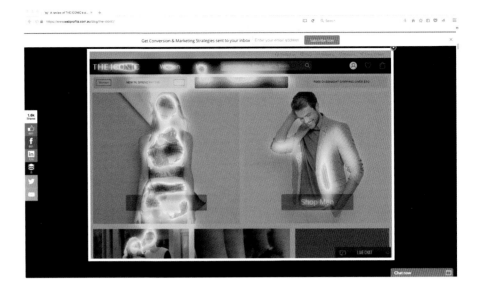

Right Eye-tracking technology shows where visual attention is concentrated when a viewer looks at an image.

Other tests

Other tests that are becoming more common are:

- Electroencephalographs (EEG) monitor the electrical activity in the brain and, therefore, measure the actual level of attention to, and emotional engagement with, advertising messages.
- Galvanic skin response (GSR) tests can measure the amount of electricity conducted by the skin via moisture released by the sweat glands, which indicates the strength of the respondent's arousal by a message.

The cost and intrusive nature of such testing is decreasing, allowing neuromarketing companies to provide these services alongside eye tracking to add scientific data to verbal recall and recognition testing.

MEASURING THE EFFECTIVENESS OF PR

Traditionally, PR companies or in-house operations collect press cuttings from magazines and newspapers as evidence of successful PR. For fashion brands, it is possible to measure what level of publication is featuring articles on the brand and assess whether fashion editors are praising the range or the direction of the brand, or talking about the brand rather than the ranges. The value of editorial publicity in the form of text or image can be quantified by the advertising value equivalent (AVE): the cost if the company had had to pay for that space in a magazine or newspaper in the form of advertising. Celebrity gifting and endorsement (see p. 98) are extremely effective at converting coverage to ROI; stockists will be keen to hear if any such coverage has been published, and can help to report the increase in footfall. The effectiveness of hosting events or organizing stunts is much harder to quantify directly, since data capture at an event may ruin the chance for a member of the public to enjoy genuine two-way dialogue and creative interaction with a brand. However, this interaction is invaluable for brands and builds longer-term credibility rather than immediate response.

MEASURING THE EFFECTIVENESS OF SOCIAL MEDIA

As with all the communication tools, when using social media it is especially important to revisit the objectives, which frequently include building a community of followers or increasing online engagement with the brand. Each brand should consider how it will measure and monitor social media activity. It may be more advantageous to monitor likes or shares that spread narrative about the brand, or creative input, or the positive or negative content of comments. Since social media is time-consuming both to operate and to manage, tools such as Hootsuite can suggest message content and track and monitor activity effectively across all social media platforms.

However brands choose to evaluate or plan their campaigns, a well-planned series of integrated communications should result in the desired rise in sales. It is also important that both new and established brands monitor traffic to check that the hard-won brand identity matches the brand image viewers have in their minds, and to make sure that viewers have access to an informed and engaging narrative that they can share with others as a result of their involvement with the brand's messages.

MEASURING THE EFFECTIVENESS OF SALES PROMOTIONS

Sales promotions are by nature delivered over a short amount of time and designed to entice the receiver to act before an offer expires or the chance escapes them in another way. As such, they provide a focused flow of responses via return of coupons, registration of interest, attendance at sale previews, visits to or an increase in impressions on a webpage, or entries to competitions that, whether online or offline, can be simply counted.

CONCLUSIONS AND ADDITIONAL THOUGHTS ON CAMPAIGN DESIGN

Several themes have emerged throughout this book.
- Strong brand identity informs all communication tools, especially a brand's tone of voice across digital channels.
- The term 'celebrity endorsement' has widened to incorporate trusted influencers such as Matthew Zorpas (see p. 100), who act as a new type of endorser with a valuable direct path to their followers.
- Previous strategies to isolate the online and offline elements of campaigns have changed so that brands are now considering where the consumer is located at all touchpoints in receiving messages. Initiatives such as Sportsgirl's interactive billboards (see p. 72) make every opportunity a shopping opportunity, even a closed store.
- Similarly, smart brands and retailers are analysing the success of e-commerce and bringing tools via apps or other technology into bricks-and-mortar retail to create a seamless, holistic experience for the visitor.

- Brands and retailers are making an incredible effort to democratize previously exclusive information to benefit and boost the profiles of followers.

To add to this final point, one event stands out as a model for involving audiences in the future. This was not a marketing exercise, nor a fashion-related happening, but it had elements of both. In 2014 HBO Documentaries made a film of the British street artist Banksy's month-long self-proclaimed residency in New York in October 2013, entitled *Banksy Does New York*. Each day for a month the artist, who is known for his social and political comment, aimed to create a work of street art in the birthplace of graffiti. A teaser appeared on Instagram every morning, followed by a picture on an accompanying website, with no way of identifying the location. The site was set up with an audio guide to each piece, as if followers were listening to an art-gallery commentary. The first work was covered up within two hours, and so there followed what was variously

Left Crowds gather to photograph a Banksy installation of 2013 featuring a security guard watching over two artworks (created in collaboration with the Brazilian artists Os Gêmeos) and a wine-filled water cooler. The work created an impromptu art space, set provocatively in the gallery district of New York.

described as a 'treasure hunt' or 'hipster scavenger hunt' for followers, who communicated with one another on Twitter as they attempted to locate the work. Banksy created a mixture of installations, stencil artworks, videos and live performances that were poignant, thought-provoking and witty. The pieces drew art followers to areas of New York they would not normally visit, and involved residents who would not normally have the chance to comment on street art. The interaction of the followers, dubbed 'Banksy Hunters', became part of the event, which was described as an integration of street and social media. Followers' images and videos included people attempting to steal the works, other graffiti artists tagging the work and people becoming impromptu street-gallery owners. The 'residency' culminated in the police being called to a fight as fans tried to stop the theft of the last piece. The event was a thought-provoking disruption of ideas about the way public art is viewed, the value of street art and the role of participants in observing art.

Largely, however, it was the sheer joy of involvement in a happening of significance that came across. People described observing only good, joyful feelings, and one Bansky Hunter involved from day one said: 'I feel like chasing these pieces. It reminds me of when I was a teenager chasing that new pair of Jordans that came out on a Saturday morning. I wake up early to catch these.'

It is this joy of involvement that promoters must provoke, by providing genuine online or offline content with which to boost the follower's own social media profile, rather than just their involvement with the brand. Promoters should not forget this last ingredient – the creation of content that allows an opportunity to connect and create something with similar followers – whatever method of communication and tools the brand uses.

REFERENCES

ASA.org.uk, 'About Regulation', 2015, www.asa.org.uk/about-asa/about-regulation.aspx

Dahlén, Micael, Fredrik Lange and Terry Smith, *Marketing Communications: A Brand Narrative Approach*, Wiley 2010

Egan, John, *Marketing Communications*, 2nd ed., Sage 2015

Fill, Chris, *Marketing Communications: Brands, Experiences and Participation*, 6th ed., Pearson 2013

Keller K.L., Apéria T. and Georgson, M., *Strategic Brand Management: A European Perspective*, Prentice Hall 2008

Lea-Greenwood, Gaynor, *Fashion Marketing Communications*, Wiley 2012

Smith, Paul R., and Ze Zook, *Marketing Communications: Integrating Offline and Online with Social Media*, 5th ed., Kogan Page 2011

FURTHER READING

Committee of Advertising Practice, 'Advertising Codes', 2015, www.cap.org.uk/advertising-codes.aspx

Moukarbel, Chris, *Banksy Does New York*, HBO Documentaries in association with Matador and Permanent Wave Productions, first broadcast 17 February 2014

UK Direct Marketing Association: www.dma.org.uk

US Federal Trade Commission: www.ftc.gov

DISCUSSION

Have you ever mistaken paid-for content for a personal post on a blog or social media? Did this make the brand seem more or less likeable?

Which three communication tools would you prioritize if the budget is tight?

Which would you choose with an unlimited budget?

GLOSSARY

@ handle or social handle is the unique identifier of an individual or company, by which they communicate across *social media* platforms. This can be dictated by name, desired perception or availability. It is recommended for brands that the selected handle is the same or very similar across all platforms.

above the fold The content the viewer sees on opening a webpage without having to scroll down.

advertising value equivalent (AVE) The value of a piece of free, or low-cost publicity compared to its equivalent value as paid-for advertising space.

affiliate channel An arrangement between complementary online organizations that pay an agreed rate of commission to generate traffic, registrations or final sales from one site to the other.

ambient marketing A wide term that refers to the use of advertising in out-of-home situations. It can encompass an unusual treatment of a billboard, advertising on humans, sides of lorries, in fields along the motorway or on shopping trolleys.

banner The space across the top or down the sides of a webpage, which can be used by online retailers to draw attention to specific offers, trends or items of interest. In online magazines, news forums and some blogs these are often given over to advertising space and referred to as banner or display ads.

bounce rate The rate in which viewers of a webpage get bored, frustrated or distracted by the content or usability of a website. This is around five seconds for 75 per cent of users.

brand ambassador An actor, sports personality, model, reality TV star or increasingly a style *influencer* that a brand has selected to 'endorse' their products for mutual benefit. The term includes unofficial arrangements when a celebrity achieves publicity for being associated with a certain brand, and formal endorsement agreements whereby an ambassador is contracted to appear wearing or using a certain brand. In the US the term also includes employees who promote the brand in sales situations.

brand narrative The transferable 'story' behind a brand, which forms the relatable content to consumers and is used to inform *marketing communications*. This can relate to the founder of the brand, the nationality of the brand or the personality the brand wishes to convey. The narrative is vitally important to create a *Point of Difference* for brands.

bumper Sponsored TV advertising shown at the start and end of an ad break. This helps the advertiser establish a brand with the ratings for a particular TV series.

business-to-business selling (B2B) When a brand or manufacturer sells its products to a retailer who will be responsible for selling directly to the public.

business-to-consumer selling (B2C) When a retailer sells directly to the buying public.

buyable Pin A shoppable function of Pinterest. Tapping on a blue 'price tag' sign on items on a Pinterest board takes viewers through to an option to buy from the supplier.

buyer persona An enhanced portrait of an ideal customer or segments of customers created using measurable online behaviour to build on the geo-demographics, and *psychographics*, of the desired consumer.

call to action Direct-response marketing material that requires completion by the consumer (name, address, email and so on) to initiate an enquiry, register interest or take up an offer.

Casual A member of the Casual sub-culture popular in Britain in the late 1970s and early 1980s. Casuals invested in expensive, rare sportswear and designer labels to wear to football matches as part of sartorial one-upmanship among rival team supporters. The movement saw the growth of labels such as Fila, Ellesse, Lois, Lacoste and Kappa in the UK.

characteristic The internal and external attributes of a brand that contribute to its *Points of Difference*. These can be expressed in the same way as human characteristics to make a brand more relatable.

circulation figures The number of copies of magazines and newspapers printed in one edition.

clutter Messages competing for attention when a brand is communicating to an audience.

consumer-driven database Databases concerned with the acquisition of potential consumers and the retention of existing ones, aimed at targeting them with engaging, personalized communications.

content A wide term for all the online material individuals and companies generate to engage their followers. This includes blogs, *social media* feeds, competitions, trend news and views, product descriptions, insider information and any other editorial copy the brand chooses to share.

content marketing The consideration of *content* as an ongoing strategy to increase consumer engagement with a brand.

control A statement of how a brand or company will know when a communication objective has been achieved. Used in conjunction with *SMART* objectives it helps companies keep to realistic, measurable goals.

cost per mille (CPM) / cost per thousand (CPT) These terms are used interchangeably to calculate the cost (to an interested party) of 1,000 *impressions*, or single page views, by a web user of a piece of online advertising.

culture jamming/culture hacking Terms used by Adbusters, an organization that urges members of the public to protest against advertising culture, for example by intervention with billboards or posters, or by taking part in 'buy nothing' days.

customer relationship management (CRM) The strategy, processes and technology needed to manage customers effectively. Also, all customer-facing departments in an organization.

direct marketing (DM) The strategy and tactics by which a company communicates on a regular basis to build a personalized relationship with the consumer.

dyadic Communication on a one-to one basis where two parties interact to achieve a mutual goal.

editorial publicity Published coverage of a brand, label or retailer by a respected third party such as a fashion magazine or style *influencer* who has used their space to recommend the products to their readers.

enhanced product placement When the inclusion of a product in a film or TV has been paid for by the brand or label.

entity A wide term that is used to denote the type of product or service a brand offers. The term also has legal connotations and is used to imply the potential market value of the brand.

equilibrium A state reached in analysing the effectiveness of a campaign, when the *share of voice* is equal to the percentage share of the market they hold of the same category.

extrinsic attributes Factors such as *marketing communications* and reputation that, along with *intrinsic attributes* such as product, fit, performance and so on, shape the consumer's idea of the brand.

forward order An order placed from sample ranges for delivery 5–6 months later. This means the supplier makes the goods against secure orders. This decades-old system is under pressure to change from store buyers' desire to commit to trends later in the season, unpredictable weather patterns, and *'see now, buy now' culture*.

fragmentation Breaking down; widely used to describe consumer behaviour ('consumer groups have fragmented, meaning brands have to build an individual picture') or the choice of purchase channel ('consumer buying behaviour is fragmented across in-store, online and m-commerce'). Also used to describe the way in which information is received ('the rise of social media influencers and online news forums has fragmented our opinions of who is an expert').

fully responsive design Consideration of how a webpage will look and function across all devices: a desktop computer or laptop, a tablet and a mobile phone.

Gantt chart A useful visual planning tool that plots a sequence of activities in blocks of time against a required timeline.

gifting Giving away samples to personalities, bloggers or style commentators in the hope that they will be photographed wearing the product or will comment positively on the brand or label.

go viral The spreading of an item of interest online until it seems almost everyone is talking about it.

gross reach A count of each possible viewing of a piece of campaign material, regardless of multiple viewings via overlapping media channels, for example the same campaign being seen in several fashion magazines in one month.

guerrilla advertising Placing advertising material in unexpected or even controversial places with the aim of creating impact and generating additional publicity.

half-page unit (HPU) A unit of space in online advertising, this is a large block of space along the side of a webpage.

home page Also referred to as a landing page, this is the page the viewer sees on opening a website.

humanize To ascribe human qualities to something, in this case to a brand. By developing a brand that has human characteristics such as being hard-working, and recognizable personality traits such as playfulness or adventurousness, brands are in theory made more relatable to us.

ident In television, a graphic device used in advertising in association with a brand in the same way as a *bumper*.

immersive communication Using technology to fully engage and involve the participant in a branded experience, for example via virtual reality.

impression In online advertising and online marketing, the number of views by a user of a single webpage. Used as a chargeable rate for advertising or to calculate web traffic.

inbound telemarketing When customers ring a retailer or brand for customer service or sales support.

influencer A person with a large online following who is noted for the credibility of their style commentary rather than paid-for content.

influencer marketing A planned strategy of working with selected *influencers* to promote a brand.

integrated marketing communications (IMC) The consideration of the available mix of communication tools and the media by which they will be broadcast, to create the most effective and cohesive message of the campaign to its audiences.

integrated product placement Where the product placement is integral to the plot, for example James Bond and Aston Martin. The link between a film or TV series and a brand will be strengthened by advertising campaigns.

intrinsic attributes The functional features of a branded product, such as its fit, fabric, performance and style, separate from the image or identity of the brand.

key performance indicator (KPI) A variable used to measure the success of a company initiative.

landed price The price of a product from a supplier, including manufacturing, shipping, insurance, customs charges and delivery.

landing page see *home page*

last season An item from a previous season; in fashion, can be used in a derogatory way to describe something out of date.

leader board In online advertising, the *banner* space across the top of a webpage.

live text / HTML text Webpage copy that appears as text rather than an image. This helps where internet access is limited and for ease of copying information between devices.

long tail In online searches, the specific words or phrases a consumer may enter when attempting to narrow down a general search. If a product description matches these, the brand or retailer will be placed towards the top of the search-engine rankings.

lookbook An online or printed brochure or series of images of a company's styles for the coming season. These represent the brand identity at trade shows and in-store, and are a means of communication between brands, the fashion press and the end consumer.

marketing communications mix The array of communication tools by which brands and retailers choose to communicate with their *B2B* and *B2C* audiences. This includes advertising, PR, *sponsorship*, *product placement*, endorsements, *social media*, *direct marketing*, sales promotions, personal selling, catwalk shows, trade fairs and the retail environment.

media pack Information made available to potential advertisers relating to their selected media, for example *circulation figures* for a magazine or viewing figures for a TV channel; the customer profile of the viewer/reader; and the advertising rates to appear in different positions or at different times.

megatrend A trend that achieves a long-lasting impact. 'Sports Luxe' or 'athleisure' for example began as a fashion catwalk trend, but now it forms part of the everyday style of the millennial generation.

meta-tagging Meta tags, also referred to as meta elements and meta keywords, are snippets of further descriptive text attached to webpage content. They do not appear on the page but are written in code and are identified by search engines. They are another tool in *search-engine optimization*.

mid-page unit (MPU), known as medium rectangle (MREC) in the US In online advertising, a rectangular *banner* space on a webpage.

Modern In this book, the Modernist era between 1900 and 1960 and prior to the *Postmodern* era. Modernism saw huge progressions in all areas of design and was generally an optimistic period.

monthly active users (MAU) The number of unique users over a 30-day period, used by *social media platforms* as a measure of their popularity.

multi-brand Of an online or offline retailer, selling a number of different brands as opposed to own-label merchandise.

national brand A brand associated with the popular perception of a nation or country. This may not necessarily be its country of origin. Neutrogena, which features the Norwegian flag and mentions its Norwegian formula (with which we associate hard-working qualities in tough conditions), is actually an American brand.

native app An app developed for use on a specific platform or for a specific device. It can therefore be used by brands or retailers to interact with other software already in use on that platform, such as GPS tracking.

neuromarketing A series of evaluative tests that measure the body's reaction to a stimulus such as campaign material. These include eye tracking, measurement of electrical activity in the brain and measurement of electricity conducted by the skin.

non-recognition photography Photography in which it is not possible to recognize the model and associate a given face with campaign material.

off-schedule Choosing to show 'off-schedule' is to show a range at the same time and location as a known fashion week, but outside the scheduled timetable of catwalk shows.

omni-channel The availability of product through multiple channels. This includes in a bricks-and-mortar store, via an e-commerce website, via m-commerce, through shoppable *social media* channels, via a catalogue or increasingly through a blend of experiences such as events, workshops or concept retail that bring the product to the consumer.

opt-in email Email by a brand or retailer only to parties who have agreed either at point of purchase or via the company's website to hear from that brand.

outbound telemarketing Where employees of a company call a target database of potential or existing customers with the intention of increasing sales, or generating interest in a brand.

outdoor advertising Advertising outdoors or in expected out-of-home locations. This includes billboards, bus stops, on transport itself and train and subway stations. See also *ambient marketing*.

pay-per-click advertising (PPC) An online tool used to drive traffic from one site to another. An advertiser pays a website owner or search engine to place advertising on their host site or via an automated matching system to sites with viewers of similar preferences. The price paid for the advertising space is measured in clicks of interest through to the advertiser's site.

pen portrait A description of an ideal target consumer that includes age, gender, location and occupation, but also an indication of interests, motivations and behaviours.

persona The brand character that is perceived by others.

point of sale (POS) Promotional material used in retail to inform and persuade shoppers, and to delineate different brands. These include posters, showcards, shelf markers, swing tags, packaging and carrier bags.

Points of Difference (POD) In brand positioning, the factors that are unique to, and therefore an advantage to, the brand in question against those of its competitors.

Points of Parity (POP) In brand positioning, the factors that are similar to the brand in question and its direct competitors. In a statement of positioning a brand would acknowledge these factors and highlight how they are better.

post-demographic consumerism An overarching *megatrend* noted by trendwatching.com that acknowledges how sophisticated consumers now are. They no longer slot neatly into expected behaviours of age or gender. Post-demographic consumerism sees a fundamental shift in how brands need to be relevant to their customers.

Postmodern The era beginning in the early 1960s and typified by artist Andy Warhol's placing of advertising material in an art gallery.

postponement A strategy to reduce the manufacture of large quantities of potentially unwanted items. Manufacturers will defer production until there is evidence of consumer or shop-floor demand. In fashion this can involve securing base fabrics that are ready to dye as colour trends crystallize.

post-postmodern A broad and complex term under much debate. For the purposes of this book, we assume that post-postmodernism means breaking down of previously held norms. Our increasingly online existence is a state of post-postmodernism intensified.

PPC see *pay-per-click advertising*

Prada Epicenters Designed by Rem Koolhaas for Prada, technologically enabled flagship shopping, gallery and office spaces.

press pack An online or physical pack containing *lookbook* images and a press release, used by brands and retailers as a snapshot of the forthcoming season. These are sent to fashion editors, *influencers*, trade press and other news forums.

proactive PR The seeking of editorial publicity or wider exposure through credible third-party channels such as fashion magazines, *influencer* feeds, celebrity gifting or endorsement, *product placement* or *sponsorship*.

product A single item or range of items produced by a brand, retailer or designer label.

product placement The inclusion of a particular brand or label in a film, TV series or reality TV show as if that product would be there naturally.

promotional mix see *marketing communications mix*

prospect In *direct marketing*, the different levels of consumers in accordance with their status as a sales prospect for the company. The levels range from members of the public who are similar to the customer profile, to those who have purchased in the past but need tempting back.

psychographics A combination of a consumer's demographics such as age, gender, location and job, with their motivations, resources and behaviours by type. This creates a more rounded picture than demographics alone.

public relations (PR) PR in fashion is used to raise or maintain awareness of designer labels, brands and retailers using newsworthy items such as events, collaborations or celebrity involvement, via coverage written by a respected third party. PR is also sought in response to negative coverage to explain or apologize on behalf of the company.

publicity see *editorial publicity*

pure play Retailers or brands who are online only. Their products are not available in bricks-and-mortar stores.

push notification A message to a consumer that pops up on a smartphone. Brands and retailers that have apps can send these at any time (if enabled by the phone owner), and they appear regardless of the user being in the app at the time.

QR (Quick Response) code A barcode that can store more information than standard barcodes. Commonly used in marketing for their ability when scanned to provide quick access to a brand's website. They can also be helpful in tracking items through the supply chain.

ratchet effect A term put forward by Egan (2015) to describe how an integrated strategy, for example using *direct marketing* to deliver a discount offer, is more effective. In other words, the effect is 'ratcheted up' from just using advertising or sales promotion alone.

reach Also readership figures. An estimate of the number of actual readers or viewers of a campaign. Printed magazines and newspapers are passed on for others to read, making their reach figures greater than their *circulation figures*.

reactive PR *Editorial publicity* that is sought in the event of the brand, retailer or label receiving negative publicity or becoming involved with an adverse news story. The company may seek to apologize or make their position clear.

readership figures see *reach*

ready-to-wear (RTW) Also prêt-à-porter or off-the-rack. Garments manufactured in standard sizes, as opposed to bespoke or couture garments that are tailor-made.

real-time bidding (RTB) The practice of buying and selling advertising material (such as *banner* ads and promoted posts, or even key words and phrases on its value per impression, in real time), via an instantaneous auctioning system.

recency, frequency and monetary (RFM) model A model used in online marketing to assess a brand or retailer's most valuable customers in terms of when they last bought, how often they buy and how much they spend.

resources In this book, personal resources such as levels of energy, self-confidence, impulsiveness and so on, which are assessed as part of the VALS (values and lifestyle) consumer *psychographics* model. These work with a person's primary motivators (ideals, achievements and self-expression) to predict their likely behaviour as a consumer type. The term also refers to an indication of the time, people, materials and budget required to carry out a given activity.

retail atmosphere Elements such as colour, sound, scent, and tactile surfaces, combined to create a pleasant and welcoming experience for shoppers.

return on investment (ROI) A measurement of the financial gain (or loss) in relation to a specific investment made into the company.

robocall Contact from a recorded message, which can be generated by a marketing company using an automated telephone dialing system. The effect is of being spoken to by a robot.

sales revenue Also sales turnover. Total sales income before other outgoings, such as cost of stock, are deducted.

salesmen's samples A range of samples made from the original prototypes, given to each salesperson or field agent. This means each sales agent will have the whole collection to sell from.

search-engine optimization (SEO) Techniques to enhance a brand or retailer's rankings in a given consumer search. These can be *content* related, such as using descriptive key words and phrases about the brand, its expertise and its specific products; using a blog or *social media* posts to reinforce these phrases; and inviting external parties to reiterate those phrases. Technical SEO is paying a search engine to bid for key words and phrases to raise their rankings, depending on what those phrases are worth in real time.

search-engine PPC The use of a specific search engine such as Google, Yahoo or Bing for a *pay-per-click* advertising arrangement.

Secure Socket Layer (SSL) Installed on a payment page, an SSL encrypts valuable information (such as credit card numbers) from plain text as it is transmitted between a browser and a server. This security reassures online shoppers.

'see now, buy now' culture A term coined after Burberry made their Spring/Summer 2016 collection available online and in-store directly after the catwalk show. Since adopted by Tom Ford, Ralph Lauren and Tommy Hilfiger, this is a radical change to meet consumer demand.

seeding The placement of a product, brand experience or brand message with the right *influencers*, bloggers, vloggers, celebrities and so on, to ensure the word will be spread among a credible and relevant network of followers.

self: ideal self, actual self, social self The facets of self-concept. Psychologists Carl Rogers and Abraham Maslow popularized the idea that we operate a complex system of 'selves' in our representation of ourselves and how others see us. Our ideal self is the person we hope and aspire to be, our actual self is who we really are, and our social self is how we believe others see us. A person is said to have reached a state of self-image congruence if these states are equal to each other.

share of market (SOM) The market share held by a company (usually expressed as a percentage) of a particular category such as occasionwear or tailoring.

share of voice (SOV) The amount a company spends on communication (usually expressed as a percentage) in relation to the total spend in a particular category, indicating how likely a company is to be 'heard' in the market.

SMART model A system of objective-setting designed to help a company create specific, measureable, achievable, realistic and timely goals.

social media The collective term for websites, apps and messaging systems that are dedicated to community-based input, interaction, content-sharing and collaboration.

social media platform A specific *social media* site, app or messaging service such as Facebook, Instagram, Snapchat and Whatsapp.

social network Interactions and personal relationships conducted on *social media*.

sponsorship A commercial agreement between two companies whereby one invests in the other for greater exposure to desired target markets.

spot advertising A TV advertisement broadcast during a specific slot or 'spot' within a scheduled break between programmes.

strategy A plan of action designed to achieve a specific aim.

subtrend A trend which sits within, and is typical of, a *megatrend*. A subtrend may be subject to more frequent changes and evolutions.

subvertiser Someone who subverts advertising; the term, from *guerrilla advertising*, encourages the use of interference such as applied slogans or debranding the message of intended advertising. See also *culture jamming*.

synergy In *integrated marketing communications*, a measure of when the tools used as part of a campaign are in harmony with the overall message.

tactics The specifics of a strategy, such as which *marketing communications* tools will be employed to carry out an objective.

tailored online cross-selling Whereby a holding company of a number of brands can collect data on consumer preferences and use that to suggest items of specific interest from its other brands.

thresholds The way in which stores are divided by buyers, merchandisers and floor managers into a rating scale of desirability for a shopper's attention. A first threshold, for example, is near the entrance.

tile Online, a square or rectangle of space containing text, images or both that is designed to be clicked on to direct a browser to a specific item of interest.

tone of voice The way in which a brand 'speaks' consistently to its audiences and embodies the brand personality.

'Tribes and Lives' (trend) An older trend identified by trendwatching.com that suggested the segmentation of audiences by lifestyle groups, and enabled a better brand understanding. Now replaced by *post-demographic consumerism*.

trunk show An intimate event hosted by a designer instead of, or in addition to, a catwalk show, to take advance sales from valued clients.

turnover see *sales revenue*

two-up page display A recommended layout for a press release in .PDF format, with one page of text and one page of images.

unique selling point (USP) Also unique selling proposition. A brand's distinct *Point of Difference* from its competitors and therefore the reason for a store or end consumer to buy into it.

user experience (UX) In online marketing, a user's engagement or interaction with web content. Findings can result in images or text being moved to better effect.

user-generated content (UGC) Content submitted by followers of a brand or retailer, such as themselves wearing a particular product, in response to campaign material, a competition, or the desire to promote or review that product.

video in print (VIP) technology The implanting of technology such as a small LCD (liquid crystal display) screen, which is able to play video within printed material.

visual merchandising (VM) The display and layout of product in-store and in the windows, to attract shoppers and provide an effective journey through the store.

wholesaling *B2B* selling whereby a brand sells a product into a store, for retail directly to the public. Wholesaling requires establishing a wholesale price, which is the cost of production plus a mark-up for the wholesaler. The retailer adds a mark-up to cover their own overheads.

INDEX

PICTURE CREDITS

Page 4 above Victor VIRGILE / Gamma-Rapho via Getty Images; 4 below courtesy Dries Van Noten; 5 courtesy howies and Carter Wong Design Ltd; 7 left courtesy G-Star; 7 right Skechers / Splash News; 8–9 main image courtesy All Saints; 8 below The Dreslyn / Land of Women / Ian Flanigan; 8–9 below Open (notclosed.com); 10 left photograph by Barbara Graham; 10 right courtesy All Saints; 14 The Dreslyn / Land of Women / Ian Flanigan; 15 Rex/Shutterstock; 16 above courtesy Levi's; 16 below Ted Polhemus / PYMCA; 18 above courtesy Keizo Kitajima; 18 below courtesy Lunn Farrow Media; 19 above courtesy Jean Paul Gaultier; 19 below courtesy Vivienne Westwood; 21 above Open (notclosed. com); 21 below courtesy trendwatching.com; 22 and 23 left courtesy trendwatching.com; 23 right courtesy Happiness-Brussels and Pimkie; 24 courtesy Domino's; 26 courtesy Cos; 26 right courtesy Alice's Pig; 27 courtesy Fred Perry; 28 Gilbert Carrasquillo / Getty Images; 29 Pat Greenhouse / The Boston Globe via Getty Images; 30 WENN Ltd / Alamy; 31 left Vanni Bassetti / Getty Images; 31 right Shutterstock; 33 courtesy Havaianas; 34 courtesy Nike; 35 left and right courtesy Shepard Fairey; 37 above and below courtesy Alice's Pig; 38 image 1 courtesy Tiffany; 38 images 2–5 courtesy Fred Perry; 39 top image Rea Lilliard; 39 clockwise from above left: courtesy Diesel, courtesy Timberland, courtesy Nike, courtesy Gas Jeans, courtesy Dior, courtesy Norse Projects, courtesy Calvin Klein, courtesy Ferragamo, courtesy Braintree; 41 courtesy House of Fraser; 42 left courtesy Cos; 42 right courtesy Havaianas; 44 above and below courtesy Lacoste and Rita Productions; 45 Tristan Fewings / Getty Images; 47 above courtesy Wanda Productions; 47 below (both) courtesy Lacoste and Rita Productions; 48 left Tristan Fewings / Getty Images; 48 right courtesy Chrisaboveher Kane and David James Associates. Photo by Harley Weir; 49 left courtesy Barbour and Sean Conway; 49 right courtesy Paul Smith; 50 above left Peter Macdiarmid / Getty Images; 50 below left courtesy Paul Smith; 50 centre courtesy Charles Tyrwhitt; 50 right courtesy Gap; 51 all courtesy Boy Bastiaens; 52 and 53 courtesy Above Shop; 55 Derrick Santini; 56 above image by Pauline Goetz and Anna Szymanska; 58–59 main image courtesy Diesel; 58 right courtesy Above Shop; 60 courtesy DKNY; 62 above courtesy Above Shop; 62 below Matthew Stone; 64 image 1 courtesy Diesel; 64 image 2 Natan Dvir / Polaris / eyevine; 64 image 3 courtesy Iro; 64 image 4 Splash/L'Agent/Liz Collins; 65 image 5 Amos Mac for & Other Stories; 65 image 6 courtesy Benetton; 65 image 7 photograph by Barbara Graham; 65 image 8 courtesy Diesel; 65 image 9 courtesy The Kooples; 66 Giannoni / WWD / REX / Shutterstock; 67 courtesy Missguided; 68 courtesy Ralph Lauren; 69 courtesy Havaianas; 70 courtesy Dolce & Gabbana, BVDO and Americhip Inc.; 71 above and centre Daily Billboard Blog; 71 below Joe Armao / Fairfax Syndication; 72 both courtesy Kenneth Cole and Ready Set Rocket; 73 above left and right courtesy adidas; 73 below courtesy Moose; 74 courtesy Adbusters Media Foundation; 75 courtesy Dazed Digital; 80 courtesy Facebook; 81 above courtesy Luluemon; 81 below courtesy Snapchat; 84 above courtesy Harrods Magazine, photography by Ishi; 84 below courtesy Sephora; 85 Ryan Thwaites / Splash News; 86 courtesy Marie Claire, photos by nohalidedigital.com; 88 courtesy Ben Rayner; 89 above courtesy Cosmopolitan; 89 centre courtesy Love-Aesthetics; 89 below right courtesy The Blonde Salad; 89 below left David M. Benett / Getty Images for Mulberry; 90 courtesy Sephora; 92 photography by Willem Jaspert; 93 above and below left courtesy Net-A-Porter; 93 centre courtesy Acne; 93 below right courtesy Mulberry; 94 above courtesy Superdry; 94 centre Gareth Cattermole / Getty Images; 94 below courtesy Noon by Noor; 95 above Alfredo Piola; 95 centre courtesy Harrods Magazine, photography by Ishi; 95 below courtesy Vogue Japan; 96 below Deanpictures / Dreamstime.com; 97 left Carolyn Cole / Los Angeles Times via Getty Images; 97 right Jonathan Hordle / REX / Shutterstock; 98 left Toby Melville / WPA Pool / Getty Images; 98 right Kevin C. Cox / Getty Images; 99 courtesy Material Girl; 100–102 courtesy Matthew Zorpas; 103 above Gareth Cattermole / Getty Images; 103 below Splash News / Balmain; 104 above Ryan Thwaites / Splash News; 104 below Shaun Botterill / Getty Images; 105 above courtesy Benetton; 105 below Christof Koepsel / Getty Images; 106 above Anthea Simms; 106 below left OLIVIER LABAN-MATTEI / AFP / Getty Images; 106 below right ZUMA Press, Inc. / Alamy; 108–109 above Splash News; 108 below courtesy Karl Lagerfeld; 109 below courtesy Burberry; 110 and 111 both courtesy Ralph Lauren; 113 courtesy Missguided; 114 above Ruaridh Connellan / Barcroft Media via Getty Images; 114 below and 115 above courtesy John Fluevog; 115 below courtesy Unilever; 116 above courtesy Burberry; 116 below courtesy AboveShop; 117 Splash News; 118 above courtesy afashionfix. co.uk; 118 below courtesy Michael Kors; 119 above courtesy Pinterest; 119 below courtesy Oscar de la Renta; 120 courtesy Burberry; 121 above courtesy Diesel; 121 below courtesy Missguided; 122 Kirstin Sinclair / Getty Images; 124 above courtesy Diesel; 124 below courtesy Karl Lagerfeld; 126–127 below courtesy Tom Walsh Design; 127 above courtesy Nineteenth Amendment; 128 above courtesy Net-A-Porter; 131 both courtesy Diligent Commerce; 133 courtesy Tom Walsh Design; 134 above courtesy J.Crew; 134 below courtesy Anthropologie; 135–136 all courtesy John Fluevog; 137 courtesy Nineteenth Amendment; 138 both courtesy Net-A-Porter; 142–143 below Kay-Paris Fernandes / Getty Images; 142 above allfive / Alamy; 143 above Eusike Fukumochi / Studio Arthur Casas; 145 above Kay-Paris Fernandes / Getty Images; 145 below Yongkwan Kim; 146 courtesy Trapstar; 147 allfive / Alamy; 149 left Richard Young / REX / Shutterstock; 149 right courtesy Apple; 151 courtesy Emily and Fin; 153 above left Martino Lombezzi; 153 above right courtesy Stone Island; 153 below courtesy Selfridges; 154 above courtesy Selfridges, photo by Matt Writtle; 154 below courtesy Uniqlo; 155 above courtesy & Other Stories; 155 below courtesy Pro Direct; 156 Eusike Fukumochi / Studio Arthur Casas; 157 above courtesy A1 Architects; 157 below courtesy LN-CC; 158 courtesy The White Company; 159 main image courtesy Paul Smith; 159 below courtesy Hotel Chocolat; 160 courtesy Oki-Ni; 161 both courtesy Paul Smith; 164 courtesy The White Company; 165 courtesy American Express; 166 both courtesy Diesel; 169 both courtesy Hotel Chocolat; 171 courtesy Kurt Geiger; 172 above both courtesy Next; 172 below courtesy WhatsApp; 174 above courtesy Racil; 174 below PATRICK KOVARIK / AFP / Getty Images; 174–175 blelow Copenhagen International Fashion Fair RAVEN, Bella Center, Copenhagen, Denmark; 175 Joshua LOTT / AFP / Getty Images; 176 all Pixelformula / REX / Shutterstock; 177 above Lee Oliveira / eyevine; 177 below Larry Busacca / Getty Images; 178 PATRICK KOVARIK / AFP / Getty Images; 179 Stuart C. Wilson / Getty Images for Burberry; 180 left Joshua LOTT / AFP / Getty Images; 180 right Dave Benett / Getty Images; 182 and 183 above courtesy Premium Berlin; 183 below Copenhagen International Fashion Fair RAVEN, Bella Center, Copenhagen, Denmark; 184–186 courtesy Racil; 188–189 photographs by Barbara Graham except background image courtesy Fuseproject; 191 above CRISTINA QUICLER / AFP / Getty Images; 191 below courtesy Net-A-Porter; 192 courtesy Zara; 193 courtesy Vente-Privee; 194 courtesy Lane Crawford; 195 REUTERS / Kim Kyung-Hoon; 197 left courtesy H&M Foundation; 197 right Bertrand Rindoff Petroff / Getty Images; 198 courtesy Nordstrom; 200 above courtesy Pinterest; 200 below left courtesy Millimetre Design; 200 below right courtesy Kuyichi; 201 all photographs by Barbara Graham; 202 courtesy Fuseproject; 203 above courtesy howies and Carter Wong Design Ltd; 203 below courtesy Gucci; 204–205 courtesy House of Fraser; 204 main image courtesy Mango; 205 below and 206 courtesy Nike; 207 courtesy Mango; 215 courtesy The Iconic; 217 Noam Galai / WireImage / Getty Images.

ACKNOWLEDGMENTS

Both authors would like to extend their thanks to all the interviewees, brands and retailers that spent time with us and agreed to be part of this book. Your thoughts and contributions have shaped our content to be as forward thinking and industry specific as it possibly can be.

Thanks also to the people who mined their contacts to help us locate the right people, including George Graham, Jean-Philippe Olgiati, Duccio Frosini, Tristan de Souza, Debby Baxter-Bruce and Nick Cannons.

A big thank you to our Commissioning Editor Sophie Drysdale for your belief in this book from the start, the endless patience of our Development Editor Anne Townley and the drive and organization of our Senior Editor Clare Double. Thanks also to the picture researcher Heather Vickers who tirelessly tackled quite simply a mountain of images.

From Barbara:
Thank you so much to my husband George, your love and support has meant everything. I would like to dedicate this book to the memory of my mum and dad who would have been proud and pleased to see it.

From Caline:
In memory of my beloved papa, who once said to me, 'never forget the good values that are planted in your soul'. For Sara, you are the apple of my eye; I love you to the moon and back and a few more (π x d) around the world.